D1022566

FIFTH EDITION

ON DEADLINE

FIFTH EDITION

ON DEADLINE
Managing Media Relations

CAROLE M. HOWARD
WILMA K. MATHEWS

WAVELAND
PRESS, INC.

Long Grove, Illinois

For information about this book, contact:
  Waveland Press, Inc.
  4180 IL Route 83, Suite 101
  Long Grove, IL 60047-9580
  (847) 634-0081
  info@waveland.com
  www.waveland.com

10-digit ISBN 1-4786-0340-2
13-digit ISBN 978-1-4786-0340-5

Printed in the United States of America

7 6 5 4

*This book is dedicated
to all the bright young students and professionals
who are following in our footsteps and branching out beyond*

CAROLE M. HOWARD, PRSA, ABC, is an award-winning author, speaker and public relations counselor. She is the retired vice president of public relations and communications policy for The Reader's Digest Association in New York, where she had worldwide responsibilities and staff in 15 countries. She also was president of the Reader's Digest Foundation and served on the corporate Management Committee. A former reporter, she worked for AT&T in Seattle, New York and New Jersey for 18 years in various public relations and marketing positions. In addition to being co-author of "On Deadline: Managing Media Relations," she has written scores of magazine articles on global PR, employee communications, marketing and management, and has contributed chapters to eight other books. Her speeches have been published in Vital Speeches and in three textbooks. She has served as a contributing editor of Public Relations Quarterly and served on the editorial boards of several other magazines. An accredited member of the Public Relations Society of America and International Association of Business Communicators, Howard is a past member of Women in Communications, Inc. and National Press Women. She has a BA from the University of California-Berkeley and an MS in management from Pace University, New York City. She is listed in the Who's Who of American Women and the World's Who's Who of Women. In 1990 she was named one of the top 40 "Corporate PR Superstars" by Public Relations Quarterly. With experience on the Board of Directors of a public company and several nonprofit organizations, as well as 45 years in communications and marketing, she brings a broad perspective to the practice of media relations. She lives in Southwestern Colorado with her husband Bob and cat Mac. Email: tailwinds1@aol.com

WILMA K. MATHEWS, ABC, IABC Fellow, with more than four decades of experience in domestic and international public relations and in communication management and implementation, has held positions with a global corporation (AT&T), a public university (Arizona State University), a medical center, a chamber of commerce, a monthly magazine and a weekly newspaper. A Fellow and accredited member of the International Association of Business Communicators (IABC), Mathews currently serves as chair of the IABC Ethics Committee. She previously served as chair of the IABC Research Foundation and the Accreditation Council, and twice was a member of the IABC executive board. She is a Gold Quill winner for media relations and writing. In addition to co-authoring "On Deadline: Managing Media Relations" (1st–5th editions), she is the author of "Effective Media Relations: A Practical Guide for Communicators," the principal contributor to "How to Get Results with Publicity," the author of "How to Create a Media Relations Program" and a contributor to magazines, newsletters, books and reports. Mathews has spoken before numerous professional, civic, government and academic audiences in the U.S., Canada, England, Hong Kong, New Zealand, China, Malaysia and Australia. She contributes articles to trade and professional journals, and provides counsel to organizations on strategic and media relations planning. Mathews is a member of the Rowan University PR Hall of Fame. For seven years she has taught "Writing for PR" at the Walter Cronkite School of Journalism & Mass Communications at Arizona State University (ASU). Mathews serves on the advisory board of "Communication Briefings," is president of the Friends of the Phoenix Library and on the board of the ASU Retirees Association. One of her greatest moments in life includes being a sponsor for a young boy in Indonesia.

CONTENTS

EXPERTS ENDORSE "ON DEADLINE"

Every student of public relations, whether a seasoned practitioner or a first-year student, should read this book. The reason is simple. The advice these two most highly regarded and experienced professionals give is too valuable to miss.

Is it new information? Perhaps not. But it's what every public relations professional must hear again and again. What the authors do is try to make everyone from media relations practitioners to senior management realize that the working press is not their enemy. Their theme: Don't try to beat the press; you need to meet the press — on their deadline. Be prepared — always. Help — don't hinder. You won't find better advice or a better book.

Don Ranly, Ph.D.
Professor Emeritus
Missouri School of Journalism

Few professionals actually have directed and participated in so many precedent-setting and successful worldwide public relations activities as the authors, so their recommendations are sound. Readers will benefit from their experiences on behalf of The Reader's Digest Association, AT&T, Arizona State University and other clients.

Their practical advice can be put to use immediately whether you work for a huge corporation or a smaller nonprofit association, are a novice or an experienced professional. For the authors' unstinting sharing of this information, the entire public relations profession is in their debt.

"On Deadline: Managing Media Relations" is virtually an encyclopedia of media relations.

Chester Burger (deceased)
Life Member, Counselors Academy
Founding President, College of Fellows
Public Relations Society of America

PREFACE

We were training a new person who had transferred into our media relations group when a colleague mentioned a similar situation at his company. "He's pestering all of us for hints on how to do his job," our friend said. "Why isn't there some book I can give him to read?"

"It sure would have been nice if someone had written it all down for us," we joked. And then, "One of us really ought to write that book." But even two robins do not make a spring. The conversation veered off in another direction, and writing the book became a dormant topic.

Shortly thereafter we responded to a late-night query from The Wall Street Journal after the leak of a layoff announcement. We had to coordinate responses to internal and external queries with spokespersons in 20 locations across the country. At one point a public relations manager in a manufacturing plant remarked, "You really ought to write this up — it would make a perfect case study."

Some time later we canceled plans for dinner together, one to write a speech on corporate media relations to a Public Relations Society of America chapter in Louisiana, the other to plan a workshop on media relations at the International Association of Business Communicators annual conference. At each of these functions we heard similar comments from the audience: "You have had so many different experiences with the news media you really ought to write a book." Thus, the idea came to life.

The fundamental tools of our trade are words. How flattering — and how humbling — to be told there is a need to sit down at your computer to tell the story of how you spend your working life.

Globalization, Technology and Social Media Prompt New Editions

Successful sales of the first edition of "On Deadline," initially in hardcover and later in paperback, led to another request — to produce a second edition that included a separate chapter on global media relations because of its growing importance to our profession.

Five years later it was time for a third edition. The Internet had rapidly changed the way we communicate with each other, and e-business was transforming entire industries. Measurement had become more sophisticated than merely counting press clippings or website visits; rather, it involved tracking changed opinions and modified behaviors. And globalization had become even more important for almost all organizations, large and small, in our worldwide, interdependent economy. After six more years, continuing strong sales and ongoing dramatic changes in technology prompted us to publish a fourth edition.

Now here we are, 28 years after the first edition, experiencing another revolution. Social media have transformed the way individuals, organizations and the media share information. It's hard to believe that this phenomenon has grown exponentially and is widely used on personal and professional levels since our fourth edition was published only seven years ago.

In this fifth edition you will find all new case studies that share best practices by describing how leading practitioners are using social media to achieve their media relations goals.

How This Book Can Improve Your Performance

Education and training, even of a very high magnitude, are not enough. You also need experience. Our approach in this book is to cite anecdotes and case studies from our combined nine-plus decades as public relations practitioners in the corporate and nonprofit worlds and from the experiences of others who have generously shared their knowledge with us. We hope you will find in them a freshness of vision that will enrich your own insights.

We look at the media relations job from both a tactical and a strategic point of view. We temper our advice with knowledge gained from our days as working reporters — and currently, as bloggers.

The fifth edition of "On Deadline" gives you the basic tools to plan and implement a media relations program appropriate for your organization. You'll find a detailed description of setting goals and measuring results, for only with such operational systems in place will you be treated as equal members of the business team by others in your organization. You'll also find tips on how to get your management's approval *before* you begin and keep them informed of your progress and any changes in external or internal conditions as you proceed, so that your contributions are appreciated by the decision makers in your organization.

 We look at the media relations job from both a tactical and a strategic point of view.

Architect Mies van der Rohe once said, "God is in the details" — and this is no less true of our profession than it was of his. With that in mind, we offer specific suggestions on how to improve your relationships with reporters. We provide instructions on how to background both your organization's spokespersons and reporters before a major interview, because the preparation you put in before they meet often makes the difference between success and failure. We set out detailed criteria to help you plan for crises well before they happen and to operate ethically 24/7. As well, we guide you in becoming a part of the decision-making process within your organization.

Who Should Read This Book?

We have written the fifth edition for a broad audience. Students of journalism and public relations should find insight into your fields no matter which side of the profession you choose. CEOs and other key spokespersons for organizations may find that parts of the book offer valuable background on how the media operate and a handy reference before an interview with a reporter. Perhaps even reporters will find it interesting to glimpse the inner workings of the world of media relations. It may make them understand why we practitioners view ourselves — when we are doing our job well — as performing a valuable service that makes us not barriers to information but rather indispensable translators of the needs of both reporters and our organizations.

Most of all, we've written the new edition for those of you who are, or plan to be, responsible for an organization's or client's day-to-day relationships with the news media. Whether you work for a bank wanting to publicize expanded financial services, a utility explaining the complexities and benefits of deregulation, a social service agency desiring to generate attendance at a new job-counseling clinic, a trade association lobbying for legislation or a large corporation marketing a new product, the media's coverage — or lack of coverage — of your news will be an important factor in getting the desired results.

Becoming a Media Relations Professional — and How It Changes Your Life

A natural avenue into the world of media relations is to join a company or organization after a few years of experience as a reporter or blogger. For those of you who fell victim to the siren's song of journalism, the transition should not be difficult. Dealing with the media from this side can be just as stimulating as chasing after a story and a byline. Indeed, we would argue it is more so, because you now have the opportunity to influence decisions and activities rather than just communicate them.

On the other hand, for people who have not spent time as reporters, producers, editors or bloggers, a move into media relations can be an abrupt change, requiring flexibility not only in *your* lifestyle but also in your family's as you strive to adapt to the media's sense of urgency. The workday's planned activities are forsaken when a reporter asks for information on your agency's fundraising expenses, as it takes you several hours to gather the facts, arrange an interview and brief a spokesperson. A dinner party is interrupted when you receive word that there has been a chemical spill at the plant and reporters are clamoring for information. A weekend outing is canceled when you must move up your planned news conference by a week because of a leak that has surfaced on the Internet. A night's sleep is lost when the clock is stopped during union bargaining as your organization works to negotiate a contract and avoid a walkout.

If you like order and predictability and prefer to take a great deal of time to enunciate your views orally or in writing, media relations is not the job for you. But if you are stimulated by being at the center of action, enjoy responding to stimuli from several directions at once, can rapidly formulate thoughts and clearly articulate positions, and find it exhilarating to bring definition to ambiguity, then media relations should give you as much job satisfaction as it has for us.

Your energy and your ability to learn will be tested. The job requires people who can remain calm and focused in a crisis — and above all, keep a sense of humor and perspective. Your reward comes from the people you meet and the events you influence — and the fact that most of the time your job will offer you adventure and fun.

We hope the fifth edition of "On Deadline" will help present and future media relations practitioners to do a better job of walking the tightrope as you strive to balance a reporter's demand for fast and accurate information with the organization's need to guard competitive secrets and avoid violating the privacy of employees; to become as adept at bringing valuable information into the organization as at getting the news out.

 For the beginner, this is a textbook; for the more experienced, a reference.

For the beginner, "On Deadline" will serve as a textbook; for the more experienced person, it will be a valuable reference. For neither should it be dull. Media relations is an exhilarating field. If our prose reflects the excitement of being part of news events as they unfold — and contributes to more accurate coverage of the activities of corporations and other organizations — then we will have achieved our objectives and served our profession.

Carole M. Howard and Wilma K. Mathews
March 2013

ACKNOWLEDGMENTS

Deciding whom to thank when you work with colleagues and journalists who are so willing to share ideas and experiences is a very difficult task. However, there were some who were especially helpful with editorial advice, manuscript reviews and unflagging interest from the time we got the initial idea for the book to the day the first edition of "On Deadline: Managing Media Relations" was published. These include Chester Burger, Bob Burke, Hal Burlingame, Bill Cooper, Bob Ehinger, Roy Foltz, David Manahan, Brian Monahan, Bill Mullane, Elizabeth Park, Jack Sauchelli, Deb Stahl, Mike Tarpey, Al Wann and Candy Young. We also want to pay tribute to Mary Sokol, whose magic fingers kept us on our toes as well as on schedule.

For support and suggestions on the second edition we gratefully acknowledge the contributions of Stephanie Carpentieri, Carol Cincola, Lesta Cordil, Helen Fledderus, David Fluhrer, Chris King, Craig Lowder, Linda Milone, Martha Molnar, Lynn Munroe, Tara Phethean, and Dr. Don Ranly. Valuable assistance for the third edition came from Barbara Griswold, Chris King, Lynn Munroe, Debbie Tully and the staff of the Pagosa Springs, Colorado, library. As well, Mac and Molly provided close and much appreciated supervision of the manuscript.

For insight and information for the fourth edition, we thank Bish Mukherjee, Katie Paine, Fraser Seitel, Dr. Melvin L. Sharpe and his public relations graduate student committee for the 25th anniversary Vernon C. Schranz lectureship event at Ball State University, and Ed and Pat Nieder from the Arthur W. Page Society.

For their input, expertise and help with this fifth edition, we are grateful to Ed Block, Lesta Cordil, Richard Edelman, Bob Ehinger, Mark Estes, Michael Fanning, Debra Gelbart, Bill Hudson, Karl Isberg, Fay Davids Kajee, Jim Lukaszewski, Mary Ann McCauley, Art Merrick, Liz Dingwall Mueller, Melissa Munroe, Ed Nieder, Dr. Don Ranly, Phil Rogers, Jo Roper, Ruth Savolaine, Bonnie Venton-Ross, Sarah Wincott, Dr. Donald K. Wright and Candy Young — and special recognition goes to Chris King and Dick Martin for so generously sharing their social media experiences.

As always, special thanks to Bob Howard, who is our greatest supporter and most constructive critic. We also remain hugely appreciative of the ongoing counsel and major contributions of the Waveland Press editorial and marketing team — Tom Curtin and Jeni Ogilvie — who have become both publishing partners and good friends over the years.

CHAPTER ONE

GETTING STARTED

Setting Up Your Program

Getting started in media relations means understanding your role and your objectives and sticking to both. But what is your role? Referee? Propagandizer? Shuffler of news releases? Senior counsel?

One fact that few executives or organization leaders seem to appreciate is that your role is to make a journalist's job easy, to help that journalist meet his/her objectives and, at the same time, to help your organization meet its objectives.

This tightrope-walking exercise means that when you speak to a journalist you are representing the organization, and when you speak to the people in your organization you

1

are representing the journalist. You do not need a split personality to achieve the balance but you do need a sound understanding of everyone's goals and objectives. The reporter's objective is to get a story to help his/her editors meet a goal of having a newspaper that will sell or a television newscast that will attract viewers or a website marked "Favorite." Now, what are your goals and objectives?

What Kind of Program?

There are two possible kinds of media relations programs: (1) passive or reactive and (2) active or proactive. A passive program means that your organization has determined, for whatever reason, not to seek the attention of the public eye. A passive posture may be initially frustrating to reporters. Once the word gets around, however, the organization generally is left alone, except in crises. Any other mention in the media about the company often is speculation. Privately held companies sometimes engage in this practice and can do so because they are not required by law or regulation to divulge earnings or other financial data.

 Active means that you plan, implement and measure.

If, however, your organization wishes to have an active media relations program, you need to know that active does not mean: issuing a tweet every five minutes; churning out a release every hour; taking reporters to lunch frequently; holding a news conference at the drop of a hat; scheduling all of your subject-matter experts on every radio and television talk show in your area; referring reporters to your company's website; counting inches of copy or seconds of air time as the sole measurement technique; or creating glitzy video news releases.

Active means that you plan, implement and measure a well-conceived media relations program that supports your organization's goals and objectives. The way to do this is to set up your own media relations goals, objectives, strategies and timetables.

Developing a Communications Policy

South African educator and public relations professional Dr. Amanda Hamilton-Attwell[1] defines communications policy as "the rules that will determine the behavior of the communications professionals and the management of the flow of information." The communications policy not only determines the content of the media and the responsibilities of the communications professional, it also provides guidelines on the way the leadership on all levels must deal with communications to ensure engaged internal and external stakeholders.

Beyond designating the official spokespersons, a communications policy sets the tone for all your media activities. The policy needs to be endorsed by, and disseminated from, the leadership of your organization. Early in his tenure, Theodore Vail, the first president of AT&T, wrote a communications policy that has withstood the test of time:

> The only policy to govern the publicity [of AT&T] is that whatever is said or told should be absolutely correct, and that no material fact, even if unfavorable but bearing on the subject, should be held back. When we see misstatements, make certain that those making them are given the correct facts. This will not only tend to stop the making of them, but will lessen the influence of them by decreasing the number of misinformed, and any excuse for misstatements. Attempted concealment of material facts cannot but be harmful in the end.[2]

You should not be creating your communication policy while the reporter is waiting at the door. If your organization does not have a clear communication policy that covers publicity, it is your responsibility to write that policy and get it approved by your organization's leaders.

 A communication policy sets the tone for all your media activities.

The basis for your communication policy can be found in the guiding tenets of your organization, such as its code of conduct, mission statement or rules of ethical behavior and business principles. It can also be found in communication disseminated by management to employees, as well as in CEO speeches and advertising.

Your policy should address — in clearly understood words (skip the legalese here) — your organization's proactive or reactive stance,

Debra Gelbart, principal at Gelbart Communications, a Phoenix, Arizona, communications and public relations firm, offers 10 solid suggestions to guide you in formulating your media relations policy:

1. **Be cooperative.** Recognize that news people and feature writers face constraints and expectations that most of us never dream of, and that if you say "yes" to a request for information or an interview, you are making their job much less of a hassle.

2. **Be accessible.** Don't even think about restricting your availability to the media to regular business hours. Give out your cell phone number freely and encourage reporters and editors to call or text you whenever they need to. If your organization is a 24-hour-a-day operation and someone else can handle routine inquiries after hours, it may be perfectly acceptable as a matter of policy to direct those routine media calls to that person. But if the reporter calls you first, don't ask him or her to jump through hoops by saying, "Why don't you call so-and-so?" Provide the answer yourself and suggest that the next time, the reporter call the person on duty. Let the reporter know that you are always available if a question cannot be answered by someone else satisfactorily. Try to return all phone calls and emails from the media within an hour.

3. **Be direct.** When you can't help a reporter, say so, and explain why. Don't be defensive, don't sound annoyed and above all, don't display arrogance. You should be genuinely sorry that you can't help a reporter, because it is a missed opportunity for both of you.

4. **Be fair.** Don't give opportunities for in-demand interviews only to certain media outlets and not to others. If your CEO is suddenly thrust into the spotlight, for example, and agrees to just one block of time for an interview, don't offer that time only to the news organization screaming the loudest.

5. **Be a resource.** If you can't arrange an interview or answer a question for a reporter, whenever possible suggest someone else who can. It is always better to end a conversation with a reporter by giving him/her another direction to pursue instead of a dead end.

6. **Be an authority.** Learn all you can about your organization and its industry — history, accomplishments, financial condition, goals, mission. And learn everything you can about how newsrooms — both print and broadcast — operate. In addition, get to know what bloggers who write about your industry are interested in. Your goal should be to

inform news people and commentators of important trends as well as converse knowledgeably with them about their business.

7. **Be an educator.** You need to educate two very different constituencies — your coworkers and media representatives — about each other. Hold workshops, informal meetings and media training seminars as appropriate, to defuse distrust and misunderstanding.

8. **Be an advocate.** It's sometimes tricky to walk that tightrope between two sets of clients — those within your organization and those in the media. Although one of your primary responsibilities is to present your organization favorably to the media, it is just as important to reinforce the value of the media to your organization.

9. **Be a strategist.** This where "proactive" media relations comes in. Don't make the mistake of thinking that if you're not out there pumping up the organization's agenda every time you have contact with a media person you're not doing your job. Be selective in what you promote.

10. **Be a team player.** This rule is really the internal version of Rule Number One. You'll find that becoming a team player is a great way to let your organization know how successfully you are practicing the preceding nine rules. Seek out information from key people throughout your organization so that you can stay informed about critical developments. Keep others in your department who don't work in media relations apprised of your activities. What does all this lead to? Building relationships and credibility — both inside and outside your organization.[3]

guidelines for disclosure (what is proprietary and what is not) and who will be authorized spokespersons for the organization. The communications policy must be understood, approved and endorsed by the senior management of your organization. More important, the policy must be adhered to at all times. The strength of a communications policy will be tested during a crisis or negative coverage.

With a policy in hand and mind, you now can focus on more detailed guidelines and plans.

Writing It Down

First, thoroughly know and understand what your organization is and does. What is its purpose? Its history? Is it regulated? By whom and for what? Who are its customers, clients, shareholders, suppliers, competitors? What is its structure, temperament, philosophy? Is it local, national or global? Finally, what are its overall growth strategy and goals?

Look at each of your organization's goals carefully. Then write down all the ways in which you can help your organization meet those goals. For example, if your organization is like most, it will have a goal concerning finances. It may be a declared statement about the amount of return on investment, or it may be a desire not to have to raise members' dues or it may express the need for a fundraising campaign to meet community needs. Your support could include conducting a series of briefings for financial analysts; placing articles relating to organizational growth in magazines that reach investor audiences; or making sure the public knows of the many services and programs your organization provides.

Another organizational goal relates to human resources — the intention to maintain a well-trained, well-paid employee universe with a low turnover. If you think this is an internal matter only, ask yourself where the employees come from. They come from the public at large and the world at large. Your role in this area can be to make sure the public is aware of your organization's hospitable environment by creating a page(s) on the company's website to issue announcements and photos (or, if appropriate, videos) of environmental awards, employees' service projects in the community, corporate donations, tuition reimbursement programs, on-site day care centers, promotions, long-term service anniversaries, suggestion award winners and company plant/office improvements.

 Gather work plans and goals/strategies from other departments.

This exercise of writing down ideas helps you marshal your thoughts, ensures that you truly do understand your organization's key objectives and helps you recognize how you can fit into the overall structure. You may find it beneficial to create a spreadsheet of your ideas listed and cross-listed with departments and ideas.

Next, gather work plans and goals/strategies from other departments, such as marketing, community relations, product development, labor relations and legal affairs. Your media relations plan also should support — directly or indirectly — these departments. You may find it helpful to create a separate media plan for each department so that individual departments and you agree on what is expected and who will do it.

Even if you're not in a position to provide direct support to each department, having their plans helps you anticipate possible issues, schedule media events around key activities or serve as an advisor to the department. At a minimum, knowing what is in these plans prevents you from unknowingly causing harm or conflict.

The Formal Structure

There are numerous ways to structure your media relations program. Select the way that best suits the day-to-day management techniques, language and operations of your organization. The following example may be of help.

Media Relations Programs: XYZ Company

Goal 1. To support the company's goal to attain financial stability through increased investments by the public.

First Objective: To help financial media have a better understanding of the organization's future.

Tactics:

1. Select three key financial writers who reach an influential target audience.

2. Arrange for each writer to interview a selected specialist in the finance department. Each interview should occur at separate times and cover separate topics.

3. Send updated information to all financial journalists on your distribution list.

4. Develop a special "Financial Information" section on your company's website.

5. Create a special "Financial Trends" blog linked to the company's website to discuss industry-wide financial news.

Second Objective: To provide the financial media with timely, accurate earnings information.

Tactics:

1. Work with your investor relations colleagues to develop a "Financial Information" section on your company's website.

2. Establish contact with a key person in the finance department who will provide information to the media relations department on a prearranged schedule.

3. Create a checklist of financial reporters in general, as well as business and trade publications, financial websites and blogs that reach targeted audiences.

4. Prepare questions and rehearse answers in advance of inquiries by journalists about the organization's finances.

5. Issue earnings announcements each quarter.

6. Provide detailed briefings for financial reporters at the annual meeting.

Third Objective: To help encourage targeted audiences to invest in the organization by making them aware of the solvency and growth of the company.

Tactics:

1. Determine the key investor audiences by working with the investor relations department.

2. Determine which publications or types of publications, websites and blogs those audiences are likely to read.

3. Attempt to place six articles, which reflect the growth of the company, in those publications and on those sites.

GOAL 2. To support the organization's goal of hiring and maintaining a well-trained employee body with low turnover.

First Objective: To inform targeted audiences of the employment opportunities and benefits of XYZ Company.

Tactics:

1. Work with the human resources department to make sure the "Working at XYZ Company" website section is both functional and attractive.

2. Notify industry media of the employment information on your organization's website.

3. Pitch specialized stories to newspaper sections, such as "Living," "Education" and "Business," and to blogs that focus on employment opportunities.

Second Objective: To show the organization as a good corporate citizen.

Tactics:

1. Compile a list of all employees involved in civic and volunteer activities.

2. Develop a list of all organizations benefitting from XYZ Company employee service and support.

3. Work with service organizations to have them include XYZ Company in their news releases on corporate support.

4. Create and link the "XYZ Company Community Service" website section and/or blog to the company's home page.

5. Develop a data profile of the company's community activities (number of employees involved, number of hours in service, dollars saved for service organizations, etc.); distribute the profile to the media and place it on the company's website.

While the XYZ Company example is somewhat simplistic and altruistic, it does show that a media relations program can be planned by writing concise goals, objectives and tactics. Of course, each tactic should have a specific time frame and budget included with it, as well as the name of the person responsible for that tactic.

When the plan is completed, share it with key executives in your organization for their review and comment. This action serves several purposes. First, it shows your top management that you are attuned to the workings of your organization because your departmental activities are geared to support the entire organization and its objectives. Second, it allows each person the opportunity to have some input to the plan. Everyone likes to be asked his/her opinion of something; most people like to respond with a suggested change or two. A word of caution: Do not automatically incorporate all suggestions into your plan. Look at each suggestion and, as objectively as possible, consider both its source and what happens to related activities if it is incorporated.

The reason to take some time with these suggestions is that not everyone sees the world in the same way. The vice president of labor relations will have concerns that are quite different from those of the chief financial officer who, in turn, will focus on issues that aren't the same as those of the vice president of marketing, who will see things very differently from the organization's attorney.

 Share your plan with key executives for their input.

Understanding each person's viewpoint will help you understand the suggestion he/she made. At that point, you can see what the implications might be if you automatically incorporate that person's suggestion about your media program. You may find that all suggestions are actual improvements on your plan. Or, you may find that none of the suggestions will improve the plan because they reflect territorial concerns rather than overall organizational issues.

Of paramount importance is making sure you and your organization's legal counsel have a clear understanding of your individual roles, and a good working relationship. You need cooperation and mutual respect to be effective.

After incorporating any new data, make sure these same people see the final document dated and labeled as your "working document." This is the plan from which you will work day by day. This also is the basis for the measurement of your program and your individual performance. Each person on the media relations team should have a copy of the final plan as well. It should be referred to often and updated regularly.

Provide quarterly updates to your key executives, including progress, challenges, delays, deletions, etc. Also plan to provide a mid-year and year-end report based on your plan.

Preparing Your Office

Generally speaking, not enough effort is spent outfitting a media relations office. Much time and frustration could be saved if more preparation were put into the hardware and software needed in your work area.

The physical equipment for media relations may be determined by the way in which your business operates. You may need the latest in computer software, website development, professional video production, top-of-the-line smartphones, tablets and an email system with lots of broadcast capability and storage space. A multifunction copier/scanner/fax is essential for those items not easily transmitted by computer. And, those seemingly "old-fashioned" filing cabinets are still necessary for storage of large materials such as annual reports, legal documents and other items not easily available online.

Among the library items you need access to — either in hard copy, on your computer or online — are:

- An up-to-date dictionary
- A style manual (your own or one such as "The Associated Press Stylebook")
- Thesaurus
- Your organization's annual reports for the past five years
- Professional/academic journals/books/websites related to media relations
- Company-produced material, such as recruitment brochures, product promotional material and benefits booklets
- Copies of your organization's internal publications
- Media directories, including local/global/online/industry-specific directories
- Organization charts
- Calendars of events for the organization (earnings releases, product announcements, speeches to be given by the president or CEO, trade shows, annual meeting, seminar, fund drives)
- Hard copy and online information kits consisting of — for example — the most recent annual report, a fact sheet about the company's products or services, the president's or CEO's most current or best speech
- Business cards
- Corporate goals and objectives/media goals and objectives
- Atlas
- Editorial calendars

All of this material will be used in some way at various times. Reporters can ask obscure questions and you have to be ready to reply as quickly as possible. In addition to the above, you should subscribe to the online or print publications with which you'll be dealing, and set up a monitoring service for broadcast and online media and a clipping service for print.

Of key importance is the compilation of your organization's statistics. Journalists adore numbers: They are easy to read, easy to compare, work well in headlines and impress readers. Get a head start on potential questions involving numbers by composing such questions yourself. The result should be a file on statistics, a special page/screen on your organization's website and/or a company profile that can answer questions about:

1. **Employee numbers.** These could be broken down by management/ nonmanagement, union/nonunion, male/female, percentage increases in different universes, location/geography, ethnic growth and distribution over the years, numbers hired and laid off in the past year and the last five years. Member profiles in nonprofits and professional associations can follow a similar pattern.

2. **Facilities.** How many sales offices or office buildings or manufacturing facilities or service centers do you have? In what states? Countries? What is manufactured at each facility? What are their website addresses? Are you adding or reducing the number of facilities?

3. **Miscellaneous information.** What are the key dates in your organization's history? What is your best production/service record? Who is the founder of your organization?

4. **Executive information.** What are the biographical data on each of your organization's executives? What are the percentages of males/ females, members of ethnic groups, locals/nationals/expatriates in management positions? What about your board members? Who are they and what are their credentials?

5. **Financial statistics.** In addition to the earnings and other information available in an annual report, compile information on how much payroll your organization paid out in the last year. How much in federal/state/local taxes? How much to suppliers — both inside and outside the country? How much to minority suppliers? How much did your organization contribute to community or service programs?

6. **Environmental statistics.** How much did your organization spend to meet environmental standards? How much did the company recycle in paper/trash/aluminum/plastic? How many employees were involved in some environmental clean-up campaign? How many campaigns did the organization sponsor?

7. **Community outreach efforts.** How many, and what kind of, local nonprofit organizations did your organization support? How many employees joined in a companywide volunteer challenge? How much money did your company and employees donate to United Way campaigns?

8. **Products/services.** How many/what kind of products does your company produce? Where are they listed on your website? What services does your nonprofit provide to which community/communities? How many people buy your products/use your services?

Because you do not know what might be on a reporter's mind until the phone rings or you get an email alert, it is best to start compiling a list of subject-matter experts now and to keep adding to it and updating it constantly. Convenient ways to store material are in your computer (with backup) or even in easily accessible indexed binders to facilitate use by others when you're not around or when your computer is down. Whichever method you select, remember the object is to have material at hand so that you can get to it quickly and easily when a reporter asks you a question. A reporter will remember you if you are able to respond immediately without having to say, "I'll get back to you on that."

 The reporter does not know the people in your company — that is your job.

This is also a good time to begin compiling a list of subject-matter experts within your organization. When reporters call for an interview or general information, they do not begin by asking to speak specifically to "Mr. Jones, the manager of personnel statistics." Instead, the reporter is more likely to ask for an interview with someone who can talk about personnel statistics. The reporter does not know the people in your company — that is your job.

Start a list of subject-matter experts by thinking like a reporter and asking yourself: Who is knowledgeable about pricing policies? Labor relations? Purchasing? Individual products? Transportation services? Food services? Financial statistics? Sales? Member services? Global markets? Quality? Environmental affairs? Government affairs? If you list the subjects alphabetically and then beside each entry the subject-matter expert (with email address, office/pager/smartphone numbers), you will find your job much easier the next time a reporter calls. Use this information to develop a directory of your organization's experts and, with your company's permission, make it available both online and in hard copy to the media.

Baruch College, one of 10 senior colleges of the City University of New York system, provides an example of an online listing of subject matter experts: http://www.baruch.cuny.edu/pressroom/sme.htm. The experts are listed by category, with their area(s) of expertise, fluency in another language (if any), direct email address and a photograph, all of which make it easy for journalists and others to find the specialist they are seeking.

Introducing Yourself

Now that you have a media relations plan and a well-coordinated office, it is time to start letting the media know who you are. With your media relations plan in mind, select the reporters and others whom you need to meet. Do not assume that you have to know all the editors and program directors at all the newspapers, magazines, online news sites, and television and radio stations in a 500-mile radius or around the world.

You should select only those media, and only those editors or reporters or bloggers, who can help you meet your goals and objectives. Those are the people critical to your efforts. Once you have made that list, do not rush out and attempt to call on all persons at once or immediately call or email them and invite them to lunch. Instead, take the time to think about what you want to do and plan your activities accordingly. If none of the editors or key writers or bloggers knows you because you are new on the job or new to the area, then your primary reason for contact is to introduce yourself to them and get to know each other.

 Let the media know who you are and how to reach you.

Select your list of people and begin contacting them to set up times when you can drop by and introduce yourself. Make sure you call at the least busy times in their schedules: after the newspaper has been put to bed, after the television crews have received their assignments and have gone on location, after the radio newscast, after the bureau chief has filed the latest report. When initiating these contacts, you should ask for just a brief amount of time. Moreover, don't try to crowd all you appointments into the same day, otherwise you might not be on time for each appointment.

As you meet each person, present him/her with some basic material about you and your organization: the information kits mentioned earlier, several of your business cards, and URLs for the various categories on your organization's website, including direct sites for photos of your company executives and company history. Also include URLs for your organization's logo and graphic standards, blog, photos and news sites.

Taking Advantage of Social Media

Social media are broad and varied, dwarfing the reach of the largest legacy media while remaining highly targeted to the interests of their individual users. Dick Martin, a business writer specializing in marketing and public relations who is the former head of PR for AT&T, advises that there are three ways to use social media in media relations:

- **Pushing out news.** Many organizations initially treat social media as just another placement platform that has the added benefit of going around reporters and their pesky questions. For example, anyone with a video camera — which is everyone with a smartphone — can post to YouTube. A classic example of YouTube's power is Blentec's series of "Will it blend?" videos. CEO Tom Dickson claims that the company's sales of kitchen blenders soared 650 percent since he started posting a series of 50 cheap videos of his blenders chewing up everything from marbles and golf balls to an iPad and a full-sized garden rake. Of course, it's foolish to think you really can go around reporters. Anything that a company posts on a social media site is fodder for the reporters who cover its industry. Blentec has been profiled in publications ranging from Esquire to The New York Times, based largely on its blending stunts.

  Smart media relations people recognize that most journalists these days are writing for multiple platforms. In addition to the traditional news release and fact sheet, you should provide nontext content, like infographics, high-resolution photos, video, background interviews, podcasts, audio clips, links to related content and interactive elements.

- **Gathering intelligence.** Social media have not only opened new channels to customers, they have also empowered customers themselves. Practically every website worth its bandwidth has incorporated some form of social networking into its pages, allowing readers to ask

15

questions and post comments or making it easier for users to share parts of the site with others. Consumers are using social media to collaborate with each other on everything from building support for social causes (http://act.mtv.com and www.change.org) and attracting business investors (www.kickstarter.com) to advising each other on purchases (www.tripadvisor.com and www.epinions.com), selling and trading goods (www.ebay.com and. www.craigslist.org) and sharing photos and videos (www.flickr.com and http://instagram.com). Sometimes people simply are socializing with each other (Facebook and MySpace) and sometimes they are extracting revenge for perceived offenses (www.my3cents.com, www.complaintsboard.com and www.pissedconsumer.com). Mobile-enabled blogs let users post photos or videos from anywhere, tagging them with labels like "BadMcDonaldsExperience" so search engines can find them more easily.

You should keep tabs on issues and growing controversies in the online world that could affect your organization. What's said in the blogosphere can be significant and more timely than what appears in the mainstream media. Make a point of monitoring the online postings of journalists and influential bloggers who follow your industry. Twitter and Facebook can give you a real-time view into the stories and issues that are of interest to the journalists who follow your organization and your industry.

- **Building relationships.** Social media represent an opportunity to build relationships with a vastly broadened category of media — the reporters, producers and editors of the legacy media as well as the bloggers, posters and special interest communities of the online world. The first step in building those relationships is to become familiar with their work. Read their stories, contribute to relevant discussions (always clearly identifying yourself and your organization) and provide information they find useful on a regular basis. This will help you get on their radar and, as you gain their trust, position you as a potential source.[4]

Summary

Setting up your media relations plan and program requires research about your role, your organization's intentions for media relations and you, and a clear understanding by both parties of what can and cannot be achieved through effective media relations. Setting up also requires attention to the practicalities of the job, from setting policy to developing a functioning office, from writing a plan to writing news briefs.

Sadly, too many novices believe that sending out a news release is all that's necessary to being a media relations specialist. The effort you put into developing an outstanding media program will separate you from them.

CHAPTER TWO

NEWS

What It Is and How It Gets to the Public

Times change. And along with them, definitions change. Trying to pin down what is "news" becomes an endless exercise, with as many definitions as there are public relations practitioners, tweeters, journalists, bloggers and academicians. Or even playwrights. George Bernard Shaw opined that "Newspapers are unable, seemingly, to discriminate between a bicycle accident and the collapse of civilization."

Trying to define news today is an exercise in understanding the shifts in populations, media as profit-making business entities and ... social media. Every person with a phone is a reporter, as evidenced by the shaky, but real-time, images of a shooting at a university or people running from a tsunami or an accident on the highway. Tom Bettag, producer of the "Rock Center with Brian Williams" weekly news magazine on NBC TV, opined in "Evolving Definitions of News":

• News is what people say they want to know about.

• News is what makes money.

• News is anything you can get a camera to do.

• News is anything you can cover live.

• News is what fills the pipeline.[1]

But the number one characteristic of news remains: Conflict.

An objective news story will offer both sides of the conflict but it is the conflict itself that is of interest. Conflicts can be intellectual (evolution vs. creationism), financial (employee layoffs vs. CEO compensation packages), economic (trade imbalance vs. free trade), political (drill for oil vs. protect the environment) or legal/bioethical (right-to-die vs. life-sustaining treatment).

David and Goliath conflicts can be of special interest (the big corporation vs. the well-intended whistle-blower), while conspiracies or conspiracy theories can be of even more public interest. Conflict is easy to create and often comes from disgruntled employees, competitors, special interest groups, proposed legislation or rumor.

Observers of the media continue to bemoan the obsession of all media with "infotainment," a hybrid of news and entertainment, designed to hold viewers and listeners longer. Is this the definition of news?

The original definition of "news" is thought to come from the four points on a compass; North, East, West, South. But that definition doesn't mean that all information from all points on the globe are newsworthy. For readers, scanners, viewers and listeners, "news" is what they personally are interested in. A long-ago rule-of-thumb definition stated that the importance of news varied inversely as the square of the distance from the reader. Example: "Two people killed in a local factory explosion in Cincinnati" gets more play than "100 people killed in a landslide in India." Readers are especially interested in those things that do or may affect their pocketbooks, safety, employment, health or environment.

News is what the editor or webmaster says it is.

Sometimes, though, the simplest definitions are the best: "News" is whatever the editor — or producer — or webmaster — or blogger says it is.

If information does not get past the final authority's desk, it does not get printed, it does not get read on radio, it does not get viewed on television and it does not get posted online — and, thus, it does not become reported news.

Editorial processing of information is not unique to the news media. All of us make decisions each day — about which pieces of information we will keep to ourselves and which pieces we will share with peers, subordinates, superiors, families and friends. In our hands, this is a benign process; when in the hands of news media, the process seems to be a show of power with a blatant disregard for the "real" truth or the "most newsworthy" stories.

Media Relations and News

For the media relations professional, the task is not the delivery of news to an editor. A more accurate characterization is the delivery of properly prepared material that might be passed on by an editor to become news. What criteria do editors use in determining whether material will become news?

For as many editors as there are, there will be the "definitive" check-list citing what constitutes news. The definition will vary depending on your organization … is it for profit, not-for-profit, global or local? What are the products, services, prominence, roles in the community?

In "What Makes Something Newsworthy," Tony Rogers, who blogs at journalism.about.com., lists the following factors:

- **Impact or consequences.** Generally, the greater the impact a story has, the more newsworthy it is. Events that have an impact on your readers, that have real consequences for their lives, are bound to be newsworthy.

- **Conflict.** If you look closely at the stories that make news in any given day, chances are most of them will have some element of conflict. Whether it's a dispute over banning books at a local school board meeting, bickering over budget legislation in Congress, or the ultimate conflict — war — conflict is almost always newsworthy.

• **Loss of life/property destruction.** Any story involving loss of human life — from a fire to a shooting to a terrorist attack — is bound to be newsworthy.

• **Proximity.** Proximity has to do with how close an event is geographically to your readers or viewers. A house fire with several people injured might be big news in your hometown newspaper, but chances are no one will care in the next town over.

• **Prominence.** Are the people involved in your story famous or prominent? If so, the story becomes newsworthy. Prominence can apply to politicians, movie stars, star athletes, CEOs — anyone who's in the public eye.

• **Timeliness.** The news business tends to focus on what's happening this day, this hour, this minute.

• **Novelty.** Another old saying in the news business goes, "When a dog bites a man, no one cares. When the man bits back — now that's a news story."[2]

A dictionary such as Merriam-Webster's also provides descriptors of "news":

• **Negativity.** Bad news is more newsworthy than good news.

• **Unexpectedness.** If an event is out of the ordinary it will have a greater effect than something that is an everyday occurrence.

• **Personalization.** Events that can be portrayed as the actions of individuals will be more attractive than those in which there is no such "human interest."

• **Reference to elite persons.** Stories concerned with the rich, powerful, famous and infamous get more coverage.

• **Continuity.** A story that is already in the news gathers a kind of inertia. This is partly because the media organizations are already in place to report the story, and partly because previous reportage may have made the story more accessible to the public (making it less ambiguous).[3]

For the media relations practitioner who has been given the edict to "Get this news out right away," determining if that material has a chance of becoming news is not as intimidating as you may think. Your information must be good enough to meet the ultimate definition of news: It's whatever the editor/webmaster says it is. However, there are questions you can ask yourself about the material. These questions correlate well with what most journalists believe to be news criteria:

- **Is the story local?** Does it have a local "hook" to it, something that will interest readers or viewers in your area? For trade or specialty publications, and websites or blogs: Is the material of interest to the targeted audience?

- **Is this information unique or unusual?** Is it the first, the latest, the last, the fastest, the biggest, the oldest of something?

- **Is the material timely?** Is this something happening now or that will happen in the near future? Does the material relate to another item that is currently being discussed publicly? Is this a new trend?

- **Is it timeless?** Is this a topic with a long shelf life, such as the environment, terrorism, jobs or the government?

- **Does this information concern people?** Our curiosity about the lives and events of others is evidenced by the strong sales of periodicals devoted just to people and by the growing number of "reality" shows and talk shows on television.

- **Does this material create human interest?** Pathos? Humor?

- **Does this information have consequences that affect lives?** Does it educate/inform? Is it of moral/social importance?

- **Are the people involved famous or prominent?**

- **Does this story have strong local/regional/national/international interest?**

- **Is this news of the widest possible interest** to all those who are within the scope of the medium's distribution (print or electronic)?

If the answer to any of these questions is yes, chances are your material will get an editor's attention and perhaps be placed on the first screen of a major news website or in the newspaper or on the evening news.

What News Is — From the Reporter's Perspective

James E. Lukaszewski, ABC, APR, Fellow PRSA, is president of The
Lukaszewski Group, a division of Risdall Public Relations, management
consultants in communications. With extensive experience in media relations, including coaching and counseling organization leaders in myriad
media situations, he has developed this list of the items all reporters look
for as they write their stories:[4]

1. Affects people, animals or the environment
2. What that effect is
3. Change
4. Conflict:
   - From outside
   - From inside
   - From organized opposition
5. Confrontation
6. Danger
7. Editorial perspective (What the editor wants the reporter to get.)
8. Extremes
9. Failure
10. Mistakes
11. Reporter's interests (Try to get the reporter into the story.)
12. Secrets
13. The unusual
14. Vulnerabilities
15. Weaknesses

Looking for News

Whether you practice media relations full-time, part-time or as a volunteer, the way to find news in your organization is to become a reporter. If you think as a reporter or journalist trained to ask questions, you will find that you are constantly coming across story ideas.

Do not just accept the existence of your company's software development or engineering departments, for example. Why are they there? What role do they play in the accomplishment of overall organizational goals and objectives? What relevance can they have to current issues such as the environment, global warming, education, poverty, elder care or literacy? Why does the organization invest in these areas? If you look closely, you will find a mine of interesting stories.

 Think as a reporter trained to ask questions.

Do not assume that personnel news would not be used. Promotions are newsworthy not just to the business, financial or trade media but also to the person's hometown media, alumni magazines and professional society journals. Some of these items, depending on visual appeal, could interest local television as well. All of these items are good fodder for your organization's internal communications and news page on your website.

An excellent source of story material about your organization is the internal newsletter, whether in print or online. Emailing this publication to editors in your area often generates a flow of activity as the media seek to expand a story or get a different angle on it. Items covered in an internal newsletter that could interest journalists include:

1. **Service projects sponsored by the company.** More and more organizations are being judged by the external service they provide to the community. The stories still need to be unique in order to be considered news. Having a toy drive is not unique, but refurbishing homes for military veterans is.

2. **Construction news.** If your organization is building a new facility or renovating your headquarters, information about the progress may be welcomed by the general and business media as a possible visual story or, at the least, a reminder that a story will be coming when the work is completed.

3. **Introduction of new technologies, equipment or software.** Technology advances have brought, and continue to bring, an abundance of items about new, labor-saving, information-sharing, global-connecting devices and software, all of which can have a direct effect on a company's bottom line and a community's well-being.

4. **Production records.** Turning out the zillionth widget can be an item worth noting if your organization is the first to make a zillion widgets, or if you did so in record time. This seemingly simple story provides reassurance to a news audience of a healthy business. For the nonprofit area, production records can be noted in terms of number of families in shelters, record-breaking blood drives or a successful fundraising campaign.

5. **Company-sponsored blood drives.** Your organization's blood drive statistics — such as the employee who has donated the most units, the employee who needed blood donations to combat a rare disease or the ranking of your company among other companies locally in the number of units donated — have great internal and external appeal.

6. **Organization milestones.** There are always anniversaries of one kind or another to commemorate; often, these dates are relevant to the community or offer an opportunity to reflect on changes brought about by your company or service organization.

7. **Visiting dignitaries.** If a home-office executive or your senator or the president of your Asian subsidiary is visiting the local facility and can make appearances or be available for interviews, the media would like to know. The same holds true for national or global officers of civic or professional organizations.

8. **CEO and executive profiles.** Business and other journalists like to profile key leaders in the industry and/or town. They also like to call on these leaders for quotes about business trends, the economy and related issues.

9. **Organization awards.** Government agencies, service groups, vendors and others often present awards to local organizations for achievements in such areas as conservation, quality and community support. Both groups benefit from publicity on the award.

10. **Suggestion award winners and entrepreneurs.** Rewarding an employee for ingenious thinking makes for a good story beyond the company gates, as does a story about an employee who acts as an internal entrepreneur.

11. **Unusual jobs.** Not all jobs are glamorous, nor are they all dull and boring. There are, within most organizations, jobs that do not fit the normal mold. For example, who puts the jelly in the doughnuts? Washes windows on a skyscraper? Is a telemarketer for a cemetery?

12. **Seasonal events.** Special activities planned for major holidays should be brought to the media's attention as soon as possible. There are more organizations wanting to highlight their activities than there are media slots in which to place them. Look for what makes your activity different or unique. Humanize it.

This list is far from complete, but it shows the possibilities for news that already exists within your organization.

Coming up with a list of story ideas that can be presented to editors is like preparing a menu: There will always be regular offerings for customers, and there should also be daily specials to entice customers to return. Do not be discouraged, however, if the editor decides he/she does not want anything from your offering today; tomorrow that same editor may decide that your fare is the best in town.

Directing Your Story to the Right Medium

Too many media relations professionals forget that websites, television and radio newscasts, newspapers and magazines are businesses and not services. As a result of this initial misunderstanding, these professionals often try to market the wrong story to the wrong medium — with the wrong outcome.

 The media are businesses, not services.

As a start, locate online your target outlets' media kits. These kits, used by media sales staff to attract advertisers, provide demographic data about that medium's desired audience. For example, the newspaper you think you want to target may have a demographic of female readers, age 50+, with a college education and disposable income. If you want to reach male readers, age 25–34, with a college education and in middle management, look elsewhere.

Another way to help direct your stories to the best possible medium is to break that medium down into its component parts — or products. Understanding the selling features of a medium's product will help you more carefully place your story. Editors will appreciate your understanding of their marketing process and will doubly appreciate that you are not wasting their time. Starting with the five main media categories, you can develop your own selection list for the particular media you wish to attract.

1. Television

Because television offers both sight and sound, because the industry has fragmented its audiences through hundreds of cable television channels, and because television channels now double up with their own websites, you should approach this medium with a unique perspective.

Most people believe they get their news from television — and many do. Even though TV news viewership has been declining for years, it remains the number one source of news for most Americans. However, television news shows account for only a small percentage of the station's offerings. Supporting the newscasts are network shows, locally produced variety/entertainment/talk shows, syndicated specials, documentaries, movies and network-produced, live coverage of events. Even the news show itself is so fragmented that only 8–10 minutes of a 30-minute program can be called "news."

Unless you are in charge of national media for your organization, you should be concerned primarily with locally produced shows for your story and news offerings. Local news and talk shows are the prime targets for your releases. Assignment editors at the television station determine which stories will be covered for the morning, noon, evening and late-evening news. They make that decision based partially on the real news value of the item, partially on its visual qualities, and partially on the station's demographics. Also, providing the editor with video clips on your organization's upcoming walkathon or a still shot of your company's new headquarters can give your announcement an edge.

Local talk shows provide an excellent medium for your subject-matter experts — if they have received media training — to talk about, demonstrate and respond to issues. The show's producer can provide detailed information about the requirements for the program, audience demographics, time needed for booking guests and capability for live demonstrations.

Cable television provides channels devoted to health, sports, news, popular music, history, biographies, travel, religion, country music, movies, cartoons, lifestyle, culture, kids, documentaries and shopping. There are hundreds of cable channels, each with its specific viewing audience. Before venturing into this area of television, work closely with your company or client to determine if the narrow viewing audience is what you want and/or need.

2. Social Media

For some companies and organizations, and especially small businesses and nonprofits, adding social media to — or substituting social media for — traditional media is challenging. But, if your website is getting email that asks, "Where is your Facebook page?" or "How can I find you on Twitter?" then it's time to change. Brian Solis, author of "The End of Business as Usual," offers social media tips with the admonition, "Starting now and forever, technology and empathy are now part of your business strategy."[5] His priorities include understanding:

- Social networks from Facebook to Twitter to Google and how they're connecting to influencers and businesses.

- How your consumers [are] using mobile devices today and what apps they're installing.

- The online presence your business produces across a variety of platforms such as tablets, smartphones, laptops and desktops.

- The consumer click path based on the platform consumers are using.

- The expectations of connected consumers, what they value in each channel and platform, where they engage and how your business can improve experiences and make them worthy of sharing.

Getting down to the specifics of social media business practices, Craft, Creative Marketing posted the following guidelines for "6 Social Media Best Practices for Business"[6]

1. Create a social media policy. Include your purpose for social media, your privacy policy, acceptable topics and language, which voice will be used — employee(s) or the brand — and, who owns your account and followers.

2. **Set a schedule.** Post regularly; post when your followers are the most engaged.

3. **Include a call to action.** Download, re-tweet, share, pin, post, follow, RSS, like, bookmark, forward, comment. subscribe, re-blog, check in, watch.

4. **Promote yourself.** Tell people where to find you. Use the logos of your connecting sites (Facebook, Twitter, etc.) on your website, in your e-sig, all print materials, even a sign at your front desk. Make sure people know you're social!

5. **Build relationships.** Have conversations. Follow others. Guest blogging goes both ways. Don't sell!

6. **Track results.** Understand who visits your pages, where visitors come from, what they do and where they leave, which keywords bring traffic, why people follow you, when your posts get the most attention, what percentage of your visitors are engaged, your "virality" and reach.

The evolution to social media is essential for a long-term, successful media relations program. "Our strategy," says Grad Conn, chief marketing officer at Microsoft U.S., "is to evolve from 'social marketing' which simply pushes a message through social networks to a 'social business' approach where we use social networks to build relationships and foster conversations with our audiences through listening engagement."[7]

3. Newspapers

Whether published weekly, daily and/or online, newspapers follow a similar formula by being divided into sections of national/international news, business, sports, entertainment, home living, real estate, cars and regional activities.

Knowing who makes the decisions for each section, what the requirements are for that section, and the schedule for the section's production are prerequisites to deciding where you should attempt to place stories. It is possible that one story might have several angles and could be of interest to several section editors. For example, the business editor would want to know the financial impact of your company's new product announcement and how it relates to the local business community. If it is a consumer product, the home or leisure editor would be interested in knowing what the product does for the customer. The lifestyles editor might want to know of your organization's new services. Each editor serves a different constituency and is interested only in what each story means in terms of the interests of that constituency.

Newspapers also have columnists, local and/or syndicated, who specialize in topics that may support the sections or reflect the general editorial stance of the newspaper. Columnists can be strong, selling features for newspapers, so getting to them is important.

A columnist writing on economics is a good target for an in-depth explanation relating to new pricing policies for your industry's products or services. The columnist in the family section who provides household hints wants only "how-to" material and cannot use detailed or lengthy background information. The columnist catering to farmers and gardeners would be interested in your company's new herbicide. A medical columnist might welcome information about your organization's counseling and referral services. And all of these columnists need almost-daily grist for their online versions.

When marketing a story that has several angles or possibilities, make sure each editor, columnist or writer knows you are talking to the others. You should never assume that internal communication on a newspaper or magazine is at peak efficiency. If your story appears twice in the same edition, you have lost your credibility.

4. Radio

Radio is perhaps the least complex of the media and, very possibly, the most overlooked medium of the new communication era. While other media have scrambled to change to meet the demands of a technology-driven society, radio has remained stable and traditional. Significant numbers of listeners continue to tune in to AM/FM radio, which relies heavily on on-air advertising for its financial stability. By contrast, HD radio failed to succeed, but satellite radio continues to gather audience appeal.

The broadcast range of radio stations is an important factor for you to know. The stations with the widest, most powerful ranges are the ones you need if you have an emergency, such as an urgent call for blood donors at your hospital or the need to update the public on an oil spill near your town.

Radio stations follow the trend of print by specializing and appealing to distinct, segmented audiences. This audio specialization produces a good product for the radio station but can frustrate the media relations professional if you do not take the time to thoroughly investigate the medium. There are all-news stations, all-classical stations, all-country stations, all-easy-listening stations, all-sports stations, all-talk stations and all-financial stations among the hundreds of options.

5. Magazines

As the capabilities and offerings of the Internet and online media increased, many print magazines fell out of circulation. However, specialized magazines have continued to appear in print and online, with themes, from brides to home improvement, sports to travel, and news — such as The Economist and Time.

The proliferation of specialized print and online magazines is making placement in this medium easier in terms of identification but more difficult in terms of a large audience reach. The first step is to identify which magazines and webzines reach your particular audience. You may have to compile several breakout lists if your media operation is extensive. For example, you may need magazines that reach your customers by level of decision making, by geography, by financial status, by industry (with specific areas such as technology, services, support) or the public at large (for business, leisure, product or consumer issues).

Like newspapers, a magazine may then be divided into sections: finance, technology, opinion, manufacturing, arts or people. However, because the magazine itself serves a special constituency, there may not be as much subdivision. The same rules of careful analysis that apply to newspapers also apply to magazines, with one added feature: photography. Magazines are candidates to run professional-grade photographs and graphics provided by you. Often, a photograph of a new product or one representing a new service may be run as a stand-alone piece if there is not room for the entire story. Check the magazine's requirements carefully, to avoid sending a product photograph to the print version that never uses photos but that may have an online version that will accept them.

Many magazines have special issues or annuals in conjunction with trade shows, fairs or seasonal events (e.g., back to school, fashion or holidays). You may decide to target these special issues instead of bombarding the publication with releases throughout the year.

Online Directories Are Useful Resources

Tracking the media, their editors, writers, production schedules and posting schedules may be the most challenging aspect of managing your media relations program. With a world of media outlets at your doorstep, keeping on top of those media that are most important and relevant to your client or company can be overwhelming and time-consuming.

The good news is: Media directories are online, updated regularly, available by subscription and easily accessible. The bad news is: There are tens of thousands of directories posted online, listed by medium and by category. There's a directory for each radio and television station, magazine, newspaper and/or newsletter. Comingled with these media listings are listings of organizations that promote their subject-matter experts available for reporters' inquiries. This overabundance of information is valuable but also can be time-consuming unless you are clear about your target audience and/or the media that best reach that audience.

 Ultimately, you will want to create your own media directory.

It is imperative that you have identified your target audience in as many ways as possible: male/female, age, business, geography, non-profit, print/online/radio/television, etc. The more specific your target audience identifiers, the easier it will be to find the right directory listing. Will you need to reach your audience through television, radio, print (newspaper daily/weekly or magazine), online media or all four? Is your audience narrow — for example, donors to a specific type of medical need or all with a college degree? By defining the variables, you will be able to more easily search your directory.

Ultimately, you will want to create your own media directory. In doing so, create the listing in a way that best reflects your media efforts. For example, if you deal almost exclusively with business news, you'll want to create a list that includes business media in print, television, radio and online (websites and blogs). Add to the basics of each listing the pertinent information you've gathered: name/email/phone numbers of journalists with whom you most closely work; key topics for that outlet; deadlines for submission of materials, special editions, opportunities to provide business experts on news and/or business shows; and so forth.

Matching Your Story to the Media

Analyzing all the factors related to each medium will help determine where to send your message. One story idea may not appeal to all media, whether hard or soft news. Quarterly sales results, for example, are considered hard news, but figures and percentages should be seen to be best understood. Newspapers and magazine may have the space to run this material but a television assignment editor probably will decide the information does not warrant the effort it takes to create graphics well suited to television. Radio editors have no means of conveying visual information and may decide the material would require too much explanation in an already crowded newscast.

Conversely, a story idea about a picnic for disabled children may get excellent response from television because of its visual capability, no response from radio because of lack of imagery capabilities, and mild response from print media because of the amount of space needed to create empathy with the project through feature writing or still photography. The key, of course, is to carefully determine which medium should be connected with which piece of material.

Even if all your efforts fail for getting your material on mainstream media, make sure that you post your story, photos and videos on the news page of your organization's website. You can post as much material and as many images as you like, providing your followers with a complete story.

Clearly, determining what news is — and isn't — and where news should be directed involves more than just writing a release and posting it to every medium in your area. Careful analysis of the information itself and the media to which it should be directed will help you achieve your media goals.

CHAPTER THREE

TOOLS OF THE TRADE

From ANRs to White Papers

The tool kit list for media relations professionals hasn't changed much over the years, but the delivery and research systems are dramatically improved, expanded and more efficient. In this chapter, we review these tools and show how they can be used to do the best job of getting your message to the right audience in the right way at the right time and through the right media.

Audio News Releases (ANRs)

An audio news release is exactly what it sounds like (pun intended): a news release prepared for the ear — for radio. This audio version of a news release used to be called an "actuality"; now, the "actuality" is a part of the ANR, known as a sound bite. A typical 60-second audio news release will have an introduction, two or three succinctly written sound bites and then a closer or recap of the main message.

Just like a video news release (VNR), the ANR is generally produced and distributed online through a vendor that has a good track record knowing the industry and selecting the right placements based on your selected targeted audiences, message, time lines and other variables. The key to developing a successful ANR is having "newsworthy information about a timely issue, upcoming event or interesting news feature."[1]

Other key features for a successful ANR include: using only stories that can be told in 60 seconds; knowing your target audiences; selecting the right voice for the ANR; and accepting that ANRs are difficult to measure for overall effectiveness.

Backgrounder

A company/organization backgrounder is a summary of your organization's history and a status report on your current condition. While much of the backgrounder will include institutional history (when the organization was created, the types of services/programs it provides, the names of its key executives, where it is located, what audiences it serves, etc.), the important part to most reporters will be business basics. These include the latest financial report, data on market growth and service, number of employees, historical background and names/titles of company leadership. Financial and business reporters often use backgrounders when they are covering a story about the company or organization.

Make sure your backgrounder is easy to find on your company website by placing it under several headers.

Briefings

Sometimes a topic may be too complex or too broad to handle in a single news release or even a news conference. In this case, you may want to consider briefing key journalists and/or editors before an announcement. The briefing allows time for detailed explanations about a new economic plan, consolidation of services and programs, proposed rate hikes, or similar topics.

The briefing can take place in person and/or with a tele- and/or videoconference. The purpose is to help journalists better inform their audiences about the upcoming announcement. You'll want to cover the issue from the beginning (history), the current status and/or scope of the issue, how this issue can/will affect the public and your company's role in this process.

Blogs

Organizations use blogs to communicate with customers, clients, memberships and even parishes. Perhaps most important, companies can use blogs to build lasting relationships with those audiences so vital to the company's or organization's success.

"When bloggers represent an organization, they must fully disclose both who they are and the nature of their relationship with the organization. Good blogs are informative, informal and frequently updated. They include links to other information sources."[2] An organization's blog should address many aspects of the organization such as: leadership, finances, community outreach, stockholders, workforce adjustments, and the latest company statistics.

As a media relations practitioner, you need to be on top of blogs that are posted about your company or organization — know who is saying what and why, and decide if you should respond.

Make sure your company's blog is easily accessible to customers, clients, employees and other audiences. Examples of highly rated company blogs include Coca-Cola at www.coca-colaconversations.com and Southwest Airlines at www.blogsouthwest.com.

Editorial Board Visits

At least once a year, you and your CEO, CFO, a key subject-matter expert or some other company leader need to visit the editorial boards of the media you use most and that cover you the most. These visits are not intended to result in stories (although that can happen). Rather, they are used to update the editorial board on the status of your organization, provide a general look at the plans for the year ahead or even give a heads-up on some upcoming challenge. Not all media have editorial boards, but they may respond positively to your request for a visit with the creation of one for a special reason or occasion.

The protocol is simple: Your CEO, or subject-matter expert, gives a brief presentation and then sits back to answer questions. The result: a better relationship with the media and a better understanding of what makes your organization tick.

The Wisconsin Tobacco Prevention & Control Program posted a media tip on its website to help members build relationships with local media. Their advice included:

- **Who should attend?** Limit the number of people to no more than three.

- **Come with a plan.** What is the primary purpose for the visit?

- **Listen carefully.** Let the editor speak; listen carefully to what the editor is saying and asking.

- **Know what you're going to say.** Be prepared to discuss your issue knowledgeably and concisely.

- **Leave behind fact sheets.** Leave-behinds are a great way to help them understand issues.

- **End with an ask.** Would the paper consider publishing a guest column on the topic?[3]

FAQs

In preparing for any major announcement or event, anticipating post-crises questions, or even issuing a simple release, you can best be served by preparing frequently asked questions (FAQs) before issuing that release or announcement. These questions will most likely be asked by the media or financial analysts or shareholders or neighbors or community leaders or political officials.

Anticipating their questions — and getting agreed-upon answers — will make your post-release life much easier. Don't stop with the basic five Ws and the H (who, what, when, where, why and how); go further into cause and effect.

In advance of the event or announcement, share these frequently asked questions with other members of the public relations team and officers of the organization.

Feature Releases

An often overlooked tool is the news feature or feature release, a hybrid piece that combines the essence of news and the style of feature writing. News features are pieces written about aspects of your business or organization that are interesting, informative and entertaining, but they are not necessarily "must have" news.

These features can describe jobs or behind-the-scenes "how to" operations or focus on one employee or volunteer. Neighborhood newspapers and locally based magazines often are interested in features because they seldom have the staff to research and write their own features. Also, weekly or monthly publications cannot compete with immediate, hard-hitting news, and features fill much of their editorial space with nontimely material.

Dr. Anthony Curtis, a professor of mass communication at the University of North Carolina, Pembroke, has broad media experience that includes newspapers, magazines, broadcast, books, public relations, advertising and online. He highlights popular types of feature stories:

- "Human Interest ... that discusses issues through the experiences of another.
- "Profiles ... that reveals an individual's character and lifestyle.
- "How-to ... helps people learn by telling them how to do something.
- "Historical Features ... commemorate important dates in history or turning points in our social, political and cultural development.
- "Seasonal Themes ... address matters at specific times of the year.
- "Behind the Scenes ... views of unusual occupations, issues and events"[4]

Keep in mind that feature stories aren't just for print media. Broadcast journalists and newscasters use human interest stories, seasonal items as well as profiles and humorous items to round out their programs.

Interviews

The interview, whether individual or at a news conference, is a highly successful tool. However, its sophistication calls for serious study and preparation. Chapter 5, "Spokespersons: Training and Briefing Them for Their Role," provides the material you need to conduct a successful interview.

Letters to the Editor

A letter (hard copy or email) to the editor should not be written every time a minor error, misquote or suspected bias appears in the publication or on its website. A letter to the editor to clarify a serious inaccuracy is welcome, for journalists are as concerned with accuracy and professionalism as you are. On the other hand, a letter written out of spite or over a minor error comes across as petulant and naïve, and is treated accordingly. As with op-ed pieces, letters to the editor should be used judiciously.

These letters are generally in response to specific articles in the publication and can be used to clarify a point or refute one. Letters can also be used to try to create interest in a subject that has not been covered by the media. Your letter should state the situation, give the background and offer a solution to the problem or a change.

Dr. Tom Seekins and Dr. Stephen B. Fawcett are heavily involved in community health promotion and development issues. Following their guidelines will increase the odds of your letter being published:

- Tell why you are writing the letter — state the problem or issue that concerns you.
- Tell why this is important — how it affects you or others.
- Praise or criticize what someone has said or done about the issue.
- Tell why this is good or bad.
- State your opinion about what should be done.
- Make a general recommendation.
- Sign the letter; address and mail.[5]

Letters also must be signed before being considered for publication. To make sure the editor and the intended audience understand that the issue is of serious concern to your organization, have the letter signed by the CEO, if possible. This is a stamp of credibility an editor would find difficult to ignore.

There is no guarantee your letter will be used, nor is there a guarantee that the letter, if published, will appear in a timely manner. Finally, there is no conclusive way to provide — to yourself or your organization — evidence that the letter accomplished anything.

News Conferences

Not all news announcements from your organization need — or deserve — a news conference. You must be judicious in how you use reporters' time and for what purpose, whether that conference is live at your business or all online. Regardless of the method of transmitting your news, you should pay the most attention to the news itself and the value it should have with the media. So, before calling for a news conference — virtual or in real time — take a look at these guidelines:

- Make sure your proposed announcement is worth the time and effort needed to produce a virtual and/or real-time news conference. Ask yourself some questions:

  1. Is this announcement something that will have significant impact on the reading/viewing/listening audience? Examples: natural disaster updates, dramatic change in company leadership.

  2. Is this a major product announcement? You can only *announce* a product once; after that, you promote and publicize the product.

  3. Is this a complex issue that cannot be explained with a release or on the company website? Does the issue demand a forum so that reporters can ask questions? Is the issue better discussed during a news briefing?

  4. Does the occasion involve a new chief executive officer, football coach, celebrity or head of state from whom the media would want quotes?

- Always consider whether you can adequately give the information to the media via some other method, such as a news release, online through Skype or some other link, telephone call, email, briefing or editorial board meeting, before calling a news conference.

- If you decide to conduct a news conference, you need to bargain for all the time and support you can get. A major product announcement should come only when all the parties are ready to deal with the questions and demands that will result from the announcement, such as product orders, requests for information and product/service demonstrations.

The logistics of a news conference are critically important:

Location. A news conference does not have to be held in a hotel ballroom. Journalists will go to where the conference is, if the event is worthy of the time and effort. A product announcement could be held in the manufacturing facility, laboratory, warehouse or trade conference site. A medical announcement could be made at a hospital or laboratory. Announcements introducing new leadership should be made at the business, university, government or not-for-profit location.

Wherever you hold the conference, make sure it meets the needs of the journalists. There should be plenty of room for the cameras as well as chairs for the reporters. Make sure any power needs are met as well as any special lighting needs. Check the acoustics so that, if you have to, you can help set up microphones for better coverage.

Online/e-conference. A news conference online can be easier on the pocketbook and easier on reporters' time. Instead of providing space in a facility, you create space on the Internet by setting up a special website just for the conference. Instead of giving directions to an in-person conference, you give out the URL for the website where you have incorporated streaming video. Instead of making copies of releases and supporting material, you load the information onto the company/organization website for easy access and quick links.

Your online conference can be audio-only or include live video and automatic graphics. You can also archive the conference for future reference and follow-up.

A key benefit in having online or e-conferences is being able to include your global journalists and/or presenters.

Timing. With media operating globally 24/7/365, the timing of a news conference no longer has to dictated by time of day or day of week. Consideration still needs to be given to your primary media and their schedules, but national or global conferences, especially if they are online or globally live, can occur at any time.

Notification. For an in-person or online news conference, notify the media several days in advance, and remind them once. Your notification should show the importance of the conference to their audience(s).

Protocol. For any news conference, greet reporters when they arrive or log in. For in-person conferences, show reporters and crews where to sit and/or set up equipment; for online conferences, have a preset list of procedures, agenda and links for information.

Start the news conference on time. Just as your speakers have other commitments, so do journalists. Stay within the specified amount of time for presentations and don't let the question-and-answer period linger beyond the point where questions become sparse or irrelevant.

Finally, thank all attendees for coming and participating. Don't assume they know how grateful you are for their appearance.

Available material. The material you provide the media before or after the conference is critically important. Online and print news kit information should include only essential items such as the primary news release, supporting material (fact sheets, FAQs, time line, etc.). Include photographs only if they are essential to the news announcement, such as a product photo or mug shot of the new officer. Additionally, provide reporters with the link to your company news site where these photos — and others — reside.

Online material can be extensive but don't overload the online attendee with too many hyperlinks, Web page references, attached photos or graphics or other materials.

For television, you can electronically send your video of the news conference and/or refer TV reporters to the proper location on your website. If you have an audio of the news conference, or even just a few actualities from the conference, send them electronically to the radio station(s) and/or place them on the company website.

Create your news kit to fit the occasion, with CDs, DVDs or USB flash drives that include photos, sound bites, bios, time lines and other materials that support the announcement.

News Releases

Of the many ways to get into the media, the most commonly known and the most often misused is the news release. An editor's

"Delete" button is always in use to clear out news releases that aren't useable.

Most releases are not different or special, according to editors, who cite horror stories of grammatical and typographical mistakes; out-of-date mailing lists; lack of a local angle; missing information; an abundance of meaningless management commentary; and information that is out of date, too long, contains indecipherable corporate jargon, is sent to the wrong media outlet, and contains bad grammar and/or punctuation.

News releases are not designed to take the place of a reporter. Instead, a news release is a for-your-information memorandum to an editor. A release simply acquaints an editor or journalist with the basic facts of a potential story, just as a memo would. The editor can then decide if the proposed story warrants attention; if so, a reporter is assigned to gather more information and rewrite the material to fit the format of the print or Internet publication, or radio or television broadcast.

The idea behind the news release is to get editors to read the release — a difficult task when editors are bombarded with emails, faxes and pieces of paper thinly disguised as news. Just as a memorandum should be short and to the point, so, too, should a news release. Additionally, there are some prerequisites:

1. **Have some news to report!** Unfortunately, the definition of news is not always the one we want to hear: *News is whatever the editor says it is.* So, it's critical for you to know the audience you want/need to reach and attempt to reach them through the right medium. If you don't, the editor you approach will decide that your information isn't news.

2. **Pay attention to the Ws.** Which of these is most important: Who? What? When? Where? Why? How? And don't forget the sixth W: Who cares? Answering each of these will help you determine if you have real news and also the best way to position it.

3. **Leave the fluff at home.** A news release is not an advertisement, nor is it a marketing piece. Adjectives and adverbs should be used wisely and well so that the core of the news release is clear to the editor. "To be a successful news release writer, you must focus intensely on what journalists like (and what they dislike) in news stories.[6]

There also are basic components to a news or feature release:

1. **The name of the organization.** Whether the news release is on paper, in an email, posted on the news page of your organization's website or faxed, it is essential to use your company/organization letterhead. The name tells the recipient the source of the release and gives credibility to the information.

2. **Contact name, numbers and addresses.** At the top of the release should be the name of the person to call/email for additional information. All pertinent contact information (telephone numbers for office, cell, home, pager, fax) should be listed (don't forget the area code or an "800" listing) as well as an email address. The media do not operate in a uniform nine-to-five day; even if they did, they are not all in the same time zone or the same country, so they need all this contact information in order to reach you. Place your contact name, email address and telephone number on each page/screen of your news release.

3. **A headline or subject line.** This piece of information gives the editor a capsule phrase summing up the essence of the release. The headline tells the reader if this is something that needs to be attended to right away or if it can wait. For email releases, you may want a subject line that pulls strong visual attention. "A good headline includes local interest and summarizes the story's main point. Whenever gracefully and logically possible, mention your organization's name or product in the headline."[7]

4. **A release time.** This information, also at the top of the release, says when the information can be published, broadcast or posted. It can read: "Release upon receipt" or "Release immediately" or "Release Friday, December 16, 20__." A word of caution: Do not embargo information unless it is required. Editors know that embargoes on stories about a company open house are coy attempts at making the information seem more important than it is. There are times when embargoes must be honored; editors know and respect those times.

5. **A date.** Include the date you are issuing the release; repeat the date in the release instead of using "today."

6. **An ending.** Of course a release ends but, editors, copyreaders and reporters are accustomed to looking for a -30- or ### mark to say that the release is ended. Otherwise, a release that comes close to the bottom of the page or screen could be misconstrued as only part of a longer story.

Those are the components of a release — the building blocks, as it were. Of equal importance are types of news releases, what the release says and how it says it.

Types of News Releases

- **General news.** Announce a general news item to create interest and earn exposure for the company or organization issuing the release. Example headline: *"ABC Company Wins Customer Service Award Three Years in a Row."*

- **Launch.** Create buzz around the launch of a company website, campaign or initiative. Example: *"The launch of ABC Company's Campaign for Education Concludes with National Teacher's Day."*

- **Product.** Give details and specs for a new product, and accompany with photos whenever possible. A product news release can also relate to a product recall, or a new or upgraded product version. Example headline: *"New Software Application by ABC Company Available in August."*

- **Executive or staff announcement.** Announce staff changes, especially in upper management or at the executive level, and include biographical information and photos. Example headline: *"Vice President of Operations Named at ABC Company."*

- **Expert positioning.** Showcase a company or organization's individuals as go-to experts for the media. Or focus on a report, statistics or results to show expertise of the company as a whole on certain topics or industry trends. Example headline: *"ABC Company's Vice President of Operations, Abby Brown, Talks Logistics within the Ever-Changing Software World."*

- **Event.** Outline the who, what, when, where and why of an event with the goal that the media will talk about it and/or attend themselves. Example headline: *"ABC Company's Annual Golf Tournament for Local Schools to Take Place on Friday, June 7."*[8]

What the Release Says and How It Says It

- **Follow an accepted journalist style of writing.** Get a copy of the latest edition of the "Associated Press Stylebook and Libel Manual" and use it! It is especially important to use this text (or a similar one) as new words, social media and new definitions and usages are challenging even the best of writers.

- **Go easy on the length.** There are no hard and fast rules about the length of a release; however, two typewritten pages, double-spaced, or one screen, also double-spaced, is considered the appropriate length. If your release is several pages or screens long, you may wish to consider either breaking it up into several releases, each dealing with a specific topic, or issuing a short release with a longer fact sheet accompanying it.

- **Avoid breaks.** It makes for easier reading if you do not split words at the end of a line or split a sentence at the bottom of a page or screen. Write "more" at the bottom of page 1 of the release to indicate there is a second page or screen. With online releases, make sure recipients can tell when the copy stops by using -30- or ###.

- **Clear Writing.** Writing a release in corporate jargon, legalese or lazy language makes as much sense as preparing a release in Mandarin and sending it to people who speak only English. Why? As a business executive once cautioned writers: "I have used lawyer-talk out of what seemed to me to be necessary care for accuracy and safety. And it comes out the other end as a credibility gap." *Keep it simple, keep it factual, keep it error free.*

- **Remember the pyramid.** The inverted pyramid style of writing is not used just for news releases. The same style applies in writing personal letters, memos, briefs, white papers and other material. *The important information or the conclusion is given first*, with less important information following and, finally, the least important information at the end. Using the pyramid calls for a bit of taste, however. Although the lead paragraph of a news release carries the most important information, it is not necessary to cram the answers to "Who? What? Where? When? Why? How?" into that first sentence or paragraph.

- **Adjectives are dangerous.** Avoid the temptation to use superlatives in describing your organization's latest product, service or new executive. Such superlatives may not be legally defensible, and the use of adjectival claims hints that the writer had nothing of substance to say about the subject so threw in the adjectives for lack of anything else. An adjective can be used in a direct quote, however.

- **Make it local.** One of the key criteria listed for what sells a release to an editor is the local angle or "hook" the release has. For example, a national release announcing a new product can be localized by telling when the product will be available in your area, through what outlet and at what suggested retail price. Or, you may want to issue a release announcing when a new medical treatment, just recently announced, will be available at your hospital.

- **Attribute the news to a person, not a company or organization.** Information is more credible if "John Doe, product manager of XYZ Co., today demonstrated the company's newest product" than if "XYZ Co. today announced it has a new widget."

- **Indent the paragraphs.** This will make it easier for the editor to read your material.

- **Select a good typeface.** This is true for hard copy and online versions of a release. You want the recipient to be able to read your material easily. For electronic versions, consider increasing the type size by 1 or 2 points and boldfacing the copy for easier reading.

- **Think twice before using a CEO quote.** Your CEO doesn't talk the way you make him/her sound in that quote. If you can't create a quote that is reflective of the way your CEO talks and sounds — as well as a quote that actually says something — then don't use a quote.

- **Check your checklist.** Before issuing any news release, ask yourself these questions:

  — Is this topic *timely*? Does it have new information?

  — Will this information *affect the heart, mind or pocketbook* of the reader or viewer?

  — Is this story *unique* — is it different from other stories on this topic?

  — Does this story involve a *well-known* politician, local business leader or celebrity?

  — Is this story *local* — geographically close to our readers/viewers?

  — Is there a *conflict* between people and other forces such as the government, nature, science, education?

News Releases: Electronic, Broadcast and Social Media

Aren't all releases prepared in the same way?

No. Not when one is for print, one is for radio, one is for television and one is for social media. Both television and radio have special characteristics that require you to handle your release differently than if the release is going to print media. Primarily, the differences are: Radio news is written for the listener, print is written for the reader, while television and online news is prepared for the viewer/ listener/reader.

Guidelines for Electronic News Releases

Of key importance is the format of an electronic news release. The authors of "Strategic Writing in Public Relations" offer these guidelines:

- In electronic news releases, the all-important subject line precedes the headings.
- Your headline should be a newspaper style headline.
- Single-space the text of email news releases. Do not indent paragraphs, instead, include a blank line between paragraphs. Just as with a paper news release, be concise: An email news release should be long enough to tell the story — and no longer.
- After the text of an email news release — but before the contact information — type -30- or ###. Include a blank line between the end of the text and that symbol.[9]

A good way to test your release before issuing it is to read it as though it were going to be read directly from your computer screen. Then, read the release aloud to someone and ask him/her to retell the message. You may find a disparity between what you said and what was heard.

Guidelines for Broadcast News Releases

Radio and TV broadcast style is not difficult. A few easy-to-remember rules will help you through:

- Along with the release time, put down a "read time" such as :15 for 15 seconds, :30 for 30 seconds.
- Because the material is written for time and not space, everything must be spelled out. There can be no abbreviations, no numerals, and all names or unusual words should be spelled phonetically.

- Sentences are short, with descriptive words before rather than after nouns. For example: "The thirty-nine-year-old vice president" instead of "the vice president, 39."
- The inverted pyramid rule is not used in broadcast journalism. In print and on the computer screen, a reader can go back and reread a paragraph or a sentence; a radio listener cannot go back. Radio and television journalism is linear. In broadcast style, the release tells what the news is, then tells it again, and then tells it again. Here's an example:

The Smith and Jones Company will build a new production plant here in Anytown. The new facility will employ one thousand people to make the latest in electronic devices. Smith and Jones' newest operation will be ready in two years, cost five million dollars and add several thousand dollars a year to the local tax base.

The fact that there will be a new facility was repeated three times to the listener.

- For television and online media, remember that the paramount consideration is visual appeal and interest. Your story about new ways to invest money for greater return sounds great and reads better but looks cluttered and confusing with its charts, graphs and a "talking head" expert. However, it's perfect for an electronic version such as your company's news website, because you have the luxury of linking to, or showing, all the supporting material. In contrast, a story about a white-water rafting trip for children who have never been out of a city reads like many other stories, sounds like a bunch of squealing children against a backdrop of rushing water but *looks* exciting, enticing and dangerous.
- The value of VNRs for a global operation is great. One message, in several languages, with country/culture appropriate visuals, is immensely beneficial to locally based media.

Guidelines for Social Media News Releases

Dick Martin, business writer and former executive vice president of public relations, employee communications and brand management at AT&T, shares sound advice on preparing social media news releases:

- Make sure news releases are online friendly.
- Include social media handles in contact information (e.g. Skype username, Twitter handle, Facebook address, etc.).

- Follow headline with bullet-list of key points in release. Keep them short so they can be easily Tweeted.
- Provide links to high-resolution graphics, multimedia material (videos, audio files, etc.), and other information such as white papers, executive bios, case histories, customer endorsements, etc.
- Make sure the most important links in the body of the release are spelled out in full, not merely hot-linked words. (For example: www.CompanyHomePage.com, not "Home Page" with embedded link.)
- Include RSS feed to relevant company blogs and news feeds.[10]

Op-Ed Pieces

Named for its position in a newspaper or magazine — opposite the editorial page — the op-ed piece provides a place for your organization to offer an opinion on a subject or perhaps take a stand on a current issue. Criteria for an op-ed piece may vary by publication or website, but there are some generally-accepted rules:

- On average, op-ed pieces are run every day in newspapers, from one article to two or three, with a length of no more than 750 words. Editors agree that op-ed pieces must have two things: time lines and creativity. The best advice is to read the intended publication to see how other op-eds have been written, and to contact the publication or website editor for specifics on the length of the piece, submission criteria, etc.
- Some editors like to discuss the idea for an op-ed piece ahead of time; others prefer to receive the op-ed with a cover letter.
- Topics for op-ed pieces are numerous, ranging from opinions and analysis of public affairs, politics, education and law to journalism, health care, religion, the military, science and lifestyles. Topics can be of a local, national or international nature. They must, however, be relevant and timely to something that is happening now or is about to happen. Some editors prefer to avoid extremely controversial issues, feeling that adversary journalism is a never-ending ping-pong game. Others encourage publication of diverse opinions on sensitive issues.
- Op-ed pieces are not to be used as a vendetta against some alleged injustice to your organization. Nor are they the forum for challenging

a reporter's techniques. The key word in considering op-ed pieces is *judicious*. Just define the issue you wish to discuss or state the problem as you see it, provide whatever background or history is needed and then suggest ways the situation can be changed or improved.

John McLain of McLain Communications notes that the best way to gain credible visibility for a client is to have that company's CEO submit an op-ed piece to a major publication and have it published. His checklist for success includes:

- Focus tightly on one issue or idea.

- Express your opinion, then base it on factual, researched or first-hand information.

- Be timely, controversial, but not outrageous. Be the voice of reason.

- Have a clear editorial viewpoint — come down hard on one side of the issue. Don't equivocate.

- Appeal to the average reader.[11]

Photographs and Videos

Digital photography, especially cell phone photography, has allowed anyone to become a news photographer. With a click on your cell phone and a hit on the "send" button, you can provide any media outlet with the latest images of a public event, a grand opening or a disaster. Don't let the technology get in the way of good images, however. The media don't want to be bombarded with thousands of unusable photos. Before deciding to be your own photographer or hiring a photographer for your event, check with the media you intend to reach to find out what their criteria and policies are for receiving digital images.

Stand-alone photos that tell a story are still useful to and desired by many media, especially those publications that must rely on outside photographers. The key to making sure your stand-alone photo has a chance of being posted or printed is to make sure the image itself isn't a cliché. Neither the famous "grip and grin" photo of two people shaking hands nor the forever familiar image of a woman sitting at a computer tells a story. Staged images are almost always trite and contrived.

While you can easily send photos to the media, giving them access to your online photo gallery will go a long way to building a better relationship with the media. Develop a gallery with the media in mind, developing categories such as "Facilities," "Company Officers," "Product Line," "Community Outreach Programs" and other areas of interest.

Videos are still highly valued for television and online media such as YouTube. The advent of cell phones and other mobile devices with video capability turned owners of these devices into instant on-site reporters. Images taken immediately after — or even during — a significant event such as a shooting at a school- or a tour-bus crash often help authorities with their investigation.

In a more proactive way, video clips are valued by the television and online media for positive stories: robotic-based manufacturing, the "amazing animal trick" video at the conclusion of the newscast, the sighting of a famous personality, military homecomings or the ground-breaking for a new hospital.

How to Pitch a Story

Having a good story or story idea is great. Getting it sold to a reporter, editor or webmaster can be challenging. They receive hundreds of releases and pitches daily and haven't the time or energy to review every pitch or email or listen to every telephone call. Author Katya Andresen says that reporters ask three questions when they evaluate a pitch: Why now? Why is this news? Who cares?[12]

To make sure you can answer those questions, you can follow the advice of Gordon Deal, host of "The Wall Street Journal This Morning," who says he looks for three specific elements in an email pitch:

1. **The pitch has to be unique.** "You have to think, 'Is our story going to improve the life or business of someone else? How unique and relevant is it?'"

2. **The pitch has to be concise.** "The subject line is your ticket in. It's got to capture the idea and the readers' interest in just a handful of words. The sooner you can make your point, the better."

3. **The pitch has to be timely.** "We're looking for people to provide relevance."[13]

Additional key advice learned from interviews with editors and conversations with other media relations professionals include:

• Find out how the appropriate editor likes to receive story ideas (phone call, email, etc.).

- Be able to explain your basic story outcome in no more than two sentences and the story idea in one to two paragraphs.
- Don't overplay your idea by making it the "greatest story of the year" — leave the embellishments in your computer.
- Be able to set up interviews immediately.
- Contact the editor only in the way and at the time she/he wants to hear from you.

"I'm not going to get to that second or third paragraph. The sooner you can make your point, the better. Use the subject line to open (the) door, and the first two or three sentences to kick the door open and get invited in."[14]

Public Service Announcements

If you work for a nonprofit organization, you might be able to take advantage of free airtime for public service announcements (PSAs) — persuasive messages aired without charge by radio and television outlets. PSAs were created after World War II by the Advertising Council and designed to influence a (then) radio audience on the country's needs during the war (blood drives). After the war, the Ad Council focused on other, national issues such as highway safety.

Broadcast media are not mandated to air a specific number of PSAs, but they must broadcast "in the public interest." The National Association of Broadcasters indicates their member stations contribute an estimated $10 billion in free time for various causes.[15]

It is impossible for stations to use all the PSAs that come to them, so you need to increase your chances of success by following some of these tips:

1. **Quality over quantity.** Because your PSA is competing with professional advertisements, you need to make sure you PSA matches that quality. It is better to have one well-done PSA that gets airtime than 10 PSAs that don't.
2. **Focus, focus, focus.** Instead of assuming that you need to contact all radio and TV stations in your area, investigate to see which ones reach your intended audience.
3. **Stop, look and listen.** Contact the public affairs or community affairs directors at your targeted stations. They can tell you if pub-

lic service time is available and in what format/forms they want your PSA.

4. **Don't get greedy.** All nonprofit organizations want to have 60-second PSAs aired, but the call for free airtime continues to increase as more and more not-for-profits have major fundraising events. Why not offer 10-, 15-, 20- and 30-second versions of your PSA and be grateful for what you receive?

5. **One at a time.** Your PSA should have only one message such as "Give blood" or "Get your flu shot" or "Donate a toy to a child."

6. **Redundancy.** When you submit an audio or video PSA, always include a printed script — just in case.

7. **Be nice.** Always thank the station for airing your PSA, even if it was at 3 a.m. If you're courteous and provide quality PSAs, you might get your PSA moved to prime time.

8. **Keep it simple.** Using flashy images or hip-hop music can often overtake the message.

9. **Celebrity spokesperson?** Use caution when selecting a celebrity for your PSA. Make sure she/he truly endorses your cause and can withstand public scrutiny.

10. **Call to action.** Make sure you ask the viewing/listening audience to do something: Donate time, money, goods. Include a toll-free number and web address to help them do so.

11. **Language barriers.** If creating a PSA for a Hispanic or other non-English audience, create the PSA in that language, don't just translate the English version.

12. **Timing.** Don't ask to post PSAs during heavy advertising times, such as just prior to elections or major holidays.

Satellite Media Tours

Satellite media tours (SMTs) have been around since the 1980s but have changed dramatically from their original stiff, talking-head format to upbeat, intricate and highly successful interactive events. SMTs often are used by corporations to provide one of their subject-matter experts to local television news broadcasts for either taped or live interviews and/or in conjunction with a video news release.

On a broader scope, SMTs have proven invaluable when making a company executive or spokesperson available for several interviews on multiple media outlets that span the country or the globe, in a short period of time. Mike Periu of Proximo International, LLC notes that "A well-planned SMT can consist of 20 to 30 interviews over a six-hour period." His recommendations for a successful SMT include:

• Have a clear message.

• Teach, don't sell.

• Work with a great production planner.

• Pick the right spokesperson

• Pitch reporter and producers well in advance.[16]

You can be creative with the set and spokesperson by having the individual demonstrate a product or engaging in some other activity.

Keys to success for SMTs include having a well-trained media spokesperson, celebrity or subject-matter expert; offering information to the audience via a website or other format; testing all link-ups before the sessions begin; and carefully selecting the right day and the right time of day (or night) to match your audiences' viewing preferences.

Standby Statements and Qs and As

If you know of an event or situation that could break into the news suddenly, there are two pieces of information you want to prepare as quickly as possible: a standby statement and a list of anticipated questions with appropriate and approved answers.

A standby statement gives the basic facts of the situation and your organization's position. It is not a news release. Rather, it is a piece the spokesperson (the media relations person or whoever is speaking publicly on this issue for your organization) will use to answer reporters' questions. Writing in the Public Relations Strategist, Joan Gladstone says, "Preparing a standby statement helps you avoid that gut-wrenching feeling that your organization has lost control of the story. Instead you will feel calm and confident knowing that you've influenced the all-important first story before it goes viral."[17]

The second piece, Qs and As, is a list of expected questions a reporter would ask you and the answers you will give if he/she does. Again, this is not material to be handed out to reporters or to be published in general employee information media. It is for use only to help you reply to questions from reporters.

To be valuable tools, the standby statement and Qs and As should meet three basic criteria:

1 They should answer the five Ws and the H that every reporter asks: Who, what, when, where, why and how?

2. They should — as much as possible — be cleared in advance so that you are ready to move quickly to answer a reporter's questions. The media's business is news, and a reporter's time frame is usually this minute/an hour/today. To get your organization's position in a story, you must meet the reporter's deadline. And you are almost always better off when your organization's view is included. In the absence of information, people "fill in" — often with disastrous results.

3. They should not be words that are cast in stone. The spokesperson should talk from the material — not read it like a script.

Subject-Matter Experts

Subject-matter experts (SMEs) can be a media relations person's best friend. It's one thing to announce a new service, product or discovery; it's another to have an expert who can answer all the questions about it. Reporters don't want to talk to the people who announce the Nobel Laureate in Economics; they want to talk to the recipient. You should create an internal list of SMEs whom you can readily contact to help you respond to media calls. Or you may want to develop a media guide of SMEs from your organization and let the media call them directly. Or, use a combination of the two.

The media guide of experts should list the topic areas on which they speak, their full name, title and contact information, what languages they speak, their availability for print, online, TV and/or radio. It is critical also to note if they can be available on very short notice for immediate response. Example: An expert on volcanoes would be needed when the volcano erupts, not three days later.

SMEs also make good authors for op-ed pieces, editorials and special reports, but you may have to work with them to convert their expertise language into average-reader language. Make sure you SMEs are well trained in how to work with all media. Depending on the subject matter, you may promote SMEs from local to global media outlets.

Katie McMurray, who runs media campaigns for major events and business owners, has devised a way to verify if selected persons qualify as a subject-matter expert. You can use these questions to test their ability:

- Have you recently spoken at conferences or given any public talks?
- Have you recently published a book?
- Do you lead workshops?
- Do you write a popular industry blog; are you considered an opinion-maker?
- Are you on any industry bodies or major boards?
- Have you been a consultant to government or major companies?
- Who are your clients? Do you have testimonials from any well-known clients?
- Have you received international acknowledgement or worked in international markets?
- Have you recently won an award?[18]

Video News Releases (VNRs)

As communication technology has continually improved, the use of video news releases (VNRs) has helped many organizations better represent themselves to the public via online and television media, but they also have pushed many small companies and organizations out of the running because of costs associated with creating a professional VNR. Introduced in the early 1980s, VNRs have helped both profit and not-for-profit organizations promote their products/services, influence or shape public opinion, announce upcoming events, or introduce a new CEO.

Often the VNR is not identified to the viewing audience as a company- or nonprofit-supplied item, which leads opponents of VNRs to describe the tool as a "propaganda technique." Regardless of the outcome of the debate, VNRs have developed a key role for many media relations programs to reach targeted audiences with unfiltered — but still newsworthy — material. VNRs also provide a benefit to slimmed-down newsrooms across the globe. Some key guidelines for VNR production and use include:

- Always use a professional firm to produce your VNR; this is not the time to try out your amateur videography.
- Make sure you have a solid news story, preferably in the venerable areas of health, safety, finance or education.
- Make sure all facts are correct.
- If using a subject-matter expert, make sure she/he is well trained for a television appearance.
- Test your proposed story idea with local TV reporters to see if the topic is of interest.
- Double-check the demographics of your intended audience to make sure the VNR will be attractive to them.
- Tie VNR distribution to national months, such as "cancer awareness."
- Discuss the pros and cons of asking for "guaranteed placement" from your VNR vendor, as that may dramatically reduce the number of outlets.
- Accept that valid measures of VNR effectiveness don't exist yet.

White Papers

Also known as "position papers," white papers explore in depth and in detail an issue facing your company or organization and offer proposed stances to those issues. White papers can advocate for a certain solution or position on a particular issue or problem. Typically, white papers are comprised of four major sections:

1. **Situation or background.** This section provides a context for whatever position will be proposed. Describing the situation or providing the background should be concise, factual and free of rhetoric. Point out problems but don't digress from the main issue.

2. **Possible solutions.** There is no limit to the number of possible solutions that might be cited in this section, although commonsense dictates that too many choices make it difficult to make clear decision. Each possible solution must be presented with pros and cons in order to assist the decision makers.

3. **Position.** From the possible solutions will come a simply stated, well-written, fact-based position. The position statement should be supported with hard data, examples and other elements that will

distinguish this recommended position from all the possible solutions that were presented earlier.

4. **Next steps.** The position statement needs action items to bring it to life. This most often involves media interviews on key television talk shows, some op-ed pieces in influential publications and online news media, speeches to the right audiences and a meeting with editorial boards.

White papers are especially useful in assisting a management team determine how, and if, to take a stand on a sensitive or explosive issue.

Summary

The media relations tool kit is filled with items you can use every day and others that are needed only on special occasions. The trick is to become familiar with multiple tools, select the best to reach your targeted audience, and understand the criteria for using each tool in real-world situations.

CHAPTER FOUR

REPORTERS

Helping Them Meet Their Objectives

A blogger wrote of his participation in a 2012 conference in Singapore and Hong Kong called Media Relations in the Digital Age: "It's interesting that an entire conference would be devoted to this subject as you might ask yourself, media relations is media relations whatever type of age you are in, let alone a digital age," wrote Andy Oliver on the LEWIS PR blog, LEWIS 360, which covers communications trends and social media. "It's clear that the core skills and approaches are untainted by the digital age. A fundamental part of our work remains unchanged, building relationships with those we want to pitch stories to."[1]

We totally agree. The emphasis in a media relations program has been and always should be on the *relations* aspect — working to build long-term relationships with the people who cover your organization. Good media contacts proliferate once they are established. They are built only gradually, based on a variety of contacts over time, and strengthened by experiences that foster growing knowledge and respect. They require you to have a thorough understanding of how traditional and social media operate on a day-to-day basis.

In the end, though, this is a people-to-people business. A media relations person deals with writers, editors, bloggers, producers and photographers — not with newspapers, television stations, radio microphones and websites. Knowing how to assist reporters and their supporting cast can make a positive difference in establishing and maintaining long-term relationships with the media — the only kind to have.

Traditional Media Demand Short Deadlines

The first thing to appreciate is that a reporter's life is controlled by very short deadlines. In every publication there is a "news hole" that must be filled by a predetermined time when the printing presses start running. Today's news must appear in today's paper — and tonight's news in tomorrow morning's editions. The reporter's success is determined by how often his/her stories appear in the paper, rather than being "killed" (newspaper jargon is "spiked" — the story was written but never printed) by the editor. If the reporter writes a particularly interesting or difficult story, he/she will be rewarded with a byline — the reporter's name appears over the story as the writer.

 The first rule of media relations: Meet the reporter's deadline.

There are equivalent (and usually, more stringent) deadlines for electronic journalism. With demand increasing for frequent up-to-the-minute reports, radio stations' past practice of carrying news only on the half-hour or hour and TV stations' traditional two newscasts an evening are obsolete. Numerous spot reports, lengthier regular newscasts, all-news programming on radio and increasing 24-hour news formats on television have replaced them.

Because of the transitory nature of the airwaves, radio stations in particular usually repeat news reports several times a day. The broadcast journalist thus must meet more numerous and tighter deadlines than his/her print colleagues. Similar to publication bylines, the television journalist's reward for an unusually fine reporting job will be an appearance on camera to report the story in person; for a radio reporter it will be an actuality where the interview is carried on the air, rather than having the anchorperson or announcer read the story.

Social Media Demand Even Shorter Deadlines

Social media provide stiff competition for traditional media because of their ability to transmit news virtually instantaneously. In response, most traditional media have created their own blogs and websites to get their news stories out 24/7. They also use social networking services like Facebook and Twitter to facilitate real-time conversations between their reporters and their audience.

Technology has created access to and demand for immediate information and frequent updates. Decisions relating to the media now must be made in an accelerated time frame with little lag time between actions and reporting. Posting your news promptly on your organization's website is essential so that a communications channel you control accurately reflects your positions at all times.

Two fundamental desires motivate the reporter: (1) to report the story well — that is, accurately and in an attention-getting way, and (2) to write it quickly. To have the story used, the reporter must meet both requirements; to meet those demands *you* must meet the *same* criteria. A cogent statement or key fact is useless to the reporter today if it was needed as an integral part of yesterday's news story.

The first rule of good media relations, then, is to meet the reporter's deadline. This usually demands a same-day response — frequently within hours, sometimes on the spot. That is easy to accept in theory. In practice, it often demands the time and authority to stop other work and devote your full attention to the reporter's needs until they are met. If clearances are necessary before you can release certain information, you also will need the authority to ask others to break their routine to support you.

Ask the reporter's deadline each time you get a request for information.

Learn the Media's Deadlines

In those cases where media covering your organization do not operate 24/7, you should know their regular and late-breaking news deadlines. For social media, you need to be available 24/7.

Some traditional newspapers have editions going to different areas; if you are interested in a rural or suburban location, that edition may close a couple of hours earlier than the final or city edition. Technology has shortened deadlines, as publications now travel via satellite rather than truck. Feature and Sunday sections close several hours, or even days, earlier. Weekly newspapers, which normally publish on Wednesdays or Thursdays, often have deadlines a few days before press day, except for major news stories.

The news desk of any publication or station will be happy to tell you its deadlines. You might want to phone those with whom you deal regularly and then make a list of the deadlines that you can keep handy when you are working with reporters.

In any case, it is a good habit to ask a reporter what his/her deadline is each time you get a request for information. This ensures there are no misunderstandings between the reporter and you and lets the reporter know you appreciate the importance of media deadlines. Over time you will come to a position of mutual understanding regarding deadlines: The reporter will learn he/she can trust you to do everything possible to meet deadlines, even the extremely short-fuse ones. In return, you will expect him/her not to "cry wolf" by creating artificial deadlines — and to give you additional time when the story is of a softer nature not demanding "today" treatment or when the request is for a large amount of information not readily available. If you cannot get all the information promptly, it is wise to call the reporter to give an update on progress in case the story is being held for your input.

Be mindful, however, to avoid phoning or emailing a reporter around deadline time with anything but critical information related to that day's news. He/she will be busy writing, talking with the editor, checking last-minute facts or working with the art department on the caption for a photograph to accompany the story — in short, getting the news out. There will be no time for chatting about a possible future feature story.

Attention to deadlines also is critical when you are issuing a news release or planning a news conference, because the hour you set almost inevitably favors some media over others. If you issue your news in the early morning, for example, noon and evening TV newscasts, as well as blogs and news websites, will be first to carry the news. If you schedule the release in the late afternoon you are giving the opportunity for first coverage to the morning paper and making it difficult for the evening TV news to carry anything but a brief mention unless your news is worthy of live on-air coverage. As one TV reporter rebuked a reluctant spokesperson who asked for an on-camera interview to be delayed: "It's the six o'clock news, sir — not the six-forty. They'll be on the air with or without us."

Announcement Timing Is Important

The media in your particular area — and your analysis of the importance of each publication, station or blog to your organization — should determine the time you schedule news releases and news conferences. A good general rule of thumb is always to set news events and schedule release times to meet your weekly's deadline if it is the leading newspaper in your community or the key trade publication in your industry. Blogs, radio stations and all-news broadcasts report just about instantaneously and repeat the news frequently, so the time you choose is not that critical to them.

 Good media relations often begin — not end — with the news release.

Another consideration: New research provides data that breaks down the digital consumer's daily news cycle. According to an article in The New York Times, the "Arc of the Day" study showed that in the morning readers want bite-sized headlines and news flashes. In the afternoon, they often are at a desktop computer and want to see a slide show or video, and at night they have time to engage in a deeper article.[2]

To meet regulatory requirements relative to release of material information if your organization is a publicly held company, always issue your news releases via news wires. Also, make sure they are posted on your company's website immediately. In addition, if you work for a public company, coordinate timing closely with your colleagues in investor relations to be sure financial analysts covering your industry get prompt and personal distribution of your news, since reporters almost always contact them for comments on a major announcement. You can issue the same news release to the financial community, but change the contact information from you as the media relations professional to the person responsible for investor relations. If you are hosting a news conference, plan a separate but identical briefing for analysts immediately before or right after the news conference.

Remember that good relations with the media often begin — not end — with a news release. You must allow reporters enough time to contact others about your story, ask questions of you and them, gather visuals to illustrate it, and generally adapt or rewrite your release to meet the interests of their particular audience.

Saturday can be a good day for nonprofit organizations to issue news releases or to hold news events. They will be covered on that evening's television news and in the next day's papers. In spite of online editions, reading the bulging Sunday paper remains a daylong activity in many homes. Also, you are less likely to have to compete for space with news of business, the stock market, the economy, the government and other organizations that operate on Monday-to-Friday schedules.

Take Advantage of Technology

Email your news release to ensure that you get your news to all the media at the same time, so you do not inadvertently help one reporter "scoop" another. Send it to a particular reporter's or editor's personal email address (as opposed to the media outlet's general address) so it quickly gets to the right person. Also, if you are sending more than one copy to the same news outlet — for example, one to the assignment editor and one to the reporter who recently wrote a story about your organization—it is a courtesy to add a brief note that says so.

Most reporters check the Internet while writing their stories, especially broad-based pieces. Make sure your organization's website is updated regularly and can be easily accessed so that reporters who regularly cover your organization and industry come to consider it a current, useful and trusted source. You will know you have a good site based on return visits, length of stay and degree of interactivity.

Be sure your website is registered on various key search engines (contact your information technology specialists if you need help). Reporters will not visit your site if they cannot get in and get out easily, especially when they are on deadline. Also, stream your news conferences and special media events on your website for reporters who cannot attend in person.

Similarly, you need to learn how to write for the Web. "News Reporting and Writing, Tenth Edition" by The Missouri Group[3] and "Strategic Writing: Multimedia Writing for Public Relations, Advertising and More, Second Edition" by Charles Marsh, David W. Guth and Bonnie Poovey Short[4] are excellent sources.

Tips re Posting Videos on YouTube

Follow these guidelines to take advantage of YouTube for posting everything from slide shows with motion to videos:[5]

- You can't upload a file longer than 10 minutes or greater than two gigabytes in size.
- H.264 (MPEG4) is the preferred file format.
- Pick a descriptive title.
- Fill out the description box to make your video easier to find via a search.
- Fill out the tags (key words), again so people can find your video more easily via a search.
- Pick a category, then designate your video as public or private.

For more details: http://www.google.com/support/youtube/

Advance Alerts Can Be Helpful

Even if you intend to keep the nature of the news a secret until the announcement event, an email advising a reporter who you think might want advance notice to keep the calendar clear on a certain day is the kind of thoughtfulness that helps build long-term relationships.

A follow-up email the day before the news event is a way to remind busy journalists of your event and to inquire if each journalist will attend so you get an idea of how many people will be present.

But do not overdo it by pestering them for a definite RSVP. Even if an editor has assigned a news team to your event, late-breaking news could result in a last-minute change in the team's availability.

Accessibility Is Paramount

Make sure key journalists covering your organization have your cell phone number. Put procedures in place to ensure the accessibility of key spokespersons 24/7. They will be useful on a regular basis — and even more so in an emergency. When you are making instant history, there is no substitute for routine procedures everyone is aware of. They are crucial whether you work for a large, multinational corporation or staff a two-person office for a trade association.

It also is extremely helpful to keep up-to-date information about your company on your laptop, mobile device or as hard copies in your home files. Descriptive and factual information about your organization — the annual report, most recent financial results, latest organization chart, product catalogues, price lists and all your recent news releases — should be readily available at all hours to save you the embarrassment of appearing ignorant of basic facts about your organization.

Sometimes the topics are too complex for you to feel comfortable handling without counsel from the person responsible for a specific area. Or sometimes a reporter wants to attribute the response to a high-level executive in your organization. Just as you want reporters to know how to get in touch with you after normal office hours, you also need the residence, cell and vacation phone numbers of key executives or experts in your organization.

You also want those executives to be able to call you day or night if an emergency arises that might result in media attention — for example, an injury to a worker in one of your facilities, a plane crash involving your employees, the death of a top executive or a bomb scare. If your organization does not have an emergency contact list, take the initiative to create one, distributing copies to all employees involved and keeping it up to date. Make sure whoever answers your office's main phone line has a copy of the list — and be certain all news media calls are referred to you or your staff first, day or night.

Case Study: Accessibility Pays Off

We frequently have been grateful that reporters have our cell and home numbers—and we in turn have the cell and home numbers of other key company people around the country. A significant case in point occurred during a period when the recessionary economy was having a big impact on AT&T. The phone rang at home at 9:40 p.m. It was a reporter from The Wall Street Journal.

He also was at home, and he was very apologetic. "I'm sorry to call so late," he said, "but some 'loony tune' just called the news desk in New York with a silly rumor that you are laying off 10,000 people and closing a factory. I know that's crazy, but they wanted me to check it out to see if there is any truth to it." As is the case with most rumors, there was a grain of truth behind it. But this reporter knew our business well, so he immediately recognized that, at a minimum, the alleged news tip was highly exaggerated. Like the good reporter he was, he called to check.

I (Carole) told him that indeed there was going to be a large layoff — 1,200 people, not 10,000 — that the news would be told to employees beginning with the night shift in about an hour, and that the company would make a public announcement the next morning. I gave him more details and then asked the key question: Did he plan to write a story? He said yes.

If you read The Wall Street Journal the next morning you might have seen a small five- or six-inch story on the layoff. But what you did not know about was the flurry of behind-the-scenes activity—both late that night and early the next morning—that the reporter caused. First and most important were the calls that night to our local public relations manager in the community where the layoff would take place. We had to alert him to the leak, to the fact that there would be a story in the next day's Wall Street Journal, and we had to coordinate answers to some more of the reporter's questions. Also, we wanted to let the PR manager and his staff know they had to move up their planned announcement to their local media. After all, it would not do much for their media relations if the local reporters read about a local layoff in the national Wall Street Journal before they heard it from our media relations people there.

Also very important were our other offices and plants around the country. We got a quick alert out to them very early the next morning, so they would be prepared to respond promptly and professionally to the inevitable calls they would get from reporters wanting to know the local situation. And we in New York got ready to handle the queries from other national publications, wire services and the trade press that we knew the Journal story would (and did) cause.

It was a busy time. But there was never any confusion or concern about what to do or how to contact the right people, even in the middle of the night. The advance planning for the layoff announcement was also vital to the calm manner with which we were able to react to the leak.

Know Journalists' Interests

Another important element in your relationship with reporters who cover your organization should be your knowledge of their special interests — either because the medium they work for has assigned them to the area or because they have a personal interest in the topic. Reading the bylined articles, columns or posts of a reporter, listening to or viewing the programs of a radio or TV commentator and visiting the blogs of journalists can give you insight into subjects on which they seem to enjoy working.

If you have an idea for a feature, try to interest a reporter or a producer in doing it, rather than writing it yourself. Similarly, if you have a good photo opportunity, call the local paper or TV station assignment editor in the hope you can get a photographer or camera crew to come out. Publications and stations are more likely to use material they have spent their people's time developing. But never talk to two journalists in competing beats or media about the same story idea or event — for example, to both the education and business reporters about a high school job fair — without telling each that you have done so.

Don't Let Failure Get You Down

Don't be oversensitive to failure when you contact a reporter with a news or feature idea. We unsuccessfully tried to interest the Associated Press national photo editor in two pictures before scoring with a unique shot of AT&T's "computer on a chip" paired with a South American fire ant. That placement resulted in the company's high-technology message appearing in more than 200 publications, with a circulation of more than 20 million in the United States and internationally.

After several turndowns, twice at The Reader's Digest Association our news releases were picked up in Ann Landers' column, which is syndicated to 1,200 newspapers with 90 million readers in the United States and Canada. One offered free reprints of a Reader's Digest article about a home eye test, resulting in 35,000 reprint requests within six weeks. The other offered consumers hints on how to detect sweepstakes fraud.

So keep trying and you'll find ways to succeed. A few strikeouts are worth it if you hit home runs like that every so often. Conversely, you should do some research before you suggest story or photo ideas. It would be embarrassing to recommend a program on controlling health care costs to a talk show host, only to be told he/she covered that topic last month.

If a newspaper is part of a chain like Gannett or Copley, which has a news syndicate, or heads its own news service like the Chicago Tribune or The New York Times, this association will also have some effect on an editor. He/she is likely to be more interested in stories affecting people or communities beyond the paper's circulation boundaries. (Incidentally, reporters frequently are not told if their stories are picked up by the member papers when they have gone out over the news service or syndicate. Thus, you often can build some personal rapport with a reporter by forwarding copies of his/her stories that your clipping service picks up — especially if they are from out of state or out of country.)

No matter how friendly and frequent your contacts with particular reporters, always remember that they have a job to do and their number-one priority is getting the story, not being your friend.

Digital cameras have made it very easy to take, store, retrieve and transmit high-quality photos to the media to illustrate your news stories or features. But there are a few cautions to keep in mind:

- Format for newspapers, magazines and high gloss-publications should be 300 dpi. Size it at approximately 6 inches wide. The 300 dpi requirement means that the camera was set at 5 megapixels or more when the photo was taken — not digitally enhanced later to fill in the dots.

- Format for blogs, Internet journals, forums and other social media can be 72 dpi. Size it also at approximately 6 inches wide.

Over the years we have had problems with publicity photos of musicians from around the world who were performing in our Music in the Mountains classical music festival in Southwest Colorado. They — and frequently their publicists — claimed that the photos on their websites were 300 dpi when they were not. Sometimes they were as low as 20 or 30 dpi — totally unusable by the print media. Also, with so many artists and other trendy people wearing black these days, too much black in the photo can be a problem for black and white publications. Choose photos with good contrast and not too much black.

- When posting photos on your website for use by the media, be sure to size them at 300 dpi (they can always be made smaller by the user) — or at both 300 and 72 dpi.

- Similarly, if you are scanning conventional photographic images for media use, be sure to start with a good quality picture and set your scanner at a high pixel count to ensure acceptable image quality.

Use Internal Media as Tools

If they carry news of more than employees' bowling scores and the company picnic, internal publications can be effective, inexpensive tools to keep reporters informed about your organization and stimulate interest in feature stories, particularly in smaller communities.

Some organizations include local media people on their mailing list for each issue of the company's employee newspaper or magazine. Others prefer to send only selected issues, with a business card or a note drawing the reporter's attention to a particular feature they think would be of interest.

In any case, it is useful to remember that what we take for granted because we deal with it every day can be perceived as news by the local media — particularly if there is a local or human-interest angle. Employees participating in blood drives, features on carpools and other employee energy conservation ideas, suggestion program winners, tutoring activities with disadvantaged children, family nights at the plant, safety and handicraft fairs — all these are feature ideas we have placed with local media. Post the best of these features on your website and they may attract the attention of browsing reporters.

 Employee media may provide feature story ideas.

It is important for your management to recognize that once an issue is covered in your organization's employee media it can easily get out beyond the boundaries of your company. If a story appears internally, you should consider it externally released as well.

You also want to have handy a standard package of materials about your organization to use as a backgrounder for reporters doing stories on your company for the first time. The annual report and a fact sheet with a list of your key products and services as well as vital statistics such as number of employees, location and unique features of your office(s) are some of the basics. You can then add other information, depending on the thrust of the reporter's story. A fact sheet should be brief (preferably no more than a page), current and carry the date on which it was prepared.

Your latest background pieces and fact sheet should be posted on your organization's website — and updated regularly. Be aware, though, that once on the Internet the information can be accessed by those other than journalists. So don't, for example, provide your home number on the website unless you are willing to receive a multitude of calls from various stakeholders.

Know How to Handle Requests for Information

If you have an active media relations program, you are likely to get calls from reporters almost every day. They may want more information on a news release you issued. They could be working on a feature story. Or they might want your organization's view on a major news event of the day. There are, of course, myriad ways in which you can respond to these queries. But one overall rule applies: If you or your organization initiated interest in the topic, you cannot duck or evade reporters' follow-up calls; if a reporter originated the contact, your response will be dictated by your company's objectives, policy and style.

As you are working with people in your organization to write and clear a news release, you want to remind them that most publications, stations and online media will have their reporters call with additional questions rather than use the release as is. That is why you should include anticipated media questions and agreed-upon answers as a routine step in your advance planning and production of any news release. You want to ensure that your internal contacts are available in person or by phone on the day you issue the release You should also brief whoever answers your phone on the proper and rapid way to handle the calls your news release generates. Reporters' normal sense of urgency quickly turns to panic as their deadline approaches. Believe it or not, media relations people actually have issued news releases and then turned off their phone to go into all-day meetings, leaving their secretaries to fend off frustrated reporters seeking additional information.

 Anticipate media follow-up questions. Be a reporter's reporter.

On occasion reporters may call you to get your organization's reaction to significant external news events, such as the announcement of a proposed change in international trade or federal tax policy or a local rezoning application for a new industrial park. Whether you are requested to comment on such public issues probably depends on the prominence of your organization within your community. Whether you choose to respond often depends on the personal style and civic involvement of your organization's top leaders. You should know or help establish your organization's general policy for handling such broad requests so that you can promptly deal with this type of media request. Follow your local media's coverage of such key issues so you can anticipate and plan responses for the types of calls you may get.

When a reporter asks for information, do not hesitate to ask enough questions yourself so you have a full understanding of the story on which the reporter is working. If you take a single, isolated question, you may not be able to give your expert enough to go on to offer a competent answer. Or the answer to the question, when relayed to the reporter, may lead to another question and you will have to go through the process all over again. Get a good grasp of what the reporter wants. Try to visualize the whole while you are talking about the parts. Anticipate follow-up questions. Be a reporter's reporter.

What you want to avoid is being perceived as a person intent on withholding information or, just as bad, a person who does not have access to information. There still remains a certain skepticism — and sometimes definite hostility — from journalists toward media relations people. The only way to overcome this is to prove yourself every time you work with the media. If reporters continually call other sources within your organization, it is because either they do not know you or you are not meeting their information needs.

Never give away an "exclusive." If a reporter develops a feature article on his/her own and comes to you for information, or is approaching a news story from a unique angle, the reporter's right to exclusive use of that story must be respected. If two reporters seek the same information, however, tell each person that the other is working on the story. Doing this may avoid a subsequent conflict and help keep you from being caught in the middle.

Test Your Knowledge and Level of Involvement

There is no sin in admitting you do not know an answer; simply say you will check it out and get back to the reporter. But if that happens very often, you should ask yourself some soul-searching questions:

- **Am I doing everything I can to keep current on company activities and industry trends?** Should I expand my regular reading or use of the Internet or blogs? Make a point of keeping in touch with people in other departments? Be more active in trade associations or professional societies?

- **Am I anticipating news and activities** in my organization that would cause media interest, and preparing to handle news queries in advance?

75

- **Am I — or is my boss — included in planning meetings and in the decision-making process?** Do I have the confidence of top management so that I am among the first to know what is happening within the organization? (If not, you cannot be considered a spokesperson; at best you may be a well-qualified reference point.)

A media relations practitioner complained that he was left out of the planning and media announcement activities when his company was awarded a major government contract in a bid against a Japanese company. But even superficial questioning made it clear he had not kept up with the current highly sensitive government negotiations on lowering foreign import barriers. Nor was he aware of the various congressional committees conducting hearings on international trade at the time. And he was not a regular reader of the trade press or visitor to blogs and websites covering his industry. So he was not up-to-date on what his company's competitors were doing or how the industry viewed his company. Little wonder his boss — and perhaps his CEO — felt that he was not qualified to be the company's spokesperson on this critical subject.

Master the Fundamentals

Equally important is that you master the basics of your craft. That means you need to be an outstanding writer and editor in all media—especially news releases and other media relations materials such as photographs, videos and news conference remarks.

Watch to see what happens to your news releases. You soon will accept the fact that reporters will rewrite your carefully crafted sentences. If they do it too often, however, you might ask yourself why. Are you following the accepted rules of press style? ("The Associated Press Stylebook" is a must as a constant reference source.) Or maybe the reporter's sentences are shorter and easier to understand than yours.

You can get informal feedback by reading blogs, online comments and letters to the editor that your news generates. While these responses are not scientific surveys, following the text threads helps you understand what people are thinking and communicating about your organization. They also may serve as an early alert to unrest among your stakeholders.

Another excellent feedback vehicle is a media audit — hiring an outside research firm to ask reporters covering your organization (and those who do not whom you would like to attract) how you are meeting their needs. If your question list is short and to the point, most journalists are willing to answer because upgrading your skills and services helps them as well as you. This also is a good opportunity to get their views on the usefulness of your website.

A reporter is more likely to get your position right — or indeed, use your statement at all — if it is a "quotable quote." Similarly, the public is more likely to agree with you if you speak in terms they can understand. It is critical that news releases and statements be written in plain English—not in "legalese," and not in corporate gobbledygook.

Know How to Handle Requests for Interviews

Many times reporters call an organization asking to interview someone about a particular topic. The natural reaction is to find an appropriate person for the reporter to talk to — sometimes a time-consuming and unnecessary effort. Often, a better response is for you as the media relations spokesperson to be the primary source of information for the majority of requests, reserving the interview for occasions when another person is needed for his/her particular expertise or when the medium warrants an executive-level spokesperson. Having you serve as the primary spokesperson enables your organization to respond more promptly and more efficiently to reporter inquiries.

 You should be the primary spokesperson for routine interviews.

When you determine that an interview with someone else in your organization is the best approach, however, there are a number of steps to follow. This section deals with deciding the forum for the interview and with your support of the reporter in an interview situation.

Decide if the Interview Will Occur Via Electronic Devices or in Person

The first decision is whether the interview will take place on the phone, via Skype, via video conference or in person. It is a good idea to ask the preference of the reporter. Radio or international reporters normally want a telephone, Skype or video conference interview because it is so much faster. Print or TV reporters' choices are usually determined by their deadlines and distance from your interviewee.

Equally important is your input in the decision, which should be based on your knowledge of the spokesperson's desires and abilities in different situations and your evaluation of the significance of this particular medium and story. If your spokesperson is just one of many sources to be interviewed for a broad survey article in a newspaper or magazine, a phone conversation is probably most appropriate. Telephone interviews are usually shorter because there is less tendency to chitchat. If your organization is to be featured more prominently in the piece, a face-to-face interview might be best. Your spokesperson is more likely to come across as a personable human being rather than a faceless bureaucrat. But you will want to exert some control over the length of the interview to prevent it from dragging on unnecessarily.

Brief the Reporter Ahead of Time

Regardless of which medium is chosen, you should provide the reporter with a biography immediately — and a photograph, if one is readily available — of your spokesperson. This also is the time to point out how the spokesperson prefers to be addressed, in person and in print; the correct spelling and pronunciation of the name; and the person's particular field of expertise vis-à-vis the story the reporter is writing. In advance of the interview, email this information, along with other appropriate background information on your organization and the subject of the proposed story. The more you communicate with and provide background to reporters before the interview, the more they are likely to get the facts straight and not waste their and your spokesperson's time with basic "How does it work?" or "What does your company do?" questions.

Tips for the Phone or Skype Interview

If you have agreed on a phone or Skype interview, let the reporter know you will initiate the call at the agreed-upon time. Elementary as this may sound, double-check the time if different time zones are involved — especially with an international reporter. Because many people object to speakerphones, it is sometimes best to set up a three-way conference call. After introducing the reporter to the spokesperson, let the reporter take control of the conversation.

Meanwhile, you should take extensive notes of the conversation — verbatim if you can write or type quickly enough. Neatness definitely does not count when it comes to these notes. The only person who needs to be able to read them is you, so that you can check a quote for the reporter if you are requested to do so or check the finished article for accuracy. If you are dealing with a particularly sensitive subject, however, you may want to write up your notes, including key questions and answers, in case there are questions later about what was said or done.

As you monitor the conversation, make notations to yourself if you feel points need clarifying or further data need to be gathered. Resist the urge to intrude on the conversation unless your spokesperson is stumbling and clearly needs you to help with an explanation, or is in danger of giving out proprietary or other sensitive information in response to the reporter's questioning or prodding.

Tips for the Face-to-Face Interview

If the interview is in person, arrange to meet with the reporter a few minutes in advance. You can get acquainted briefly if you do not already know the reporter and review plans before you go to your spokesperson's office. After making introductions you should again avoid getting involved very deeply in the conversation. Take notes and offer counsel and follow-up where necessary. You also should politely end the interview if the reporter's questions become repetitious or if the time has extended much longer than originally scheduled to a point you feel to be inappropriate. It is rare for an interview to be profitable to both parties if it lasts longer than an hour.

If a photographer is accompanying the reporter for shots of the interview, there should not be much extra coordination required on your part beyond alerting your spokesperson. But if you know the photographer wants to tour your operation to take additional photographs, and you have the staff available, you should stay with the reporter and get someone else to work with the photographer to handle critical details like photo permissions and safety and security concerns.

If a TV station wants to send in a camera crew, make sure the room where the interview will take place does not have too many windows or a busy or strongly patterned background. Most TV people consider the video far more important than what is heard, so it is worth your while to think through ways to meet the crew's needs, thus helping you get your key messages across in picture form.

After the Interview

After the interview, get the reporter's deadline for any additional data you agreed to provide and ask for a general idea when the story is expected to run. (No reporter can promise a publication or airdate. That prerogative is reserved for editors and producers.) Offer to check quotes or verify any additional information needed as the article or report is being written — a polite way of letting the reporter know you care about accuracy but understand you cannot see the copy in advance.

Once the story appears, if you feel it was a difficult subject handled well or written in a particularly interesting way, you should not hesitate to tell the reporter either in an email or the next time you meet in person. Like all of us, reporters are interested in honest feedback and flattered by positive reactions.

If the story does not appear within the expected time frame, it is acceptable to email the reporter to check the status — as long as you make clear your understanding that editors make these decisions, not reporters. If the story is "spiked," you must not protest too strongly. It is fine to inquire as to the reason, because you may learn from it and thus improve your media relations in the future. Most stories do not appear for the simple reason that news is plentiful, space and/or time is limited and editors must make judgments on the value of each story.

Know How to Handle Errors

The news media have neither the space nor the time to tell the "whole truth." Rather, they carry the part their reporters and editors think important. Under pressures of time and without detailed knowledge of your business, it is inevitable that errors will occasionally appear in news coverage of your organization. Your behavior in this situation will have a major effect on your long-term relationship with the reporter and the publication, station or blog. A natural first reaction is to demand a correction or write a letter to the editor. More appropriately, that should be a last resort. The publication of a retraction, like a double-edged sword, cuts both ways. Errors read only once may be quickly forgotten; read twice, they may stick despite the attempt at correction.

 It's okay to write a letter to the editor — but in most cases, don't send it.

Whether the error occurred in print or in electronic — analog or digital — media, when you contact the reporter, photographer or editor about the error, you will be dealing with a person who is likely to be defensive if she/he wrote or photographed the offending piece, or protective if she/he is the editor to whom the person reports.

Here, in order of consideration and seriousness, is what you should do if there is an error in coverage of your organization:

1. **Acknowledge the difference between what is *incorrect* and what you *don't like* about a story.** List the factual errors; chances are they are few in number and not all that major. Next, list what you didn't like about the story: the headline; placement of the article in the publication; the 10-second sound bite; the position of your quotes; quotes from your competitors. Make sure you're considering asking for a correction only of important factual errors.

2. **In most cases, be charitable and do nothing.** Most errors are insignificant in the context of the overall story. They probably will not be noticed by any but the most knowledgeable in the audience who would recognize that there was a mistake. Sometimes it is the headline that offends. Remember that it is written not by the reporter but by a copy editor under incredible space constraints to summarize the essence of the story in a few words. With such brevity can come obscurity or misplaced emphasis. You should not blame the reporter, who probably did not see the headline before the piece was published or aired.

3. **In some cases, email the reporter to request the item be corrected for the record.** Your purpose here is to politely alert the reporter to the error and ensure it is not repeated in future coverage of your organization. An example of a mistake warranting a correction in the file copy might be a misstatement about your product line, the size of your facility, a name misspelling or an incorrect title of one of your executives.

4. **In a few cases you will want to write a letter to the editor.** This can be done when you feel your position was not adequately stated — as compared to being incorrectly stated — and you want to use the forum of the Letters to the Editor column to expand exposure of your views. It might also be appropriate when you want to publicly and formally correct the record, as when your organization is involved in a legal or regulatory action.

5. **In rare cases you will be justified in asking the publication to print a correction.** This would occur, for example, if facts such as your earnings or other pertinent financial information affecting the price of your stock were misquoted. Sometimes a correction can be masked by the addition of updated information, such as including the time and place of the funeral in a second article when the person's name was misspelled in the initial obituary.

6. **In no case should you contact competing media to tell them of the incident and to ask them to set the record straight.** Ethical journalists will not participate in vendettas against their colleagues.

7. **If the error is critical, post the correction on your organization's website.** Remember that two-edged sword, though; many people now will see something they may never have noticed before, so be sure it is worth it.

There are differences, however, when you are dealing with the broadcast media instead of print. If you phone a radio station to complain of an error in coverage, the station often will ask to tape you over the phone then and there, giving your side of the story. They may use your comments live if the program is a talk show with a call-in format. Or they may save the tape for a later broadcast. Before you call, be prepared by writing down two or three key points to help you state your position coherently. A TV station could also ask you to appear on a guest editorial giving your position if the issue is controversial or of long-term significance to your community.

You, of course, must be even more swift in correcting any errors that go out in your materials to the media. No matter how careful you are, one day an error is going to slip through your checking and proofreading system. If it is only a typographical error, there is no need to issue a correction and a second release — although you will want to redouble your proofing efforts because even small errors reflect on your professionalism and desire for accuracy. If it is a significant mistake—a name misspelled or a factual error — you must *immediately* issue an email alert to everyone you sent the release to and offer a quick apology. Attach a revised news release with the words "corrected version" prominently written on the top of the first page.

Know When to Say No

In spite of the fact that your major role for reporters is to facilitate access to data and people in your organization, there are legitimate reasons for you to refuse to divulge information. There is, however, no occasion we have ever run across when it is appropriate for you or any spokesperson for your organization to reply to a media query with a terse "No comment." That is a desperate response, almost guaranteed to make the reporter search for other sources for the facts.

Tell the reporter *why* you can't discuss an issue in much detail — because it involves proprietary information that will divulge too much to your competitors, because as a matter of policy the company does not discuss rumors in the marketplace that might have an effect on the price of your stock, because you are in the midst of sensitive labor negotiations and want to keep discussion going around the bargaining table rather than on the pages of the daily newspaper, because it is too soon after the accident to know what actually happened, because your lawyers have not yet received the court papers, or whatever is appropriate. The reporter then has a legitimate quote from you, and you have released no inappropriate information to the public. Both the media's and your organization's objectives have been met.

When you are citing proprietary information as the reason for refusing to disclose information, be sure it really *is* proprietary. One spokesperson refused to acknowledge the existence of a new manufacturing process, only to have the reporter pull out a company brochure with a photo of the alleged secret equipment. On another occasion a media relations person refused to divulge the salary of the CEO and president until caustically reminded by a reporter that the figures were carried in the company's legally required public filings with the Securities and Exchange Commission as well as the annual meeting mailing to shareowners.

On some occasions **you may decide to say no to a reporter's request because of the time it would take to gather the information** or because the information is not available in the form the reporter wishes. These types of requests often come from editors or reporters seeking to localize news of a regional or national company by breaking down sales or financial information at the local manufacturing or sales office level. In these cases, a simple statement that it would be too costly for your organization to keep statistics in every conceivable format, combined with an offer of the information in a somewhat different arrangement, is usually sufficient. Also, many companies do not release sales and profit information for local business units, subsidiaries or product lines for competitive reasons. Reporters will understand if you cite that rationale.

There also are situations **when reporters do not seem to know what they want.** When we come upon a writer whose questions and requests for information indicate a time-consuming fishing expedition rather than a story, we sometimes politely but firmly ask him/her to determine the focus of the piece, at which time we will be pleased to help.

In extreme cases you might want to decline a guest appearance on a TV interview or radio talk show. For example, **if the host has a record of asking loaded questions** or espousing positions contrary to your organization, industry or issue, your appearance may provide a target for complaints rather than a forum for discussion. If a fellow guest is a bitter ex-employee complaining of working conditions, your appearance could tend to legitimize the complaint and hurt relationships with your current employees. If the theme of the coverage is not supportive of your objectives — the favorite recipes of a woman candidate for senator, for example — a polite no may also be the best response. Sometimes no publicity is better than frivolous publicity.

Another case where saying "no" is totally appropriate would be **requests to appear on controversial programs** with hosts who care more for ratings than facts. In these situations both the format and the mood of the program are so unprofessional that your appearance would demean your organization and yourself. In the end, your research into the program, host and other guests — combined with your gut instinct — will tell you whether to say yes or no.

Other legitimate times to say no may be those rare occasions **when you cannot confirm that a freelance writer or photographer is actually on assignment** for a publication, station or blog. If you are not familiar with a person who says he/she works for the media, it is good practice to call the news desk or assignment editor of the appropriate medium to verify the assignment. The editor in charge will be happy to take your call; no publication, station or blog wants unaffiliated people posing as their staff reporters or stringers (writers in smaller markets who occasionally are assigned news stories and features for a large publication).

There may be rare situations when you or your organization have dealt with a particular reporter on several occasions and believe **he/she has such a bias or is so careless** that almost all the resultant stories have been negative or inaccurate. A businesslike but candid discussion with the reporter's editor will usually result in the assignment of another person to cover your company if your complaint is deemed valid by the editor. This is a last-resort action that should be taken only in exceptional cases when your allegations are well documented. Editors tend to be defensive of their reporters and profession, especially when criticized by the subject of an article.

Other Helpful Hints

Here are some miscellaneous hints to help you anticipate — and thus be prepared to respond promptly to — reporters' requests:

1. **Avoid sending out news releases with embargo dates.** They can be counterproductive to your organization's relations with the news media and to your objective of getting wide coverage of your news if one medium breaks the release date and scoops the others. Unless you have a very special circumstance, it is safer to plan a release time that is good for you and the most important media covering your organization and then release the news with no embargo.

2. **When you are issuing a news release on an executive's speech, keep a copy of the full text on your computer in case a reporter asks for it.** The request may be caused by the reporter's desire to rewrite or to expand on your news release. Or, the reporter may want to file the talk for use as background or source material in future stories. In any case, anticipating such requests enables you to get the speaker's agreement in advance to release the full speech — which can be annotated, if necessary, with the phrase "as prepared" or "as delivered" if there are or could be changes to the typed text. It also is a good idea to have the speaker's biography and photo posted on your website and available on a CD or USB flash drive.

3. **Documents filed with a government regulatory agency such as the Securities and Exchange Commission or at a courthouse as part of a trial automatically become part of the public record.** You can save the reporter some trouble, buy your organization goodwill and help assure that your position is accurately carried in the story by providing such filings if a reporter requests them or supplying the URL for the information online.

4. **Set up an electronic file of biographies and photographs of your organization's key officers, managers and board members.** Create a standard form to be filled out, or write up a one-page narrative including such information. Ask for the names of each person's community newspapers if you live in a large metropolitan area; sometimes news of your managers appearing in their local paper or alumni magazine means more to the family than coverage in a big city newspaper. Update the biographical data whenever there is a job change or every two years. Photos should be formal studio shots, with new ones taken every five years. You also may want to include some candid photos of your top executives. Digital photography has made it easier to supply media with the exact photographs they want, when they want them and in what format. (Also see "Cautions re Digital Photos" on page 72.)

Advice from a Weekly Newspaper Editor

If you are lucky enough to live in a small community served by a weekly newspaper, take advantage of the fact that it can be an excellent avenue for your organization's news, both in print and online. The focus of weekly newspapers is local news, sports, people and events — and they usually are extremely well read because community journalism hits close to home, literally.

Here is advice on how to get your news published in a weekly newspaper from Karl Isberg, editor of The Pagosa Springs SUN. His paper serves the small mountain town of Pagosa Springs in southwest Colorado, and it frequently sells out only days after it comes off the presses every Thursday. Like most weeklies, The SUN also has a website. Here are the paper's procedures for submissions:

• **For nonprofits.** Our policy is to give nonprofits free coverage in the community calendar as well as news articles and photos about their events.

- **For businesses.** If a business is sponsoring a fundraiser for a nonprofit, we will include the business name in the coverage because they deserve credit for their community support. But there will be no mention of products. That becomes advertising.

- **For everyone.** As a community newspaper, we publish free notices of weddings, obituaries and cards of thanks. Many times the cards of thanks will list businesses contributing to fundraising events, and that's fine as long as products are not mentioned.

- **Letters to the editor.** We are remarkably tolerant of topics people cover in their letters and the way they express themselves. We edit only for length, libel and obscenity. Our intent is to provide a forum for the widest spectrum of ideas in the community, whether or not we agree with the writer.

- **News releases.** We welcome news releases and story suggestions as long as they are local and are not ads posing as news. The purpose of a small-town newspaper is to focus on what goes on in our community. We don't print wire service or national news. We concentrate only on local events.

- **Photographs.** We welcome photos also, as long as they are newsworthy and good quality (see box on page 72). We are extremely hesitant to publish Photoshopped work, such as promotional photos where the background is eliminated, and we won't print collages on the news pages. Here's an absolute maxim: Never alter a news photo beyond minor cropping.

Remember Your Organization's Employees

Your desire to be responsive to reporters' information requests cannot supersede your responsibility to the employees of your organization. They are your best ambassadors or loudest critics, depending on how fast they get relevant information and the context in which it is received. And they are deeply influenced by what the media report about their employer.

With the Internet, there is no such thing as "local" news. A layoff in Milan can make news in Madrid; an environmental problem in London can be posted on a blog in the United States. Tweets and negative quotes from uninformed or angry employees can quickly undo an otherwise positive news media effort.

When you are making an announcement to the external media, coordinate the release time with the person responsible for internal communications so your employees do not read news of your organization in the local paper or on the Internet or hear it on a newscast before they learn of it from management. When there is an external leak ahead of the planned announcement time, you should immediately alert the employee communications person so a decision to advance the internal release can be considered. (Your colleagues should be equally considerate of you and provide advance copies of all employee communications materials so you are aware of what is covered in case they get into reporters' hands.)

Similarly, set up a close relationship with your customer service people. Be sure they have copies of your news releases, standby statements and questions and answers, so they are giving out the same information to your customers that you are to the news media. When you know media coverage affecting your organization is going to appear, alert your internal communications person. If a positive piece is expected — for example, a feature on one of your workers or an interview with your CEO — your employees will appreciate knowing in advance, especially if it is on a blog, radio or television, so they do not miss it. If a negative piece is forthcoming, you need to ensure that employees have your organization's position on the topic in case they get questions from their family, friends and customers.

Set up a high-traffic area like the cafeteria to demonstrate your publicity efforts in cyberspace and on TV. If the media coverage is significant enough, consider an advance alert via email to your organization's board of directors or trustees, key customers or contributors, and perhaps also send them an Internet link after the event.

CHAPTER FIVE

SPOKESPERSONS

Training and Briefing Them for Their Role

In the 2011 Academy Award winning film, "The King's Speech,"[1] England's King George VI is trained by a speech therapist to overcome his stammer, a speech impediment that is both uncomfortable and embarrassing for a monarch whose public speaking engagements — from worldwide radio broadcasts to ceremonial addresses — were heard by millions of people across the globe.[2]

Most spokespersons are not required to perform on such a grand scale. Nonetheless, becoming an effective spokesperson can bring accolades from within and outside the organization, and a visibility that can be good for repu-

89

tations and careers. But, as with all high-risk, high-reward situations, there can be pitfalls. When you are dealing with the media, any mistake can be a very public one. No wonder people in our organizations react with something approaching terror at the thought of a media interview, especially on a sensitive subject.

 A vital part of your job is training your organization's spokespersons.

The skills required to be an effective spokesperson can be practiced and perfected. That associate whom you admire for the apparently natural ability to speak with clarity and confidence undoubtedly is as nervous as you are. But training and experience have helped him/her to master fear — or at least mask it. A vital part of your job in media relations is your ability to be proficient enough in interview techniques and knowledgeable enough of the organization's policies and products that you can help your spokespersons prepare for news media contacts. At best this interview-techniques training should be part of an ongoing program. At a minimum it should be included as part of the routine briefing session you have with your spokesperson before any media interview.

Choosing a Spokesperson

Before discussing the support of spokespersons, it is well to step back and talk about selecting the right one. The choice is not always obvious.

The most natural candidate — the chief executive officer of your company or organization — is not always the best one. CEOs deal with broad, general, policy matters. Rarely are they involved in the nitty-gritty of the organization enough to know the details of a specific project or issue. Unless your CEO has a personal desire to be the primary spokesperson, you are better off reserving access to him/her for reporters whose article requires comments on overall policy or strategic direction.

Nor is the head of the department involved in the topic always the right person. Promotions in organizations normally are based on outstanding technical or professional knowledge. Department heads may have the ability to make a presentation at an internal meeting or to the board of directors, but this is not quite the same as being able to meet with reporters.

As the media relations person, you should become familiar with the abilities of others in your organization so you can choose the best spokesperson for each media opportunity. Here are the characteristics you are looking for:

1. **Knowledge of the topic to be discussed with the reporter.** Only with a firm grounding in the facts can anyone speak confidently and positively.

2. **An understanding of the organization's overall objectives and strategies.** There is no way every one of the reporter's questions can be anticipated. You want someone who can think quickly and be responsive to the reporter's needs without divulging proprietary information.

3. **An ability to tell and sell what he/she knows** — in everyday language and from the point of view of the reporter and the ultimate *audience.*

4. **The confidence of top management.** This person will be representing your organization to the general public. You do not want to choose someone who is not well respected by those within the organization.

5. **A desire to do the interview.** If your proposed spokesperson demurs beyond what normal modesty and apprehension would explain, you probably should drop your request. People tend to be honest with themselves; you should take heed when people believe they are poor choices for the assignment.

6. **Overall presentation style.** It is important to select someone with presence and personality. Also, your spokesperson should reflect the personality of the organization. A person wearing a three-piece suit is out of place representing a new software company. Similarly, a woman who wears a low-cut blouse and short skirt does not match the persona of a Wall Street financial institution.

SPECIAL HINT: Over time, you will notice that some of your spokespersons are better in some media than others. Once you've discovered someone who is good with audio, test him/her in front of the camera to see how he/she would perform for a VNR (Video News Release) or a TV interview. Some people with exceptional talent in the podcast booth cannot make the transition to on-camera. But others are comfortable with both. You soon will be able to establish a stable of video commentators and radio/podcast commentators — and a few who can do it all.

Preparing Your Spokesperson

Once you have determined who will be your organization's spokesperson for a particular interview, there is a great deal you can do to support him/her. The fact that many of the steps with your spokesperson parallel those you are taking with the reporter is no coincidence; thus, some sections of this chapter are pitched at you and some at the spokesperson. Indeed, your role as the bridge between the media and your organization is amply tested in an interview situation. The quality of your work will be reflected both in the resultant media coverage and in the spokesperson's response to your future requests to talk with reporters.

Immediately after you have set the appointment and determined whether the interview will be on the phone, online, on Skype or in person, you should provide your spokesperson the following information:

1. **Date, time, place and expected length of interview.** If this is a new experience for this person, state that you will attend to take notes and get any follow-up information needed by the reporter.

2. **Type of story the reporter is working on** — in-depth feature on your organization or survey piece on your industry, for example. Has the reporter's conversation already indicated a clear point of view for the story? Or is she/he doing an overview piece and searching for a local angle?

3. **What the reporter told you he/she wants from the interview** — quotes on corporate objectives, general sales plans for a new product line, the organization's opinion of a new community development plan or whatever.

4. **What you have provided the reporter.** Describe briefly what information you already have given the reporter. Include copies as attachments to the email or memo to your spokesperson or go over them in person. Your objective here is to let the spokesperson know what already has been said to the reporter so the spokesperson can expand on it rather than merely repeat it.

5. **Background on the reporter if this is the first time the spokesperson has dealt with this particular journalist.** Does the reporter

regularly write stories on your organization, or is this a first? Does she/he understand the business, or will the spokesperson have to be especially careful to explain the terminology? What has been your experience with the reporter in earlier contacts? Does she/he take notes or use an audio recorder? It is a good idea to include samples of the reporter's recent stories or posts — or suggest that the spokesperson tune in to the appropriate program if it is a TV or radio interview and you have enough advance notice.

6. **If photography is involved, any special arrangements you are making for the photographer or television crew.** Explain the set-up time required for TV production, especially if the interview is taking place in the spokesperson's office. Or arrange to move the interview to another office or location.

7. **Suggestions on the main message and one or two key points you think the spokesperson should stress in the interview.** Here is where you make your greatest contribution, not only as a media relations professional but also as a counselor to your organization.

8. **Advice on key interview techniques.** See the section, "Hints on Interview Techniques," for a full review of such advice. It is presented as a unit so that you easily can use all or part of the section when working with your spokesperson.

9. **Insist on the need to get together to review anticipated questions and possible answers before the actual interview.** This initial backgrounding is important. If the interview is two or three days hence, this preparation helps the spokesperson focus thoughts and prepare responses. If the interview is later that same day or early the next (as so frequently is the case), it provides a framework in which to operate. Your briefing session just before the interview is likely to be more concerned with content than logistics.

Prior to the Interview

Make it a routine practice to get together with the spokesperson for a briefing before the interview. Executives' calendars are crowded — but a half-hour meeting before the reporter arrives is time well spent. It gives you both an opportunity to talk about your main message, review expected questions, constructively critique proposed answers, look at alternative ways to highlight key points, and discuss the thrust of this particular journalist and article.

It is a good idea to prepare for the worst-case scenario. Talk about the questions you most hope the reporter will *not* ask, and agree on your answers. Write them down and sharpen them until you are comfortable the spokesperson is presenting your organization's case in the best possible way without being defensive. Get others' input, including legal counsel, if the issues are sensitive.

 Prepare for worst-case scenarios and practice answers to difficult questions.

You also can work out a plan to end the interview if the reporter appears to be getting long-winded or repetitive. You should remind the spokesperson to tell the reporter that follow-up information will be channeled through you. For a phone interview, alert the spokesperson not to be unnerved by a request to record the conversation or by the keyboard sounds of a computer. Indeed, it is positive feedback that the reporter's questions are being well answered, since many journalists do not take notes until they hear a newsworthy comment.

If there will be photographs, it also can be helpful to remind your spokesperson to be tolerant of what may appear to be strange requests to move objects or rearrange poses. The photographer likely is looking for ways to get an interesting picture out of what is essentially a routine setting.

During the Interview

Your role as media relations person during the interview is to make introductions and then let the reporter take over while you take notes, interjecting only if a statement needs clarifying, a number requires verifying or a promise of follow-up information should be made. If you are physically near the spokesperson during a phone interview, you might want to pass a note if you believe the person has missed an opportunity to make a key point or has made a statement that needs further explanation.

A decision to record the interview — whether or not the reporter is doing so — should be made with care. Some reporters who consider it normal for a media relations person to take notes are offended if you ask to record the session. On the other hand, if you are reluctant to honor a reporter's request not to record because a reporter or program has a reputation for distortion, you may want to insist on recording as a condition for your spokesperson to be interviewed.

Follow-up after the Interview

Your job is not over after the interview. At the same time you are following up on your obligations to the reporter, you should devote similar attention to the interviewee.

Right after the interview you should call your spokesperson with feedback — giving both your impressions (helpful for the next time) and the reporter's (whose reaction right after the interview is a good indication of the probable tone of the story). If the reporter is critical, you will want to think carefully about how much detail you pass along — and how you communicate it.

 Provide prompt feedback to your spokesperson after the interview.

If you foresee a potential problem in the resultant coverage that you cannot resolve with the reporter, go ahead and mention it. Your spokesperson would rather be alerted in advance than blindsided when the story appears. If the spokesperson did a particularly bad job, either confusing the reporter with poorly stated points or blithely releasing proprietary information, you will probably need to find a different spokesperson in the future for that area of your operation.

As soon as the story appears, check the quotations and facts for accuracy. If it is print coverage, always get a copy of the article to the interviewee in advance of wider circulation within your organization. Offer your reaction — and get the spokesperson's.

If it is radio or TV coverage, purchase a transcript or a video from those tracking firms that sell such services.

If it is on a blog, website or other social media platform, email the link to the spokesperson.

Hints on Interview Techniques

Most reporters are too sophisticated to be impressed by style over substance. Conversely, a fine position can be misunderstood if it is not presented with clarity and confidence. Interviews are not conversations — they are highly structured situations.

 Interviews are not conversations — they are highly structured situations.

Formal media interview-techniques training — especially with an outside expert — is well worth the investment. Make sure the firm you select can provide the individualized training your spokespersons need, from television appearances to telephone interviews, from in-person to online. Even if your spokespersons have experience, they can make mistakes if they get overconfident or complacent.

Here are some interview techniques that should help you do a better job when you are interviewed by a reporter.

- **Remember your objective.** Is your purpose in doing the interview merely to *inform* the reporter's audience of some event or action? Or are you attempting to *persuade* people to adopt your point of view? *Inspire* them to change their behavior? *Motivate* them to take some particular action? Your ultimate objective will have a great impact on what you say and how you say it.

- **Prepare and practice.** Mark Twain once said it takes three weeks to prepare a good ad-lib speech. Have in mind one key message that you want to get across in the finished story. Ask yourself, "If I could edit the article that will come out of this interview, what one sentence would I most like to see?" Or, "If I could write the headline, what would it say?" Well in advance of the interview, write them out. Simplify and shorten them. Practice saying them out loud so they sound natural to the ear. Perfectly proper sentences in a written text are often too formal and cumbersome when spoken aloud. Keep your key points in front of you. Then at the earliest opportunity, try to capsulize your main points in answer to an interview question.

- **Simplify, simplify, simplify.** That is your best chance to have your message break through the clutter of competing messages and options for your target audience's time and attention. It is impossible to tell everyone everything about your organization. So do not waste effort on unnecessary baggage or battles. Simplify the message and send it with consistency and clarity.

- **Place your most important points at the beginning of each response where they will be clear and isolated.** In 15 words or less, what is the essence of your message? This is especially important for broadcast interviews because journalists often are looking for a very short "sound bite." Responses like "There are three reasons for that" invite poor editing. Rather say, "Price, performance and reliability are the key factors in our decision." Try to get your main message down to 9 or 10 seconds which, sadly, are too often all a spokesperson gets when the editing is complete.

- **It is not only what you say but also how you say it that communicates.** The effective speaker is not necessarily polished and perfect. He/she is energetic, enthusiastic and direct. A forthright, enthusiastic response to a question portrays candor and confidence — in your organization, in your position, in the reporter, in yourself. Long pauses before you answer or a stiff, flat monotone indicate either a lack of conviction or a lack of interest. If the interview is being televised, this appearance of indecision and insincerity will be magnified.

- **Do not feel pressured to respond instantly to a difficult question on a complex subject.** Although we have just mentioned the possible negative effect of a pause before answering, it sometimes is appropriate to take a moment to organize your thoughts. When you are making instant history — or instant policy — you have the right to be comfortable with the way you articulate your organization's role. In a print interview you can verbalize the pause by saying something like, "I hadn't thought of it from that viewpoint before ...."

- **Think fast but talk slowly.** If the reporter is taking notes, it will help the accuracy. If you are being interviewed for broadcast — audio or video — it will help your audience's comprehension. For broadcast, however, you will want to speak a little bit faster because sound bites are getting shorter.

- **Never forget your ultimate audience.** You are talking to a reporter, but you are speaking to the people who read the publication or watch the program — your past, present and potential customers, employees, shareowners and suppliers. (If none of these audiences is being reached by the reporter's medium, you can legitimately ask why you are doing the interview.) Frame your answers from their point of view, not your organization's. For example, say, "Our customers now have three new colors to choose from," rather than "We have expanded our color selection." Or, "If this bill becomes law there will be significantly fewer parks where you can take your family," rather than "Our industry is opposing this legislation because ...."

- **Always include the "me factor."** The Zen masters have a good approach: "Tell me what window you are looking through and I will tell you what you see." It is crucial to appreciate your audience's viewpoint in order to understand how they will react to your message. The key word is *benefit*. If you can enunciate the benefit to each individual's life or family or career or wallet, you will turn a nod of agreement into a spark of interest — and, ultimately, action. People listen and respond in terms of their own lives. What are you telling them that will make their lives easier, more fun, richer or more rewarding?

- **Choose your pronouns carefully.** Don't call the company "it"; you, your staff and your spokesperson should think of your organization as "we" and "us," and your audience as "you." These pronouns convey a personal, interactive image of your organization. "We" demonstrates your synonymy with your organization and eliminates the egotistical ring of "I."

- **Humanize your responses by giving a little bit of your own personality as well as the organization's position.** Too often when we start to communicate a business message, we freeze and start sounding more like a machine than a person. Your field is interesting to you. Make it equally interesting to the reporter. In addition to providing the reporter with a "quotable quote," you may help destroy the myth that businesspeople are stodgy and boring, particularly if you work for a large corporation.

- **Be sure your messages reinforce your organization's overall branding.** Each product or service has its own unique character and strengths that you need to articulate and build on to position it clearly with your target publics. Stay focused and pay attention to consistency. Whether communicating with reporters or financial analysts, employees or consumers, on the Internet or in traditional media, be sure your messages and key points always support the personality and performance of your brand. Learn from advertising, where repetition is a sacred tool. Repeat anything often enough —

and simply enough — and it will be *remembered*. Base it on facts and back it up with performance and it will be *believed*.

- **Do not be embarrassed if a number or detail is not at hand, and do not guess.** Simply tell the reporter that your media relations person will get it. Also, don't feel obliged to accept a figure or fact the reporter cites. Say you are not familiar with it and offer to have it checked.

- **Never have other staff people in the room with you.** Surrounded by too many advisers, you may appear to be an obedient Gulliver surrounded by Lilliputians. The reporter wants your views and comments, not facts and figures, from the interview. Your delegating such follow-up detail means your train of thought will not be interrupted and you will be perceived as an expert not concerned with minutia. As well, it explicitly reminds the reporter that the media relations person is and should continue to be the one entrance point to the organization.

- **Do not let a reporter put words in your mouth.** Whenever you hear the phrases, "Are you saying that …?" or "Do you mean …?" or "Isn't it really …?" alarm bells should ring in your head. Mishandling this type of question can result in your feeling your words were reflected back by a fun-house mirror when the final story appears. If you do not like the way a question is stated, do not repeat it in your response — even to deny it. The reporter's question will not appear in print. Your answer will. It is better to respond in a positive way, using your own words, not the reporter's. For example, if a reporter asks if one of your products is overpriced compared to the competition, don't say, "I wouldn't want to use the term 'overpriced.'" You just did! Instead, say what you would want to say: "We believe our products provide high value for the price." Then go on to list the features. This is particularly important in a television interview, when time constraints will force severe editing. You want to be sure your main point is right up front in every answer, in case you are on the air with only one sentence. Look back at this example to see what a one-sentence edit would do to you.

- **Look for the hidden agenda in questions.** If a reporter is probing your recent hiring of salespeople proficient in certain skills, the resultant article may say that your company is in the midst of a marketing buildup to launch a new product line.

- **Never say you do not know an answer when in fact you do.** A good reporter will know — or find out — that you should have known the information and may be antagonized by your claiming ignorance. If a question that is not in the best interests of your organization is posed to you, explain why you won't answer it. And, as discussed previously, avoid "No comment."

- **Keep your cool.** More and more these days, interviewers deliberately frame their questions in emotional or accusatory tones, going for "attitude" or "edge" in their story. It is just a technique to get you to say something controversial. Do not let it work.

- **Understand that the reporter may be starting out with negative opinions about you or your organization.** These opinions may stem from ongoing publicity about inflated executive salaries or by the fact that few journalists have experience in business. The interview is your opportunity to turn that opinion around.

- **Avoid tongue twisters.** We all have heard someone stumble on words like "specificity." Choose words with a minimum of S's so you do not sound like a hissing snake — an especially important hint for radio.

- **Avoid using jargon.** When a reporter interrupts with what seem to be basic clarifying questions — or, in the case of an interview with an international reporter, if the interpreter pauses and looks puzzled — it may be that you have unconsciously dropped into obscure professional or industry jargon. Look for ways to explain your point with simple illustrations or analogies from everyday life.

- **Avoid "frankly," "to tell you the truth," and "to be honest."** These expressions may backfire by raising the question of how frank or truthful or honest you have been in all the rest of your interview if you suddenly say that you are going to be "frank" or "truthful" or "honest" with the reporter now.

- **Avoid negatives.** "No, we are not discriminating against women" is not as convincing as "We have a broad program to actively recruit more women executives."

- **Consider what your words will mean to others.** Sometimes a word can have different meanings to different audiences. A terminal in the computer business is a piece of equipment — but to many people it is a place where you catch a bus. In the international arena there are classic stories of misunderstandings caused by a poor choice of words. If your organization actively sells its products or services globally, make sure your spokespersons and interpreters are very familiar with the language, including local idioms, of each country where you do business.

- **Look at each question from the public's point of view.** For example, if a reporter says, "You don't have many Hispanic supervisors, do you?" don't counter with "Our record is terrific. We're doing much better than most companies." That sounds defensive. Instead, be positive in your answers. You might say, "We are making progress. [Such and such] percent of our supervisors are Hispanic and we have these specific programs in place to improve those numbers."

- **Be realistic in your answers.** Arthur W. Page, an AT&T vice president who in essence founded the field of corporate PR as a strategic management function, taught that "while well-thought-out communications programs are vital to an organization's success, they must be based on the reality of its performance and not on Madison Avenue slogans." Page summed up his philosophy in a single sentence: "Public relations is 90 percent doing and 10 percent talking about it."[3]

- **Respond to a simple question with a simple answer.** Short, simple answers are better than long, complicated ones. A few sentences using everyday language give the interviewer less opportunity to misunderstand you. And on TV, where time is measured in dollars, this is especially important. In fact, in a TV interview you should try to make your key points in 10 or 20 seconds.

- **Never underestimate the intelligence of your audience — and never overestimate their knowledge.** There's no need to adjust your prose to the words used by high school sophomores, but you must explain your terms, especially when you are covering a difficult subject. Two hours after a recent interview, a reporter phoned the media relations person to plead for a translation: "That interview reminded me of my college physics classes," she said. "I understood it while the professor was talking but when I got back to my room, I couldn't explain it."

- **Speak in the active voice.** Avoid the passive, which places the doer of the action at the end of the sentence or sometimes eliminates responsibility altogether. Say, "We will be moving our offices," not "Our offices will be moved." You want to portray your organization as a group of interesting, concerned people who decide and do things, rather than as a faceless, inanimate group. Similarly, don't duck responsibility for difficult actions. Say, "We reluctantly have decided that a layoff of some of our employees is required," not "The economy has forced a layoff." Companies don't make decisions or establish policies — people do.

- **Do not waste your brief time with a reporter by arguing against the other side.** You may want to refute their point of view but inadvertently end up giving valuable media exposure to their position. Instead, stay on *your* message. State your case positively, without mentioning your opponents by name. If you are forced to refer to your adversaries, avoid emotional labels such as "chauvinist" or "radical." Use "less experienced observers" or "the other side" instead.

- **Do not be offended by a reporter's questions about what you consider private or proprietary areas.** But as a spokesperson, it is your prerogative and responsibility to decide how much you want to say in your answer. If the questioning moves into proprietary or confidential areas, simply explain that providing such information would be too helpful to your competitors. Broadening your response to divert attention from the narrow, personal nature of a question is a good tactic — particularly during a television interview. A female politician asked how she balances her duties to her husband, children and the public might reply: "That question clearly illustrates the problems faced by so many American women who are working mothers ...."

- **Do not respond to a narrow question with an equally narrow answer.** Take the opportunity to reiterate one of your key points. For example, if you are being interviewed on a downsizing and are asked how many people will be out of work, do not just say "about seven hundred." Instead, reply directly to the question and then immediately expand on it: "About seven hundred, and we are doing everything we can to help soften the blow. We will phase down operations gradually over the next six months. We have generous severance payments. And we are setting up an outplacement center to help our people look for other jobs."

- **Do not answer hypothetical questions.** Instead, particularize them with: "That's a hypothetical question so it is impossible to know what might happen. But let me tell you exactly what did happen in a similar case ...."

- **Never, absolutely never, lie to a reporter.** You may get away with it once or twice, but ultimately you will be found out. Then not only you but also your organization will have lost a priceless asset — your credibility.

- **Be yourself.** If you like to sit around a conference table when you are meeting with your staff, that is likely a fine place for the interview; you will feel comfortable and the reporter will have a surface on which to write and/or place a recorder. If you prefer to emphasize your points by drawing diagrams on an easel, do it. If you love sports, use an analogy from the football field to illustrate your point. If your taste leans more to music, make a comparison using an orchestra as a metaphor. The reporter wants your perspective — not that of a well-trained but impersonal robot who gives the impression of speaking fluently but formally in another language.

Interviewing Hints and Tricks

- Don't let down your guard during an interview. You are most vulnerable when you let your mind wander. Stay focused, regardless of how long the interview might last.

- Whenever you hear "What if ...?" from a reporter, know that your answer, however speculative, will be open to wide interpretation by readers, viewers and listeners. It's best to refocus the question to factual content and avoid all hypothetical situations.

- Respond to negatives with a positive. Aggressive reporters often use a negative line of questioning to put you on edge. Deflating that stance takes patience, focus and a steady supply of positive, supportive data on your topic.

- "For example, ..." are two words reporters appreciate. They are not experts in your field, so examples help bring focus to your information.

- Avoid: "As I said in my presentation, ..." "As stated in our annual report, ..." "As you know ..." The reporter may not have heard the presentation, read the annual report, and she/he doesn't know. That's why you're having the interview.

Hints for Television, Podcasts and Live Stream Videos

When you stare into the eye of a television camera and see that little red light go on, or are speaking at a news conference where the video is being streamed live over the Internet, you are reminded that there is a huge audience out there who will see and hear whatever you say. Stage fright caused by the camera's relentless gaze and TV's wide exposure is natural, no matter how frequently you are interviewed. There are many things you can do in advance to prepare for the particular demands of television.

First of all is the choice of what to wear. Blue and red are still the preferred choices for both men and women — blue shirt and blue or red tie for men, and red or blue outfit for women. But most other colors are equally good. **What you want to avoid are extremes —** either small, busy patterns or large, bold stripes on your tie, shirt, blouse or jacket. Solid colors are best, but you should leave pure white at home in the closet.

Do not wear a large amount of jewelry, especially if it is bright, because it will cause the cameras to "flare," distracting viewers with a starburst of light. Men should wear calf-length socks in case they want to cross their legs on camera.

If you have a tan, do not get a haircut just before the interview in case your tan line is uncovered. Men with a heavy "five o'clock shadow" should shave just before the event. Women should not wear too much makeup, especially eye shadow; the right amount for work is normally the right amount for television. Men should not refuse a little powder just before the cameras roll; if a TV technician makes the suggestion it means some perspiration is visible on the TV monitor's view of you — not surprising considering the bright lights and a normal amount of nervousness.

All of the techniques you practiced to present your position persuasively to print journalists apply to television — only more so. It is critically important that you speak in sound-bite headlines. Make your points short and simple. TV's formula is to use perhaps 100 words from the reporter and a "sound bite" of 10 to 20 words from the speaker.

Television is a visual medium, so what the eye sees is more important than what the ear hears. The camera magnifies whatever it sees. It sounds trite, but you should act naturally. Do not smile when it is not appropriate — you will look phony, not friendly. Do not gesture wildly or move suddenly — the camera may lose you altogether. Do not stare upward into space when you are thinking — you will look like you are praying for divine guidance.

If you are being interviewed in your office, you or your media relations person should suggest other attractive areas of your operation for shootings, or provide "already in the can" background footage.

Think visually. Television is at its best when it can show something happening. A picture of nothing but a "talking head" is visually boring. Your chances for coverage will be immeasurably improved if you make it easy for the program's producer to illustrate what you are saying.

Take a look at existing props in your office that may appear on camera if the interview is conducted there. Family photographs add a warm touch. But a plaque with two small gold axes presented as an award for an expense-reduction program can give the wrong impression if the interview is on layoffs or moving operations offshore.

Television is an intimate medium. You will be speaking not to the "general public" but rather to individual people — mom and dad in the family room, a tired worker dozing in the den, someone catching up with ironing while watching the news.

Normally a TV interview will be severely edited before being aired. Many times TV reporters will ask you the same question several times in different ways. They are giving their editors a variety of versions and lengths from which to choose. It may be disconcerting to have the reporter pay more attention to a stopwatch than to your words, and it may seem unnecessarily repetitive to be asked the same question. You should take the opportunity to sharpen your answer.

No matter how often you are asked, try to include your main point in each answer — right up front — said in different ways. When the interview is edited, only one response will be left — and you and the reporter both want it to be a clear and concise statement.

Do not be intimidated by a reporter with a microphone during a fast-breaking "spot news" situation. An unnerving interview technique is to thrust the mike at you and then pull it back when the reporter has what he/she wants. You regain control of the interview with a smile and saying, "I haven't finished answering the last question yet," and go back to making your point.

Assume you are on the air all the time when being interviewed on television. And also remember: You are always *on* the record. Bright lights and a quiet room are no longer needed for an interview.

Sometimes attempts to be pleasant and polite can backfire. Avoid nodding as the reporter talks. It could be viewed on camera as acknowledgment of the premise behind the question. Similarly, be careful about saying, "That's a good point" after a negative question. Tight editing could wipe out the rest of your response.

Hints for Radio

A radio interview has some different characteristics. Unless it is a major news story, the station will use only a very brief segment (10 to 20 seconds) of your interview — although it is likely to rebroadcast the item several times, perhaps using different sound bites each time. **So it is even more important that you make your main points succinctly.** Also, radio rarely uses the reporter's questions on the air. Before you answer you should pause a moment to be sure the questioner is finished and you are not "stepping on that person's line." You will ensure cleaner edits and warm thoughts from the audio engineer.

You are not seen by anyone, so you can have your key points written out and handy where you can see them easily.

Practice out loud. If you sound awkward or must gasp for breath, shorten your sentences and eliminate difficult phrases. Guard against sounding like you are reading a prepared response — on the air you will sound terribly stilted. You should speak in a conversational tone as you would with a friend on the phone.

During the interview, **gesture as you would during a normal conversation;** it will help both your voice and your body to relax. As well, smile when you talk; it will make your voice sparkle and also help you to relax.

Repeat your company or brand name several times during the interview. People listening on the radio have no visuals to remind them who you are and what you are talking about. You need to paint repeated word pictures for your messages to be remembered.

In our enthusiasm for social media, it's easy to underestimate an "old-fashioned" medium like radio. That could be a mistake. Gary Knell, the president of National Public Radio, said in an interview in 2012 that public radio's 35 million listeners make up a bigger audience than the top 78 national newspapers combined. And NPR's "Morning Edition" program has a bigger audience than all three network TV morning shows combined.[4] You may want to explore radio opportunities as platforms for your organization's spokespersons to promote new products or human interest stories. As well, commercial radio stations often air free Community Events Calendars that highlight local activities, especially those sponsored by nonprofit organizations.

Hints for Skype

Chris King is a PR professional with a special talent for using technology wisely and well. He offers the following tips for taking advantage of Skype based on his experience at The Reader's Digest Association in New York and with other clients:[5]

- **Skype is a little different from a sit-down interview** you'd do if a camera crew came to the site. The webcam on the computer is wide angle and is designed to record the spokesperson at "seating distance" from the screen. This affects the way the background comes across and how much depth of field you get in the shot. We found that keeping the spokesperson against a neutral colored wall worked best. We also designed a small foam-core logo and miniature mock-ups of the products we were promoting to stick up on the back of the shot, depending on the situation. In general, though, it's best to keep the background simple, avoiding the typical table with flowers and a lamp that you see on "60 Minutes," for example.

- Out of habit, most people use the laptop computer's built-in microphone when making Skype calls. But when you're being recorded at a news conference or for a TV interview using Skype, **it's better to use a Bluetooth device (or any telephone headset device) as your mike.** The sound will be much clearer — especially useful in a "live" environment like an outdoor event or the stock market floor where the computer mike would pick up all the ambient crowd noise.

- **One thing you can't get away with on Skype is the passed note.** Your spokesperson is "always on," so it is distracting if he/she has to turn away from the webcam to look down at a note that has been passed to him/her. A better alternative is to leave a chat (instant message) window open on the Skype screen. The viewer cannot see it but the spokesperson can. If someone needs to prod the spokesperson or clarify a point, the spokesperson can read the message without turning his/her head from the screen.

- **We often found it useful to walk away with our own recording of the entire Skype interview.** There are plug-in apps available for this purpose. It's a great tool for media training with your spokesperson after the fact, and it's a lifesaver for the Legal/PR team if anyone questions what was said.

- **At first, you should hire a professional agency** versed in setting up live Internet events (webinars, Skype interviews, etc.) to see how it is done and to learn best practices. If you have in-house talent, you later can take on these technical components yourself — and save a lot of money.

- **Caveats.** Be aware that some broadcasters don't like to use Skype interviews because of their below-par quality. They are appropriate for a remote news report where a single person using his/her laptop's Web cam and a wireless connection can send a dramatic and cheap message. But they are not always smooth and professional, so probably are not appropriate for a posh product launch where image is important. It is a good idea for you to check with your target TV stations to see if they want a Skype interview or would prefer a satellite media feed.

Hints for News Conferences

When you are participating in a news conference, you have the obligation not only to answer reporters' questions but also to make opening remarks giving the purpose of the conference and formally announcing the news that caused it. Answering questions at a news conference is very similar to being interviewed except that you have more than one person asking questions and you are not in the comfortable surroundings of your own office. Making the opening remarks at a conference is much like giving a brief speech. As you look out over the crowd of cameras, lights, microphones and people peering up at you expectantly, you may feel like a mother robin perched on the edge of her nest looking into the hungry, gaping mouths of her babies. Much like the mother bird, your obligation is to feed the media — that is, provide them with news in an interesting way in the shortest period of time. The same techniques you use for interviews and TV appearances will serve you well here.

Before the news conference, come to the room to familiarize yourself with the setup. Work out signals with your media relations person as cues if you begin speaking too quickly or answering reporters' questions too abruptly. Then leave, and use the time to practice what you intend to say — and perhaps to go for a brisk walk to clear your mind.

Do not show up again until immediately before the news conference is scheduled to start. Do not mingle with reporters ahead of time. Whether you are introduced by your media relations person or open the news conference yourself is up to you. In any case, ignore the many microphones that are placed on the podium.

Do not ask if everyone can hear you — it is the responsibility of the audio engineers and your media person to ensure all the mike levels are correct. Just begin your formal remarks, speaking slowly and clearly and following your text closely if it has been included in the press kit materials. Like any attentive participant, the TV camera will be focused on you. But if you become long-winded or the cameraperson's attention wanes, the camera may scan the listeners — particularly that station's reporter — for reaction shots. If things really get dull, the little red light will go off as the technician turns the camera off altogether.

After your introductory talk, open the session to questions. Use an open phrase like "Now I would be happy to answer your questions" or "What are your questions?" rather than the closed construction "Does anyone have any questions?" If you do not know them all, ask the journalists to give their names and publications, stations or blogs as they are called on. Do not pace around or the microphones and cameras will have trouble following you.

If there are no questions right away, do not panic. The reporters may be reviewing their notes on your opening remarks and framing questions that will appeal to their readers or viewers. Simply wait a few minutes (it will seem like hours) and then invite questions again. Or point to a reporter you know and say "Susan, you usually have a good question for me." If there still are none, thank the reporters for coming and say you are available for individual questions if they wish.

More likely, the questions will start popping several at a time. Once you select a reporter to ask a question, keep your eyes on her/him while you answer. This will keep other reporters from interrupting and help the reporter's camera crew get both of you in the picture if they so desire. Allow one follow-up question from that journalist — but then establish eye contact with another questioner so one person is not able to dominate. Use the reporter's name in your answer whenever possible.

Do not be unnerved if someone moves around with a hand-held camera or even crawls up to the podium on hands and knees to adjust a microphone or test the lighting with a light meter. You probably will be asked several similar questions by TV people, because broadcast editors generally like to show their own reporters on the screen asking questions. So don't hesitate to repeat your key point in answer to each question — again, only one version will appear on each channel — and be sure *not* to say, "As I said in response to an earlier question ...."

If very few journalists have shown up, you should proceed as planned. But if the small turnout is obvious, you may wish to acknowledge it with a light comment such as "Ladies and gentlemen, it looks like you will have an exclusive by coming here today ...." and conduct the session in a less formal manner.

Equally important is for your media relations person to be prepared with everything from extra chairs to additional press kits in case many more people than expected show up. But if they are nonmedia people, they should politely but firmly be kept out of the news conference room. Journalists do not appreciate an audience, which can create distractions and generate noises picked up by the sensitive TV and radio audio equipment. And you are likely to be nervous enough without having kibitzers present.

Twenty to 30 minutes is the normal length of a news conference. Nevertheless, if questions are still coming, you may decide to go over the scheduled time. You can end the conference yourself or have your media relations person do so by announcing that you have time for one more question.

Mingle afterwards with reporters in case they want private interviews or individual on-camera shots of you talking with them. Remember that everything you say during these conversations is also on the record. Therefore, you should be no less careful with your comments than you were when you were at the podium.

Interview No-Nos

Here are some topics to avoid when you are talking with reporters, since they inevitably cause misunderstandings.

- **Do not ask if you can review the story in advance.** Just as the reporter cannot expect to see your annual report or latest product plans until you are ready to make them public, so you cannot have advance access to their reporting of the news.

- **Do not mention how much your organization advertises in the reporter's medium.** Reputable media do not permit their editorial judgment to be influenced by advertising, and you may unwittingly insult the reporter's personal and professional codes of behavior.

- **Do not tell broadcast reporters you think 30 or 60 seconds is too short a time to tell your story adequately.** They are no more satisfied with the time constraints they work under than you are.

- **Do not tell a reporter you will provide written answers to questions if he/she will send them to you.** The media are not in the business of taking dictation. That type of exchange probably is too time-consuming to meet the news deadlines. In any case, it will make the reporters think you are hiding something because you will not talk face to face.

- **Do not ask a reporter to keep what you say "off the record."** The reason a reporter is interviewing you is literally *for* the record — that is, to write and produce a news story. Editors are adamant that their reporters identify their sources in all but the most unusual cases. Presidents and secretaries of state may continue demanding off-the-record status for their remarks, but it is much safer for the rest of us to assume everything we utter will be attributed. Thus, do not say anything you do not want publicly associated with yourself or your organization unless you have a long relationship and a special understanding with a particular reporter.

Advice from a TV Anchor

In his memoir "Rather Outspoken: My Life in the News," longtime CBS TV reporter and news anchor Dan Rather listed five rules he followed for interviews.[7] Spokespersons can benefit from this insight from a journalist asking the questions — and many of the tips apply to us as the responders as well.

- **Preparation is the key.** The more you prepare, the better chance you have for a good interview.

- **Listening is almost as important.** Listen actively. Many times your best questions come from picking up on something the interview subject has said. Don't be a prisoner of your notebook, going down your list of questions.

- **Prioritize your questions.** I usually separate the interview into three parts: the key group of four to six questions that I must ask; another group of the same size that are secondary but nonetheless important; and a third set if we get that far.

- **Pay attention to nonverbal cues.** Is someone avoiding eye contact, or fidgeting, or wringing their hands? How a response is given, as well as the subject's facial expression or body language, can be very telling.

- **Understand the power of pauses.** After asking a question, don't pop back with another one right on the heels of the initial response. The dead air may seem interminable, but you can always edit that out. On the other hand, I've heard a lot of interesting things that were blurted out by folks who got squirrelly in the silence.

CHAPTER SIX

ETHICS

Technology and Common Sense

Manuel V. Pangilinan, chairman of the Philippine Long Distance Telephone Company, resigned his position as chairman of the board of trustees of Ateneo de Manila University after it became known that he had plagiarized several sections of the commencement speech he had given in 2010 at the school's graduation ceremonies. It was the commencement address heard around the world.

An equal opportunity plagiarist, Pangilinan had lifted material from commencement addresses by U.S. President Barack Obama at Arizona State University, Conan O'Brien and J. K. Rowling at Harvard University, and TV talk show host Oprah Winfrey at Stanford University.

On the other side of the world, blogger Duane Lester was surprised to learn that an article he had written and shared only with friends and fellow bloggers had appeared on the front page of a local newspaper, with no source citation or attribution to Lester. The blogger learned that he could assert his copyright of the article and request a payment. Lester visited the publisher of the newspaper who, while not happy about the situation, paid the requested amount.[1]

Plagiarism and Copyright Infringement

Plagiarism and copyright infringement are the hobgoblins of the Internet world. Students in college, high school, middle school — and younger — use the Internet as their hunting ground for writing assignments, taking word-for-word the writings and ideas of others, without attributing the material to the source of the information. There is little, if any, instruction to students on the safe and legitimate ways to use the Internet, especially for school assignments.

Researchers, always under pressure to write and publish new papers, sometimes overlook the specifics of collecting and citing material from their sources, which can cast doubt on the veracity and professionalism of their work.

While it's easier to plagiarize or violate copyright protection, the overall professional damage that can come your way isn't worth the risk.

Plagiarism

The origin of the word plagiarism (Latin: *plagiarius*) means — interestingly — "kidnapped." In academia and journalism, plagiarism is now considered academic dishonesty and a breach of journalistic ethics, subject to sanctions like expulsion and other severe career damage.[2] In simple terms, plagiarism means taking material from other sources and not giving any credit to those sources.

Noted New York Times journalist and admitted plagiarist Jayson Blair, in a conversation on "CBS Sunday Morning" with host Lee Cowan, told how his first violation of plagiarism came about: "I actually just took a quote from an Associated Press story, put it in the paper and didn't attribute it to the AP." Blair briefly considered fixing the quote but changed his mind, and waited for the copy desk to discover the unattributed quote — which they didn't.[3] Blair went on to write more than 600 articles for The Times, each one of which later had to be reviewed for plagiarized material.

Both CNN and Time magazine released journalist Fareed Zakaria for "lifting several paragraphs from a New Yorker magazine essay and using them in his Time magazine column" but, after a thorough review, reinstated Zakaria saying that the review of his work had shown "the lapse was an isolated incident."[4]

Plagiarism also shows up in books. Author Quentin Rowan had a very brief run as an acclaimed thriller writer before it was discovered that his book "Assassin of Secrets" was put together from whole chunks of books by spy masters Charles McCarry, Robert Ludlum, John Gardner and Adam Hall. The publisher recalled and pulped Rowan's book.[5]

 "Employers should create guidelines to provide their employees with examples of plagiarism and how to avoid it."

Plagiarism in the office is on the rise in both small and large companies. Miranda Brookins of Demand Media notes: "Since plagiarism in the corporate world can lead to hefty lawsuits and damage the reputation of a brand, employers should create guidelines to provide their employees with examples of plagiarism and how to avoid it." In the same article, Brookins provides a checklist for possible plagiarism: using others' images, taking credit for an idea, failing to list a source, stealing blog content and reproducing an e-book.[6]

Within any business or company, it is the responsibility of the media relations professional — with assistance from the legal department — not just to be on the lookout for plagiarism but also to educate co-workers and clients about the pitfalls of plagiarism online or in print.

Copyright Infringement

According to Student Technology Services at Washington University in St. Louis: "If you didn't write it, you don't own it. If you don't own it, you can't share it, upload it or download it."[8] This simple guide-

"In 2012, it was reported that Jonah Lehrer self-plagiarized several works he submitted to The New Yorker. All five of these articles now appear on The New Yorker website with the editor's notes listing the articles' previous places of publishing, including The Wall Street Journal, the Boston Globe, Wired and The Guardian. A correction posted on The New Yorker website claims that Lehrer also misrepresented the source of a quote taken from an article by another author."[7]

For more information you can go to The New Yorker website: http://www.newyorker.com/search?qt=dismax&sort=score+desc&query=lehrer&submit=

line about "copyright infringement" is easy to remember but skips over some of the specifics, such as copyright notification information. Note the following description from U.S. Copyright Office: "A copyright notice is an identifier placed on copies of the work to inform the world of copyright ownership. The copyright notice generally consists of the symbol or word 'copyright (or copr.),' the name of the copyright owner and the year of the first publication, e.g., © 2008 John Doe."[9]

Protecting copyright on products, services or procedures, while still getting the news out about your company or organization, occasionally creates conflict, as it can take time to research material, verify quotations and develop a cogent, correct and appropriate news release.

At Cisco Systems, Inc., a Fortune 100 company and a global leader in providing networking technology for businesses, nonprofit organizations and home use, their Code of Business Conduct includes this admonition on copyright: "Be sure you have authorization before using third-party copyrighted material. It is against Cisco policy — and, in fact, may be unlawful — to copy, reproduce, scan, digitize, broadcast, or modify third-party copyrighted material when developing Cisco products, promotional materials, or written communication."[10]

Violation of copyright most often refers to written materials like books, articles, screenplays and recipes. Added to that list is blogs. Most blogs are social, without copyright protection and, therefore, subject to content theft by other bloggers. But a blog that is used as for professional or business reasons can be — and should be — copyrighted.

A popular show on Zee TV — the flagship channel of India-based Zee Network — is "Khana Khazana," which also has a Facebook page referred to as ZKK, the focus of which is food. A community of food bloggers accused ZKK of "regularly stealing photographs from food bloggers and websites for their (ZKK's) features." Of special concern to the food bloggers was the admission that the recipes ZKK posted with the stolen photographs were not tested. ZKK offered an apology while claiming its actions were not "stealth" but were used solely to raise visual appeal of the recipes.[11]

In business, issues of copyright violation are usually dealt with by a corporate attorney. Public relations professionals who don't have the advantage of an on-site lawyer can often find themselves without resources to answer their questions.

The Copyright Society of the U.S.A. provides a wealth of information on their website (www.csusa.org), including lists of organizations and companies, such as movie, software and publishing, for whom copyright infringement is a critical element of their business and success. The organization holds professional development conferences and lists numerous resources. Other resources in your area include the Better Business Bureau, local chambers of commerce and local/city/state government offices.

Conflict of Interest

"You do not have to do anything improper to have a conflict of interest; it is strictly situational," opined Dr. Paul J. Friedman, professor emeritus of the School of Medicine, University of California, San Diego, in an abstract he wrote 40 years ago.[12] His statement has become the *de facto* explanation of conflict of interest for academicians and other professionals.

The challenge is to identify if there is a conflict of interest and, if so, how to avoid or fix it. For media relations professionals, the test of conflict of interest can come up in a variety of ways and forms:

• Do you change an executive's comment to correct grammatical errors, or do you let it stand as stated?

- Do you embellish your CEO's biography, as requested by him/her?
- Do you give a "heads up" to your blogger friend about an upcoming announcement?
- Do you "forget" to invite a key reporter to your press conference because you don't like her/him?

Tootsie Roll Industries (TRI) tells its employees that a conflict of interest "occurs when an individual's personal interests interfere or conflict in any way (or even appear to interfere or conflict) with the interest of TRI." The company admits that "it is difficult to identify exhaustively what constitutes a conflict of interest. For this reason, employees, officers and directors must avoid any situation in which their independent business judgment might appear to be compromised."[13]

A Matter of Judgment

The Salt River Project, one of Arizona's largest utilities, relies on its employees to understand their potential conflict of interest as "any circumstance that could cast doubt on one's willingness or ability to protect SRP's interests."

The company's employee manual includes a section on the topic, calling it "A Matter of Judgment, Objectivity," that includes examples and test questions on the topics of Personal Financial Interest, Outside Employment, Boards and Elected Offices, and Disclosure of Conflict of Interest. The company also provides a conflict of interest disclosure statement and instructions on how to file that information; the site is at http://www.floodsrp.org/program/rules.php#2.[14]

Cisco Systems, Inc., in its Code of Business Conduct, has created an "Ethics Decision Tree," designed to help employees determine if a particular action or situation violates the company's code and work their way through an ethical dilemma.[15]

Regardless of the method you and your organization choose, providing information and situational examples to your employees about conflict of interest is a strong step toward eliminating those conflicts.

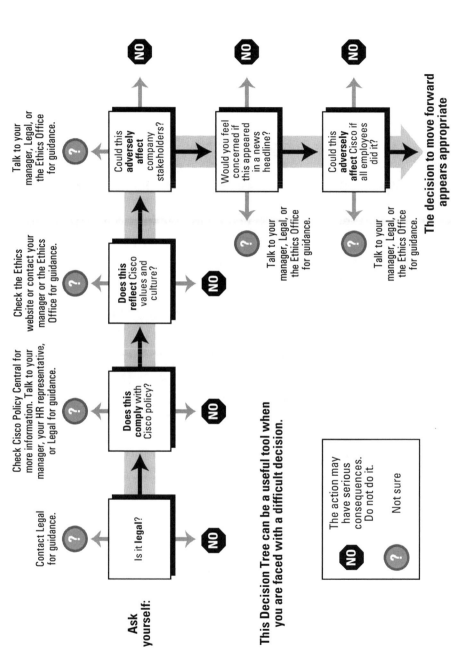

Ask yourself:

Contact Legal for guidance. 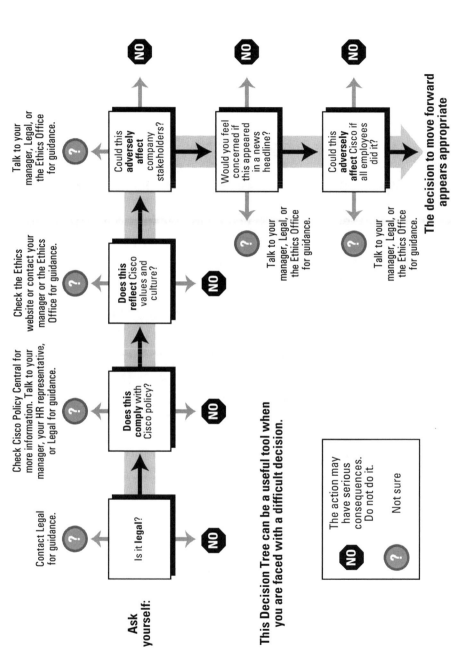 — Is it legal? — NO

Check Cisco Policy Central for more information. Talk to your manager, your HR representative, or Legal for guidance. — Does this **comply** with Cisco policy? — NO

Check the Ethics website or contact your manager or the Ethics Office for guidance. — **Does this reflect** Cisco values and culture? — NO

Talk to your manager, Legal, or the Ethics Office for guidance. — Could this **adversely affect** company stakeholders? — NO

Would you feel concerned if this appeared in a news headline? — NO
Talk to your manager, Legal, or the Ethics Office for guidance.

Could this **adversely affect** Cisco if all employees did it? — NO
Talk to your manager, Legal, or the Ethics Office for guidance.

The decision to move forward appears appropriate

This Decision Tree can be a useful tool when you are faced with a difficult decision.

NO — The action may have serious consequences. Do not do it.

? — Not sure

Decision Tree. © Cisco Systems, Inc. 2012.

To Comment or Not to Comment

Few words create more frustration for a reporter than "No comment." A key element in a reporter's job is the process wherein the reporter asks questions and the respondent answers. "No comment" throws a red cape in front of a very large and angry bull. But for you — the person being interviewed — "No comment" seems safer than saying, "I don't know what you are talking about," or "I made a mistake," or "We don't want that topic to be made public."

Reporters and the general public almost always take "No comment" to mean that whatever you're not commenting on is negative in nature. Instead of stonewalling a reporter, state why you can't comment directly on the question — for example, "We haven't made a decision on that purchase," or "I'm not the right person to respond to that," or "The situation is under review by the board and I'll call you when that review is complete."

 Gaining control is the key.

One way to gain control of a lazy reporter's "Would you care to comment?" question is to turn the table and ask the reporter: "Could you be more specific about what you want to know?" Or, you could take the question away by saying, "Yes, I want to comment. I want you to know that our company has been making and selling these products for 37 years with no failures. I will show you the letters from happy customers, and, if you'd like, I'll arrange a tour for you at our manufacturing facility."

Following is a list of sample situations with examples of ways to avoid "No comment":

1 **Rumors of imminent dividend action, stock offering, debt issue, merger, etc.** "We have nothing to announce at this time. You are well aware that there are clear procedures for any announcement that could affect our stock price or an investment decision." Or, "As a matter of policy, we never discuss or speculate on rumors in the marketplace."

2. **Sales projections, production plans and other proprietary information.** "I hope you can understand that answering that question

would give our competitors valuable information about our sales plan [or manufacturing processes or marketing strategies or whatever]."

3. **Inappropriate questions.** "Our organization has no position on that issue one way or the other" is an appropriate answer to questions about political, social, religious or other issues on which a public position might unnecessarily alienate segments of the public. Also, "We are in the business of software development [or whatever], not religion."

4. **Leaks of settlement plans or other bargaining information.** "We are negotiating with the union in good faith to resolve the issues that separate us. Certainly we all want to avoid a strike. We shall confine any other remarks to the bargaining table, where we hope they will contribute to the negotiation process."

5. **Question on a judicial or regulatory ruling.** "We will have to study the decision [or ruling or judgment] before we can discuss it in detail."

6. **Rumors of an imminent layoff.** "When we have any such announcement, I will let you know at once. I am sure you understand that our procedure is to let the employees know first so they don't learn about it from the media."

7. **Legal issues.** In an effort to make sure cases are tried in the courtroom and not in the media, many judges impose restrictions on the parties in the action, which prevents any discussion of the case with the media. However, if a reporter asks about a court case, it's safer to say: "I'm sorry but we're not allowed to discuss this case under terms agreed to in the court." You are neither commenting on the subject nor are you stonewalling. Similarly, if you are asked for details about talks between your company and another, you can respond: "I'm sorry, but we have agreed to keep our business discussions private."

On or Off the Record?

One of the most perplexing elements applied to media relations is "off the record." The phrase is not legally defensible. It has no absolute rules or guidelines. It usually is an agreement between a reporter and the person she/he is interviewing. But not always.

The phrase is attributed to President Franklin D. Roosevelt, who first used it in November 1932 at a social event in North Carolina where he supposedly said that "it was mighty nice to be able to talk 'off the record.'" The event and the president's use of "off the record" were cited in The Daily Times-News, November 1942.[16] Since that time, uses and abuses, along with definitions and parameters, have cluttered news rooms and media relations offices.

In its simplest terms, "off the record" usually means that anything that you say to that reporter cannot be used publicly and is intended solely for background or to give an explanation of an event, program or plan. That's the exact opposite of "on the record" where everything you say can be used and attributed to you. In between those two extremes is "not for attribution," which means what you say can be used but not attributed to you.

 Establishing ground rules is essential.

"On background" and "deep background" also creep into inter-views, in the misguided direction that having a subject speak in either of these areas will produce better information and the source of that information — you — will be protected. What's important to learn is that you must establish ground rules for what will and won't be "off the record" and what is/isn't "on background." Some organizations have broad rules regarding what information can and cannot be given to a reporter — ever. These might include research projects, executive suc-cession plans, possible acquisitions and similar big news items. Many organizations refuse to use "off the record" at all, claiming that the term suggests "hidden news" or "secret activities."

Once you, your media relations colleagues and your corporate attorney have agreed on definitions and usage, distribute your guide-lines within the organization.

CHAPTER SEVEN

MEDIA EVENTS

How to Make Them Work for You

Your organization may not always have dramatic new products, hundred-million-dollar new offices or a vital scientific breakthrough to attract reporters' attention. But the basic principles of announcements remain the same for all of us, and you, too, can hold an event to help your organization generate increased sales and positive media coverage.

In addition to new product or service announcements, a manufacturing plant opening, hiring a new CEO, an open house or market expansion are fine reasons to host a celebration and news conference. These media events are staged occurrences, so you usually control the timing. They are held to promote good news, so you are on the offensive, not the defensive. They tend to have a more casual atmosphere to encourage person-to-person dialogue between the news media and your organization's executives.

Working on media events can be fun. The trick is to make it profitable for your organization in terms of increased sales, positive news media coverage, improved public opinion — and maybe also a jump in the stock price. There are two keys to getting the most effective media relations results from these events. First, clearly enunciate your communications objective and then evaluate every idea by whether it helps meet that objective. Remember that when management asks what it is getting for its PR investment, it is asking for evidence that communications activities support business goals. Second, keep running lists that track progress and responsibility for all planned and possible activities. You must think constantly in generalities while at the same time living in detail. Michelangelo is said to have counseled a young artist, "Perfection is made up of details." It will be your ability to keep sight of the forest and every single tree that will make the event a success from a media viewpoint — and well worth the expense from your organization's perspective.

Remember Your Target Audiences

Look at your event from the point of view of the reporters and bloggers you will be inviting. They get invitations almost daily, so your event must be different in some way to attract their attention. It must be *unique*, to differentiate it from the competition. It must be *relevant*, to be considered newsworthy or worth being given attention. It must be *cost-effective*. And, above all, it needs to *sell* — because that is what we all are here for.

 Coordinate with investor relations and employee communications colleagues.

If your company's stock is traded publicly, you also will want to coordinate with those colleagues responsible for investor relations.

Reporters frequently call financial analysts and market experts for an outside, objective evaluation — and a quotable quote — to include in their story on a major corporate announcement. Thus, it is to your advantage to keep financial analysts who follow your company and industry fully informed about your news, preferably on announcement day. You can have copies of the media materials emailed to key financial analysts. Or you may want to arrange a separate restaging of the news conference for them. (It is normally not wise to invite journalists and financial analysts to the same announcement event. Their interests are different, and they deserve individual attention.)

Also, remember your employees. Make them feel special by live streaming the event on your intranet or website.

Announcing a New Facility

Announcing the purchase of property and the building of a new facility provides unparalleled opportunities for positive media and community relations. It also serves as a fine example of how to plan a media event. It will, however, tax your abilities if you find yourself operating in new territory — such as an expansion into a state or country in which your organization has not operated — without the benefit of established relationships with local reporters, editors and bloggers (or even knowledge of the local geography).

Integral to your planning should be the knowledge that your plans very likely are not going to be kept secret until announcement day. If the deal is a big one — in terms of size of the property, cost of construction, prestige of the company or number of potential jobs, for example — you should count on the fact that there will be a leak. Real estate agents showing property, local boards approached for zoning regulations, a hotel visited to evaluate conference facilities, a pilot hired for aerial photographs of the site provide ample opportunities for the news to slip out no matter what precautions your organization takes.

You should have an approved standby statement ready for immediate use in case a reporter calls seeking your comment on rumors. If your plans are so uncertain that you do not even have an announcement date tentatively set, you should probably say nothing more than your organization is looking at a number of potential sites for possible future expansion, but no plans are firm yet. If you have a timetable in mind, you might want to go further by adding that you will let the reporter know when a decision is made and an announcement is imminent.

You also will want to develop solid relationships early on with others involved in the project. People from such disciplines as real estate, legal and finance, either on your organization's staff or retained for this job, will become critical resources as announcement time draws near. Your involvement in the planning stages helps build their confidence in you and in your contribution to the project's successful outcome. It also makes it more likely that you can get their early concurrence on an objective and working strategy — not to mention their personal involvement in the implementation of your announcement plan.

 Develop a checklist of all activities that need to be undertaken.

Once you know the announcement is a "go" — even before you have a firm date — you should immediately develop a checklist of all activities that need to be undertaken and note any related issues that must be considered. This will be your overall master list. It will also spawn a number of more detailed "to-do" lists for many of the entries.

For a major announcement, you will probably be working with other departments within your organization or even an outside agency hired to put on this event. It is critical that you and your colleagues know who is doing what and don't overlap your work. You are in charge of the media side of the event while someone else should handle the logistics of permits, food, parking, transportation and so forth. Included on your media checklist should be the following:

1. **Date/time of announcement.** Probability of bad weather? Other conflicting events such as a holiday or an election? Best time for the local news media? Availability of key participants?

2. **Site of announcement.** At your organization's headquarters or at location of new property? On-site or in a hotel or commercial establishment? Ease of accessibility for guests and news media?

3. **Main theme/primary message.** Expansion of your organization into new territory? New business? Move from older facility?

4. **Guests and media.** Federal, state and local government officials? Key community and business leaders? Local people helpful in site

selection? News media — local? national? trade? Other VIPs? Employees? Spouses? Financial analysts?

5. **Speakers.** Only your organization's executives? Governor or top state or federal official? Mayor or local official?

6. **Type of occasion.** News conference alone? Low-key or big blast? With lunch or dinner? Reception?

7. **Media relations.** Press kit materials? Transportation to site? One-on-one interviews?

8. **Invitations to media.** Reporters and editors? Editorial board members? Bloggers?

9. **Mementos.** Appropriate? Different ones for media than VIP guests?

10. **Collateral materials.** Exhibit? Printed program? "Who we are, what we do" brochure for guests? "Working news media only" sign outside news conference room?

It is a good idea to ask others who will be involved to review your list to see if you have left anything out or overlooked any local media customs. Next, you should establish an information objective and budget, assign responsibility for each of the activities, develop an overall timetable, and set specific due dates. Then you must oversee implementation of the media plans on virtually a day-to-day basis to ensure everything gets done on time.

Guidelines for Major Media Events

Planning before the Event

1. **Make sure the objective and theme for your information effort is supportive of your organization's goals and your overall media relations plan and is agreed to by everyone involved.** It should include both your key message and target audience. Before making any decision, evaluate it against that objective. For example, when we were discussing possible speakers for the official opening of AT&T's Network Software Center in Illinois, someone suggested we invite the vice president of the United States "to get publicity" since it was an election year. Our goal was not, however, publicity for the sake of publicity. If it were, we could do something bizarre like have

an employee stage a loud demonstration in the middle of the ceremony. Rather, our objective was to get media coverage on AT&T's software expertise and its contributions to new information age services. Having the vice president speak — *particularly* because the ceremony would take place only a few months before a national election — could divert attention from our software message and focus it on politics. Thus, it might inhibit rather than support our information objectives. Better to invite the president of Bell Laboratories to join our CEO on stage so the speakers would personify the high-technology partnership that would deliver AT&T's products to the marketplace.

2. **It sometimes is good politics as well as good media relations to invite the governor of the state, or the mayor, or a high-ranking county official to make a few brief remarks.** It is wise to restrict a politician to a five-minute official welcome rather than the keynote address. This way you control the length of the program and the main message the media take away from the event.

3. **Choose your spokespersons carefully.** Then provide them with solid background information and help them practice. (See guidelines in Chapter 5, "Spokespersons: Training and Briefing Them for Their Role.")

4. **Do not let yourself be distracted by time-consuming tasks.** You don't need to worry about the menu — other staff should take care of that.

 Control your speakers to control the message.

Implementing the Event

5. **If a site or facility tour is part of your program, give the media a heads-up about the amount of time on the tour, what they will see, if photographs are allowed, etc.**

6. **Severely limit the number of officials introduced individually or allowed to speak as part of the news conference or ceremony.** "Obligatory" recognitions are terribly boring to the audience.

They also distract from the main message your organization wants to deliver. Better to have your emcee or the organization's top speaker use one general statement to thank "all the local people who made us feel so welcome" or commend "the employees whose dedication and talent made this event possible."

7. **Document each stage of a new facility — from the architect's drawings through construction and official opening.** Such a photographic history will be invaluable not only for the news media but also for your annual report, website and YouTube postings, or other external and internal information materials. Make plans early. You don't want to conceive the plan only to find construction nearly completed.

8. **Review and update your checklists often.** The ball takes some funny bounces on occasion, and the only way to track it is to keep it perpetually in sight. Conduct frequent meetings where everyone involved shares progress reports. Occasionally send brief updates to your organization's top executives.

9. **If you decide to give a memento to the media, personalize it with your logo so that recipients are reminded of your organization when they use it.** Pens or USB drives displaying your logo are useful, and they can be inserted into the press kits if you want to give them only to reporters. Tote bags or briefcases are especially good giveaways because they are carried and become moving billboards for your brand.

10. **Arrange for photography** — still and video — of the news conference and announcement ceremony.

11. **You can have first-class press kit folders and also save money by carrying a photograph or drawing of the new facility along with your organization's name on the cover** — but *not* including the date of the event. That way you can arrange for production of the folders before a final date is set to avoid rush-job printing charges, keep your last-minute duties to a minimum and avoid wasted money if the date changes at the last minute. You also can use the folders for other occasions such as open houses or background information packages for the media as construction proceeds or new reporters request materials.

12. **Target your press kits** so that each reporter and blogger has the right information for his/her audience — hometown angle for the plant site's local paper, long-term growth for the business and financial media, relationship to industry trends for the trade press, etc.

13. **Just before the event, write out a final detailed list of the media representatives expected to attend.** Give copies to everyone involved so they can welcome them and recognize them in the news conference.

14. **Supervise all aspects of the news conference personally, from the opening statement to the contents of the press kits.** Anything affecting the information effort is your business, regardless of who is responsible. You may be the only person with the complete picture.

15. **If there will be a meal after the news conference, put "Reserved for press" cards on tables nearest the podium or head table.** Do not assume reporters will stay for the meal just because they are coming to the news conference. Ask them to RSVP to the news conference and luncheon or reception separately.

16. **If possible, arrange for a separate room for private interviews between your CEO and selected reporters and bloggers after the news conference.** Allow time in your schedule for these interviews between the news conference and the meal, perhaps by scheduling a reception between the two. Schedule time-consuming online chats for the next day.

17. **Try to have a separate "working room."** This is ideal for storage of press kits, mementos and other office materials such as computers, a printer and blank news release paper in case you have to revise the release at the last minute. If your event is taking place at a commercial establishment, get permission from the manager to ship as much of your material as possible to arrive early.

18. **Bring plenty of your business cards to give to the media.** Try to find time to chat with any reporters you have not met before. The relationships you begin to develop at the announcement ceremony will serve your organization well as construction proceeds — especially if you face unfortunate events like an accident or a union problem, and if communication will be primarily by telephone because your office is not near the new facility.

19. **Understand that the primary focus of local reporters' questions will be on the economic advantages to the community in terms of jobs, taxes and related support services.** Anticipate their needs by being prepared to give out general figures and a probable timetable. Be careful not to lock yourself into a potential problem of appearing to renege on a promise a few years hence by being overly specific at announcement time. Use round numbers: "We expect to hire about a thousand people over the next few years" is better than "We plan to hire 1,083 people by next December." Also, for local taxation purposes be careful about placing a value on your project until your design and construction plans are firm and you have consulted with a tax expert.

20. **Make sure the head table and news conference setup photograph well so that you get maximum exposure for your organization's message.** The lectern should display your logo, not the hotel's. If the drapes behind the announcement area have a busy pattern or inappropriate color, put up portable curtains or an attractive sign with your theme or organization's name behind the speakers. All visuals should be simple, with copies included in the press kits and available online. View the staging through a camera's eye — literally if necessary.

 The lectern should display your logo, not the hotel's.

21. **Set up a separate table staffed by a person who will help you handle the news media.** This includes press kit distribution, requests for private interviews or any other courtesies that should be extended to working journalists.

22. **Prepare a separate package of materials for your key executives involved in the program.** Include the press kit and a detailed agenda — and also private background and Qs and As that could come up, the names of key officials and reporters deserving personal attention (with nicknames and phonetic spelling if their names are difficult to pronounce), potential local concerns such as environmental issues or union problems, and the executives' individualized itinerary and schedule, with a reminder of the times

they should be available for separate media interviews. Give a copy of this package to each executive's assistant or chief staff person — and keep a few extra copies with you in case they misplace theirs.

23. **Coordinate the agenda and schedule closely with the press secretary or chief aide of government officials and celebrities who are participating in the program.** Get on their calendars early because their schedules often are set well in advance. Also, be aware that government officials and politicians often bring staff people with them.

24. **Arrange for a setup time and personally inspect all the facilities the night before and the day of the event.** Test the sound and lighting arrangements for broadcast needs.

25. **Post the media materials on your website for reporters not attending the event.** Posting should take place at the time of or just after your news conference. Only in rare cases should you allow advance distribution, or you will hurt chances of the media's covering the event in person.

Following Up and Evaluating the Event

26. **Monitor local and industry blogs and that evening's television news programs.** Get copies of the daily papers. Within 24 or 48 hours provide your organization's top executives with samples of initial news coverage of the event, plus a videotape of the full news conference and ceremony if you made one. Consider a separate, shorter version to show to your employees and your board of directors.

27. **Promptly after the event write thank-you letters to the media for the CEO's signature.** These should be emailed to the media who came and/or covered the event.

28. **Set up a system to handle the inevitable queries generated by the news coverage of your announcement.** You will receive queries from real estate agents, relocation people, job applicants, banks and other prospective product and service suppliers. Alert those responsible so they are prepared to handle them.

29. **A month or so after the event, when all the news coverage has been gathered, put together a summary that includes objectives and a brief analysis of how they were met.** This can be done in

print or electronically. Include selected samples of news media coverage and distribute the summary to your organization's officers and board and to all others involved in the event.

30. **Compile a complete file including everything connected with the occasion, from your private memos and checklists to the press kits, official announcement speech and overall evaluation.** It will be invaluable not only as a record of a historic event but also as a model for planning future announcements.

When Your Event Is for an International Market

Chapter 8, "Going Global: How to Manage International Media Relations," contains advice on operating beyond your borders that should be helpful when you find yourself working in an unfamiliar country. In addition, here are some tips specifically related to meeting and event planning outside your home country:

1. **Consider hiring a destination management company (DMC) or international public relations agency.** They can be very helpful in introducing you to local hotels and caterers, arranging visas, setting up tours, handling local transportation and selecting appropriate off-site festivities. Before choosing a DMC or agency, check references and determine their billing methodology — per person? Flat fee? Cost plus?

2. **While one site inspection may suffice here at home, you likely will need more in unfamiliar markets.** A first-class hotel in the United States is different from one in Europe or Asia. Also, organizers must plan for differences in electrical voltage, expectations of meeting rooms and news conference sites, even the size of tables and chairs. Make sure the site is set up so you can provide an online direct feed into the press conference.

3. **Exchange rates will have a great effect on your budget and decision making.** Be flexible as currencies fluctuate during the planning phase. And talk with your finance department colleagues about the pros and cons of hedging your foreign exchange risk.

4. **Understand the VAT rules**. Where they exist, value-added taxes range from 5 to 25 percent, so they can have a great effect on your budget. Fortunately, many countries have a system in place to allow

at least some of your VAT charges to be refunded. Get local advice on the rules and how you can determine your organization's eligibility.

5. **Transportation is a critical factor.** Most journalists do not have time for lengthy travel, so you need to consider a site's accessibility to airports.

6. **Check the U.S. State Department list before settling on a venue.** This security and alert list lets you know what countries and geographic areas to avoid at any given time.

7. **Use only well-known, experienced shipping companies** — preferably those with whom your organization has a long-standing business relationship. You may need a freight forwarder who is also a licensed customs broker. Check references.

Ingredients for Press Kits at a Special News Event

Even with our dependence on the Internet, there still are many reporters who find printed press kits useful. Here are the basic pieces that should be included in the package of special materials you provide the news media, both in the press kit and on your organization's website:

• Main news release

• Other related feature or "sidebar" stories

• Flash drive or CD of photographs or graphics, with captions, and a DVD of network-quality video to TV stations as background footage if you have it

• List of names, titles and affiliations of all people on the stage, at the head table or otherwise participating in the event

• Flash drive or CD of photos and biographies of keynote speakers

• Basic fact sheet on your organization

• Annual report, brochure and other information on your organization

• Name and cell number of person to contact for additional information

It also is critical that each of the pieces in the press kit be dated — in print and online — since they undoubtedly will be separated and probably will be filed in the publication's or station's morgue for future use by any reporter writing a story on your organization.

The High Price of News Leaks

Frequently, employees are a major cause of news leaks. Sometimes they are salespeople hoping to impress customers by offering advance information about a new product, forgetting that they may be flirting with an antitrust violation by preannouncing a product. Or they are staff managers carelessly chattering about their work in public.

There is a very basic reason to keep a tight lid on new product information until the announcement day: You likely cannot afford to alienate the news media and lose the free — and probably positive — publicity they will give you. Except in rare cases, journalists will not cover the announcement of a new product as a major news event if the story has leaked out in dribs and drabs. While they understand the necessity for a trial location or two, if knowledge is widespread, reporters will say too many of their readers or viewers already know the story to make it news — and then direct you to the advertising department. As the old saying goes, "Loose lips sink ships," or make it very expensive to float them again.

Celebrity Chats Can Work Well for Product Launches

Celebrities who have endorsed your new product or service frequently are willing to host an online chat, especially if you give them good backup support.

It's usually a good idea to hire a typist to do the actual "chatting" with the audience, with the celebrity sitting nearby to verbally respond to the questions or remarks and thus communicating the pizzazz and personality the celebrity is known for. Also, make sure you have fact checkers or other subject-matter experts standing by to help the celebrity phrase his/her answers with correct facts and figures.

Make Integrated Marketing Part of Your Plan

The softening of the traditional boundaries between marketing, advertising and PR is a natural response to the economic and competitive imperatives facing companies and clients. Organizational silos are out and teamwork is in. CEOs have little interest in what function traditionally had responsibility for a given task. Rather, they want the brightest and most creative minds addressing business challenges no matter where they reside in the organizational chart. Communicating priority messages cost-effectively to journalists, customers, shareholders, employees and other target publics is necessary to an organization's survival. Integrated marketing communications can be an effective way to do that.

To create an effective integrated marketing communications program and avoid a cheerleading approach to promotions, get all the key functions together to decide on your priority messages and key selling points. Step back and look at the new product or service as a journalist would. Forget ego. Ask, what really is *news*? What is *new* or *unique*? What aspect of the product or service would have the most interest for the media's readers, viewers or listeners? Look for a human side as well as a business side to the story. Your role as a strategist and counselor means thinking through and guiding the entire publicity program, not just writing a news release.

Two Case Studies: How Do Traditional Media Use Social Media?

As you plan your media strategies for the future, you might benefit from knowing how two traditional media are using social media to achieve their goals:

A Major Midwest Metro Daily

This information is adapted from a digital tools tip sheet developed by Brad Best, the Reynolds Journalism Institute's advertising editor, and a team of Missouri School of Journalism students following weeks of analysis of how a major Midwest metro daily newspaper uses social media to interact with subscribers.[1] It gives you a feel for what a major Midwest newspaper is doing on Facebook and Twitter, and perhaps can inspire ideas useful to your organization in return:

Facebook: A useful tool to implement online discussion and develop loyalty with readers if you:

• Ask questions on the site and use it to begin discussions about events.

• Use event discussion as an opportunity to link back to your website.

• Pose questions to draw comments and stimulate interaction.

- Use visuals to brighten your page.

- Post videos to keep your page current and interesting.

- Find a balance between daily posts and conversations. Too many posts will clog users' feeds, and readers will begin to unsubscribe in frustration.

    Twitter: A useful means to communicate breaking news.

- Incorporate your Twitter feed on your home page, thus attracting readers to follow news on both platforms.

- Simplify implementation of the Twitter feed on your home page so viewers click a minimum number of times to get to their desired location.

- Create separate, specific lists that tailor to followers' interests, enabling them to choose what subjects they want constant updates about.

- Interact with your followers, replying to mentions, re-tweeting relevant information, and tagging reporters and followers in your tweets.

A Small TV Station in Canada

Melissa Munroe is senior editor and graphic designer at CHNU in Surrey, B.C., Canada. The television station serves Vancouver, Victoria and the Fraser Valley, offering multifaith programming and family-friendly comedy and drama aimed at Zoomers, "baby boomers with zip." CHNU takes advantage of social media to reach its relatively young audience. Here Munroe describes some of their strategies:[2]

As a local broadcaster we primarily use Facebook, YouTube and Twitter to reaffirm messages we have already broadcast on our channel as well as to drive viewers to watch our station, she says.

Facebook: We use Facebook to promote our programming to bring more viewers back to television. We also promote our contests and giveaways, bringing attention both to us and our sponsors. Especially successful are contests that require our viewers to upload their own images or videos to our page.

YouTube: We upload all our relevant content to YouTube, which allows people to share their opinions and provides viewers an opportunity to interact with our videographers and other on-air talent. Viewers and our YouTube subscribers are able to have a conversation about our features and news programming. If they have questions, they can ask our reporters who covered the story.

Twitter: Twitter is usually a repeat of whatever we post on Facebook — but we don't find Twitter very effective because we are television and visual.

Lessons learned: Some of the setbacks we experienced include negative and inappropriate comments. People have the freedom to complain in a much more public way. On the other hand, when you respond appropriately your fans clearly see that you provide good customer service. Although we love to communicate with viewers via social media, we need to bring their eyes back to television as that is our mandate. The challenge is to find a manner in which both methods of communication work. Our biggest lesson learned is to communicate with fans the way they want to be communicated with. If you notice that your Facebook fans are now posting with Twitter or Pinterest, it is time to rethink your social media strategy. Remember that it is all about interaction — and this means both ways. Ask questions, look for opinions and respond to them. Also, keep it simple. People are much more likely to respond to a photo than a long paragraph. Creativity counts!

Sophisticated Sequencing Maximizes Results

Too often great effort is expended on what will be said, with little attention paid as to when. Yet, sophisticated sequencing is crucial to maximizing your results. Experienced CEOs and CFOs plan asset sales and expansion activities to keep earnings rising smoothly and consistently. Similarly, all departments involved in media and marketing communications should plan so that there is a consistent stream of good news coming out of the company during the year, rather than a large number of new product and service announcements bunched together.

 Ensure your news conference precedes any advertising.

Announcement dates should be set for those strategic moments in time when they will generate the most attention — for example, before a major financial analysts meeting or at an important trade show — rather than at the whim of one person or department. Get all involved parties together and agree upon an announcement calendar for the next year or two that benefits the individual product managers and business units involved, as well as the overall organization.

Editors also frequently refuse to carry a story on a new product on their news pages or programs if your company has a paid ad running. Their feeling is that if your company had time to produce and place an advertisement, the product is no longer "hard news" to their readers and viewers and the publication is being used to provide free advertising. It is thus an important part of the media relations person's responsibility to ensure your news conference precedes any advertising by at least a day or two.

Planning Time Line for Major Announcements

Here is a planning model and time line for major new product or service announcements. It can be a tool to help you and your colleagues in your planning, especially for significant announcements of interest to a wide number of your priority audiences. Of course, all these activities are not appropriate for all products and services, and the ones you choose will depend on your organization, its culture, the marketplace and the nature of the product or service being announced.

Announcement Day minus Six Months

- Interdepartmental planning committee formed, chaired by marketing or product manager responsible for the new product or service (consider including representatives from all sales and marketing functions involved, engineering, manufacturing, R&D, distribution channels, training, media relations, advertising, promotions, investor relations, legal and customer service).
- Roles and responsibilities for all committee members defined, tentative meetings schedule and announcement timetable agreed to.
- Research, product and marketing plans shared with committee members.

Announcement Day minus Five to Two Months

- Beta tests with key customers as appropriate to get operational feedback (signed written confidentiality and nondisclosure agreements required).
- Agreement on priority messages, target audiences, key selling/positioning/copy points (consistent with overall brand strategies).

- Agreement on overall theme and visuals for all media and marketing communications materials as well as advertising, and new logo — if one was created (consistent with overall corporate identification program).
- Announcement date agreed to, cleared on everyone's calendars.
- Site selected and agreed to, hotel and travel reservations made if necessary.
- Technical arrangements made for live Internet or video hookup for those who cannot attend.
- Master to-do list agreed to, with responsibilities for each item and issue.
- Standby statements and Qs and As distributed to media relations and sales staff as well as customer service reps to respond to rumors and prevent preannouncement leaks.
- Shelter magazines, quarterlies and/or other long-lead-time publications given photos and general information if appropriate (signed written confidentiality agreement required).

Announcement Day minus One Month

- Draft announcement materials (including scripts and background-only Qs and As), circulated for comments, clearance and buy-in.
- Demonstration products loaned to two or three key reporters (signed, written confidentiality agreement required).
- Arrangements made to accommodate a live feed to bloggers, employees and other key constituencies.
- Final timetable and responsibilities reviewed and agreed to.
- Board of directors, senior management alerted to plans and schedule on confidential basis.
- Spokesperson training for speakers at news conference, analyst briefing, customer seminars, etc.

Announcement Day minus One Week to One Day

- Journalists invited to news conference, financial analysts invited to briefing, customers/distributors invited to reception relating to "important new product/service" (no specifics).
- Rehearsals for news conference and analyst briefing, at announcement site whenever possible.

- Announcement materials online, on CDs or flash drives and printed, "ready to go" at key staging areas.

Announcement Day

- Stock market alerted if publicly traded company and new product/service is material.
- Wire services notified, news conference held, press kits distributed, materials put on your organization's website.
- Financial analysts briefing.
- Announcement materials distributed to all employees, with news conference streamed live if possible.
- Notification of key customers via phone, email, reception or other special event.
- Notification of legislators, community leaders, suppliers, other VIPs as appropriate.

Announcement Day plus One Day to One Week

- Advertising begins.
- Customer/dealer/distributor seminars and executive briefings as appropriate.
- Sampling of news media coverage circulated to board of directors, management and employees as appropriate.

Announcement Day plus First Few Months

- Messages and materials adapted based on monitoring media and customer feedback.
- Products, announcement theme and visuals appear in trade show exhibits, product fairs, plant and factory tours, open houses — plus related handouts and decorations (banners, balloons, etc.).
- Announcement theme and visuals appear on all collateral sales materials including brochures, direct mail, Internet sites, point-of-purchase materials, billboards, giveaways and product training materials.
- Customer testimonials distributed as news release to business, consumer and/or trade press and posted on website.
- Customer testimonials, sampling of positive news media coverage and announcement advertising distributed to distributors, key customer prospects, financial analysts and employees and also posted as appropriate on website, blogs, online chat rooms, bulletin boards.

- Audio or video satellite media tours to save spokespersons' travel time — popular in secondary markets for interview segments on local morning and noon news programs.

- Speeches at appropriate forums such as trade shows, industry groups, chambers of commerce, Rotary, etc., with reprints distributed as appropriate.

- Employee media features on customer reaction, sales results and staff who "made the product and sales happen."

- Product placements with media personalities (local celebrities can be as powerful as Oprah).

- Product contributions to selected charity events as appropriate.

Announcement Day plus One Year

- Seasonal publicity pushes during holidays, Mother's Day, Father's Day, summer vacation time, etc., as appropriate.

- First anniversary update to news media, analysts, board of directors, employees, key customers.

Three Case Studies: How Companies and a Nonprofit Use Media

Michelin Uses Social and Traditional Media to Promote Its Guides

The Michelin Guides are world renowned for setting the bar for both everyday dining and exceptional cuisine. Chefs around the world clamor to have their restaurants included in the "Guide Rouge," as it is known in France. Adding or losing a star can mean thousands of dollars to a restaurant, determining whether or not reservation phone calls and online bookings are strong. The guides were established in France more than 100 years ago. In 2005, they ventured out of Europe for the first time, eventually offering recommendations in New York, San Francisco, Chicago, Hong Kong and Tokyo. This global expansion was matched with a re-launch of the guides, including mobile apps and online support, a reader-friendly print format and a new marketing approach.

One clear challenge for the guides was to show the relevance of its recommendations in order to compete with the variety of alternative rating systems. The Michelin approach has always been based on the experience of anonymous inspectors who visit restaurants and hotels daily to report on the experience of the average consumer — shown no special treatment, no perks, and no freebies. But the secrecy that made the guide's recommendations so authentic was a clear stumbling block to its marketing needs. After all, how can a cadre of anonymous inspectors conduct interviews or share their experiences with the media or consumers except through the guide itself?

The PR department at Michelin North America, in tandem with the global Michelin press office, took up this challenge as a way to launch the latest versions of the guides in the United States while opening up the market to a broader group of foodies in New York, Chicago and San Francisco.

Working collaboratively, the PR and marketing teams knew that social media would offer a perfect opportunity to engage inspectors directly with consumers while maintaining absolute secrecy. The result was the 2009 "Famously Anonymous" campaign that launched Facebook and Twitter accounts for the Michelin Guides, including city-specific Twitter accounts that allowed inspectors to tweet about specific activity in each city to foster a sense of community with foodies both local and global.

The campaign included inspector kiosks at the launch party in each U.S. city. At the kiosk, guests could "speak" with the inspectors live via Twitter. The Twitter accounts also maintained engagement with the target audience long after the book launch, extending the selling season and driving the highest U.S. sales (up 22 percent) since the first launch of the guide in the United States. With the introduction of Michelin Guides Facebook and Twitter channels, social conversations about the Michelin Guides increased threefold (322 percent) during the first 60 days of the launch, compared to the previous year. Chefs and restaurants quickly "followed," "liked" and "friended" the accounts, creating a true interactive community with zero loss of anonymity. Firmly established as the perfect engagement tool, the social media approach continues to garner attention and sales alike.

Lessons learned: "Social media is about authenticity," said Michael Fanning, who was vice president of corporate affairs for Michelin North America at the time of this event, and now works at the company's headquarters in France. "Don't put gatekeepers between your core public and your subject-matter experts. PR should give guidelines, training, monitor and refine but let the experts 'speak' directly to your consumers."[3]

To promote the guides, however, Fanning and the Michelin team did not reply only on social media. They used traditional media and advertising in the promotions effort as well. They ran an ad campaign with the theme, "Who's the Famously Anonymous Inspector?" And they arranged for a New Yorker magazine writer to dine with a female Michelin Guides inspector at an elegant restaurant on the ground floor of the Trump International Hotel in midtown Manhattan.[4] Both these placements reinforced the credentials of the anonymous inspectors while making it clear that they were real, live people.

Cisco's Biggest Media Event Is Entirely Online

Some companies have moved their biggest media events entirely online. Author and former AT&T PR executive Dick Martin describes a highly successful product launch by Cisco Systems, Inc., a leading networking systems company based in San Jose, California:[5]

> Instead of staging the usual hotel room news conference and a flight of ads to launch a new high-end router, Cisco created an online event to which it invited customers, bloggers and analysts in addition to the trade media. It had 9,000 attendees as compared to the traditional 100 or so. And it produced three times as many news articles as usual, more than 1,000 blog postings and an estimated 40 million online impressions. According to Cisco, the event attracted 90 times the audience at one-sixth the cost. Going exclusively online made perfect sense for Cisco not only because of its leadership in networking technology but also because the new router being announced was the product of listening to customers talk about their networking challenges online.

Small Library Uses Multiple Media to Overcome Budget Constraints

The Ruby Sisson Library, located in a small mountain community in Southwestern Colorado, hosts an extraordinary range of special events from high-tech training on digital photography and downloading e-books to LEGO contests for kids and film series for adults. The library is typical of many nonprofits that need to work wonders with limited media and marketing budgets. Its success demonstrates that even a small-town library can announce events and programs by maintaining high visibility via both traditional and social media.

The creative and hardworking staff are following a newly developed strategic plan that Director Jackie Welch says is very helpful in meeting the information needs of the library's diverse audience in the most cost-effective way. "We know our younger patrons never read the local paper, and some of our older patrons do not use the Internet," she said. "We need to take advantage of every available channel, especially free media, to get our news out at little or no expense."[6]

- The library's website is the foundation of its communications efforts. Here patrons research and reserve books they want to read and learn about library news and events. They also take advantage of multiple databases including lifelong learning enrichment classes, 84 different language courses, automotive and small engine repair tips, medical information, and preparing for most of the major academic and professional tests.

- A weekly column written by a volunteer about current classes and special events at the library, plus new books, CDs, DVDs and other offerings, appears every Thursday on the news pages of the local newspaper at no cost to the library. This column is highly popular with older library patrons who still prefer to get their news the old-fashioned way. The column also is posted on two local Internet journal sites for those who prefer electronic media.

- Facebook and a blog are used to communicate with teens about programs, books and other media aimed especially at them. Facebook also is effective as a means of keeping in touch with home schoolers, who frequently pass on the library news to their "friends."

- Free community calendar listings in the weekly newspaper and on the local Internet journal sites help provide more visibility for classes and other library programs.

- Library staff appear twice a month on the community's local radio station morning talk program to promote events coming up at the library. Printed flyers and calendars are available at the library every month with information about programs and services, especially special reading sessions for toddlers, youngsters and teens.

- "Did You Know?" paid ads about the library's programs, services and events run every week in the local paper. Several times a year, quarter-page ads announce the Summer Reading Program and the Lifelong Learning lecture series.

CHAPTER EIGHT

GOING GLOBAL

How to Manage International Media Relations

At the beginning of the age of exploration, early maps carried a warning that guided navigators heading to new worlds. Unknown portions of the oceans were marked, "Here there be monsters." Such "monsters" provided opportunities for learning, adventure and heroes. That certainly is true today for media relations specialists whose companies or clients are expanding around the world. The opportunities are great, but so too is the risk of failure. There can be trouble if you are not sensitive to local conditions, willing to ask advice and eager to learn. It takes savvy and sensitivity to succeed. Yet, many firms — not only giant corporations but also smaller businesses — are taking advantage of the huge opportunities for increased sales and profits in new markets and the cost-savings inherent in sharing resources worldwide.

If your company or client is going global, you have expanded opportunities to make unique contributions on a larger scale than ever before. You can become a vital resource in efforts to enter new markets; establish corporate reputation and brand identity; launch new products; and attract the respect of journalists, customers, investors, potential employees, suppliers and other opinion leaders. Key to being successful in each new market is finding the right balance between universal interests and local customs, taking advantage of global scale while also adapting to local conditions. "One size fits all" does not work.

Even the much heralded European Union did not result in one homogenized market. Nor did the introduction of the euro automatically eliminate cultural differences. Europeans have sharply contrasting outlooks, tastes and resources. Almost 500 million people in 27 countries[1] — yes, they have common interests but they also have distinct individual identities. The Dutch will remain Dutch. The French will remain French. And the Germans will remain German.

Being Sensitive to Other Cultures

In fact, as trade barriers come down sometimes sensitivities go up. Witness ongoing conflict relating to the North American Free Trade Agreement about which countries are losing or gaining jobs. That's what makes going global so interesting — and doing business in international markets so dangerous if you do not keep your cross-cultural wits about you.

Even little things can mean a great deal. For example, entertaining effectively often is very important to doing business successfully. In China, there is no such thing as "fashionably late." In all of Asia especially and also in other countries, protocol must be observed at banquets because rank and status are serious matters. Seating arrangements and who is at or near the head table can be major issues. Huge partnerships have gone bad because North American executives who did not understand local customs and courtesies committed seemingly small *faux pas* that cost their companies millions of dollars in lost deals and opportunities.

Global expansion offers you personal growth and career opportunities.

It is not a superficial shift. It is not business as usual. It is a major strategic refocus. As a result, you have new opportunities to broaden your perspectives and learn a great deal about cultures and traditions other than your own. With the technological advantages of the Internet, satellite hookups and global networks, you can brainstorm magazine publicity strategy in Sydney and organize a news conference in Stockholm while still keeping up with the work in your home office.

Global and Multinational Media Programs

These trends have massive implications for media relations professionals. If your company is going global, you should be at the forefront of its efforts to position itself in the worldwide marketplace. Organizations with a global business strategy also need a global media relations strategy — with agreement on objectives, priority messages, target publics and product promotion plans from New York to New Zealand, from Asia to Africa. Each country's media relations activities should not only support local operations but also reinforce the corporation's global plan. The media relations strategy must align with the business strategy.

The balance between global and local media relations programs depends on your company's or client's business strategy and organizational structure. For example, take the difference between a multinational and a global company:

• It may be appropriate for ***multinational companies*** with autonomous subsidiaries and independent strategies in each market to concentrate their communications on local plans, products, people, customers and competitors — for example, featuring local executives as the visible spokespersons and leaders while downplaying the connection to the corporate parent.

• ***Global companies,*** on the other hand, operate as one business — an integrated system in which headquarters and all the subsidiary entities are interdependent in terms of strategies and operations. Every decision — from where it is most cost-effective to manufacture each product and purchase supplies to pricing policies and profit goals — takes into account the worldwide system. The sum of the parts is a whole lot more valuable to the bottom line than the pieces themselves. Individual media plans are based on local issues, local markets and local products — but collectively they all bear a remarkable similarity to each other because they also are based on the company's global communications strategy.

Be Alert to Issues in All Markets

A media relations strategy requires more than cleverly crafting messages. You also must be alert to emerging issues in all markets where your company does business, not just in your home country.

Professionals headquartered in the United States and Canada need to remember that major issues do not always surface in North America. Although most would probably agree consumer activism began in the United States, the consumerist movement today could be considered more proactive, for example, in Europe, particularly with economic boundaries falling and harmonization from European Union laws. Your antennae must be up wherever your organization does business.

When you *plan* on a global basis, you also need to *think* on a global basis. All the *"we"*s and *"they"*s need to disappear from your vocabulary, with each decision based on what's best for the total organization — and your customers. Ideas need to be given equal consideration whether they come from corporate headquarters or a field office, from San Francisco or Singapore. Wisdom flows in all directions.

Think Global — Act Local

Key to being successful in the global marketplace is to find the right balance between local customs and universal interests and practices. The Bates Worldwide advertising agency's theme sums it up well: "Think global. Act local."

In mounting media relations programs in other countries, it is essential to understand and respect others' cultures. For example: Do not give clocks as gifts in China as they are seen as symbols of bad luck. Avoid bringing food and gifts in the Middle East lest you imply your host cannot afford them. Handle graphics carefully because symbolic abstractions in one country can be hex signs in another.

These are useful guidelines, but as we travel around the world, we find more similarities than differences. Many media relations techniques that are successful in North America will also achieve your objectives in other countries, with modifications.

Practical Hints for Global Media Relations

A basic rule of thumb as you enter the global arena might be: Stop, look and listen. The practice of public relations and all its related fields including media relations differs throughout the world. Before you develop a media plan to introduce a new product in a different country, take the following steps:

1. **STOP and read a bit about the country itself.** Get past the travel brochures. Research material that gives an overview of the history, religion, culture, government and business of the country. This basic knowledge will prevent you from asking questions that should have been studied before that important planning meeting.

2. **LOOK at the material already prepared by the marketing people.** They likely have taken advantage of extensive studies, white papers, research and on-site visits before coming up with their business and marketing plans. Reviewing that material will give you an understanding of the differences between doing business in North America and elsewhere.

3. **LISTEN to what those with in-country experience tell you about operating in the selected country.** Sometimes there is a tendency to discount advice and information given by a person who has lived or worked in other countries. This no doubt is a natural outgrowth of the typical North American feeling of, "The whole world should operate as we do back home." This attitude disappears once you get to a country and conduct business there; however, valuable time can be lost by not believing words of wisdom from those who have been there before.

Additional Tips for Media Relations in International Markets

Don't start thinking about communication plans until you have studied and understood the local business issues in each market. Take the European Union, for example. Just as U.S. or Canadian federal law has great impact on your business even if you operate in only a few states or provinces, so does EU law affect you even if you do business in only a few European countries.

Don't start communications plans until you have studied the local business issues.

Do your homework — twice. Business and marketing plans on introducing a product, service or operation in another country provide essential background. These plans will highlight government relations, trade concerns, technology transfer issues, key competitors in the locale and other information that will be very useful as you develop a media plan.

If you have no contacts in the new market, find up-to-date information on the Internet. An excellent source is World Press Encyclopedia Online, a comprehensive survey of press and electronic media in more than 200 countries that also is available in print.[2] Other sources include professional organizations such as the International Public Relations Association (www.ipra.org) or the International Association of Business Communicators (www.iabc.com), each of which may be able to give you names of contacts in your countries. Additionally, in-country public relations agencies will be able to pinpoint for you the contacts and media you need.

Get local advice. The first rule of international PR is to get local help. Seek out an in-country public relations firm or agency that has done work similar to your present needs. Major U.S.- and European-headquartered agencies have full-service, stand-alone agencies in numerous countries around the world. Make sure that the agency specializes in media relations, not advertising or political affairs.

The first rule of international PR is to get local help.

It is well worth the money to get an in-depth briefing from these local experts on how media relations — especially media relations vis-à-vis marketing — works in that locale. You'll also want local expertise to help you adapt to each market's customs while maintaining your corporate and personal ethical standards and, not incidentally, obeying your own country's and local laws. For example, "pay for press" is a common practice among many non-U.S. media operations. In one form, this means paying the publication a "publishing fee" to have your release printed. In another, it can involve picking up the costs for a journalist to travel to news conferences or come to the United States for tours and interviews. These are not bribes. They can be an economic fact of life in many countries where local media budgets are sparse.

In some countries the journalist you deal with may be a lawyer or engineer first and a journalist second. This often means the difference between a general information interview and an in-depth, detailed interview. Here again, listen to what these people say and do not scoff at a public relations practice that would not work in North America but is essential somewhere else.

Local is key to social media, too. LEWIS PR, a global PR and digital communications agency headquartered in London, has particular expertise in social media and advises you to identify key influencers in each of your target markets. Then you should "reach out to the most important and relevant bloggers in your space with relevant information, give them access to resources and (literally) speak their language." This is a more effective strategy, LEWIS PR says, than blasting the same corporate material to everyone. "Of course, it is true that a large number of the most influential blogs are English-speaking and interest-oriented rather than geographically focused. That said, it is human nature that a blogger in the U.K., for example, will respond more positively to U.K.-focused information, even if his readership is international."

LEWIS PR offers these four rules for social media content creation:

• Always bear in mind that your audience is global. Be careful of content that is irrelevant or inappropriate to certain markets.

• Don't rely on Google Translate to create local language content. Use a professional translation service and have someone who is a native speaker check it.

• Use images whenever possible. Pictures and graphics are much easier to digest for international audiences.

• Relevance is critical. For international programs, make sure you are informed about the hot topics and sensitive issues in each target market, and be sure to have local examples to offer.[3]

Study a globe. Whenever you are heading to a new country, look at a globe. A globe is better than a map because it more accurately

- Make sure everyone understands how your organization uses social media and knows the purpose of your main channels.

- Make sure everyone knows who is responsible for your social media and how to reach them, whether they hail from PR, marketing or another department.

- Establish ground rules. Who can and cannot create a social media channel on behalf of the company? Lay out what is permissible, who needs to give approval, how each channel must be branded, and what types of content can and cannot be shared.

- Establish individual use guidelines so your staff knows the rules of use for social media at work, what may or may not be said about the company in an employee's own social networks, and the consequences of breaching the policy.[4]

represents the sizes, shapes and locations of continents, countries and cities. A globe overcomes what we call the "Mercator effect" — the fact that North Americans were raised with school maps using the Mercator projection, which makes North America look bigger and more important than it is in the worldwide scheme of things.

Had companies expanding into former Soviet Union-dominated countries taken a moment to look at a globe, they might understand, for example, why people in the Czech Republic resent being called Eastern Europeans. Czechs think of themselves as Central Europeans, and if you make that mistake while you are there someone might point out that Prague is farther west than Vienna.

Read some history. It also is useful to read up on the history of each market that is new to you. That sounds obvious — but it is surprising how rarely it is done. A little history can help avoid offending local hosts. For example, in Warsaw a prominent U.S.-based company was criticized for running an ad produced in New York announcing they were "expanding into the emerging Polish market." The offended Pole was a professor at the Jagiellonian University in Krakow which has been famous for centuries for mathematics, astronomy and graduates like Copernicus.

Similarly, Westerners too often view China as an emerging market. Yet, the Chinese were making glorious silk in 1750 B.C., their ancient paintings and sculpture are among the most beautiful in the world, and they are a leading market in many industries today.

So sensitivity to local nuances and a keen respect for the richness of other peoples' heritage are essential to starting off on the right foot in a new market. You do not need dull history textbooks to get that knowledge. It is available on the Internet and in travel guides, biographies, the media, popular fiction and movies.

Meet the people. Imagine a visitor to North America believing he or she understands our values and culture after traveling only to New York, Washington, D.C. or Toronto. When you travel to a country new to you, take time to get out of the cities. Talk with people in the countryside and smaller towns. Your local colleagues should be able to arrange such dialogues. Community leaders, school teachers and students frequently are willing to answer questions and give you their opinions over lunch or drinks because it is a great way for them to practice their English and learn about North America in return.

Learn the language. There is an old joke in international circles that says someone who speaks three languages is trilingual, someone who speaks two languages is bilingual, and someone who speaks one language is an American. At the minimum, you will want to learn a few basic phrases of the country's language before you visit. You truly will set yourself and your organization apart if you take the time to learn another language or two in some detail. Language skills are essential to climbing the executive ladder at European and Asian companies, and the lack of them is a key reason why so few Americans head companies based outside of North America.

Learn about your targets. Whether your intended media targets are newspapers, trade publications or blogs, become familiar with them. Read them (in translation, if necessary) as you would a new publication in your home market to find out the slant, key writers and columnists, use of photographs and type of advertising. Do not get hung up on the circulation of a publication or the number of visitors to a blog as a key indicator of its importance. Sometimes what would be a small circulation in North America could be the most significant medium in another country or region.

Check with local offices of international business or trade publications. They can save you frustrating attempts to get copies of in-country publications. Also, both the editorial and advertising offices can provide excellent overviews of national, regional or global media and their audiences.

Read international papers and listen to/view global broadcasts regularly. This is easy to do on the Internet. "BBC World News" also is available online, on Public Radio International and on PBS TV.

Electronic media require extra study. Electronic media in other countries can be valuable to a media relations campaign. Learn the differing styles of government-owned or directed television stations and also keep in mind their similarity — a need to fill airtime. There are programs about educational, business and government issues that can greatly benefit your media relations program. Often these stations are pleased to receive background video footage — sometimes even complete programs about your company.

Don't overlook the North American community "over there." In most countries, embassies and chambers of commerce have staffs willing to help you get started. They can provide a platform for introducing your company and its products or services, and also offer excellent advice for the novice coming in.

Remember the "foreign" press corps in other countries. Just as in Washington, D.C., there is a huge group of international reporters from Jakarta to Johannesburg and from Montevideo to Mexico City; so too there are U.S. and Canadian stringers, journalists or bloggers from television and radio networks, major magazines and leading newspapers in many international capitals and other big cities around the world. Make sure they get special treatment such as private interviews if you want coverage of your news in your home country as well as the new market.

Local press clubs are invaluable resources for both learning about the country and making key media contacts. Membership often is broad enough to include public relations agencies and corporate professionals.

Work those trade shows. Trade shows offer a good way to get to know the news media from another country or several countries. If your company is exhibiting at a trade show, make sure local and visiting journalists know you are there by issuing personal invitations for a visit to your exhibit booth. Host a reception for trade journalists to meet the key company officers.

Visit all the trade publications' booths. Although you might meet only members of the advertising staff, at the minimum you can get copies of key publications, leave your business card to be passed along to the editorial staff and — most important — start building relationships. Business cards vary in size from the format used in the United States to larger, 3" × 5" cards. Most include business and home addresses and telephone numbers, as well as an email address and the company's website. In some markets, especially in Asia, information will be in the local language on one side of the card and in English on the other.

Attend international conferences. In a global economy, international conferences have become a great way for North American companies to make the right international business connections and also leverage the local and regional media to drive brand awareness in new markets. It is well worth the money to invest in hiring a local PR firm to help your organization take full advantage of the opportunity — and not make small but embarrassing mistakes like formatting documents for U.S.-sized paper that then won't print properly when you use different-standard paper in other countries. Also, you may need help to make sure that any communications technology and software you plan to use at the conference is proven to work in that country.

Know your place. After reading business and marketing plans, you may find that a media relations campaign isn't needed, at least in the early stages. Perhaps the public or government affairs department should be the key player with a behind-the-scenes strategy that does not involve the news media. If that occurs, be mature enough to step out of the picture temporarily and turn the leadership role over to someone else.

Watch your language. It is amazing how often words can trip you up when you least expect it. At The Reader's Digest Association, after half a century of *international* growth, we made a major strategic shift to become a *global* organization. In our U.S. offices we went so far as to avoid words like "domestic," "foreign," "overseas," "offshore" and "abroad." It is more than semantics. It can be an unintentional sign of arrogance that is best not to send. It also can be confusing to your listeners or readers, who must do geographical gymnastics in their minds to follow your meaning. After all, what is "foreign" here is "domestic" there. A journalist in Paris being briefed by a U.S. executive who uses the term "domestic sales" is likely to think the numbers relate to French sales when the speaker might have meant U.S. sales. Or a South African hearing about an "overseas expansion" is likely to think about the United Kingdom while a North American listening to the same briefing would think Europe or Asia.

 Avoid words like "domestic," "foreign," "overseas," "offshore" and "abroad."

Similarly, when you are preparing materials about activities around the world, be careful not to write from a U.S. perspective. When you are compiling a worldwide list, for example, do not always start with the United States. Rather, alphabetize the list, thus placing the U.S. information at or near the end.

Allow extra time for translations and all the additional checking that is required to get them right. Switzerland is an example of a potentially complicated situation. There are four official languages in that country — German, spoken by about 65 percent of the population; French, about 20 percent; Italian, about 10 percent; and Romansh, generally restricted to one area. English is not an official language but it is widely spoken. Get local advice relating to your target markets before choosing what language(s) to use.

Take care with announcement dates and times. Select announcement dates and times with the same care as in North America — but not necessarily with the same criteria. In North America you likely would avoid breaking news on Friday afternoons lest it be buried in least-read Saturday media or reporters think you are hiding something. Yet, Fridays may be great days for announcements in other countries. Holidays are different so that July 4 is perfectly acceptable in the Middle East but the days of Ramadan are not. Be alert to numerous religious observance days as well as local celebrations that might detract from your announcement.

Also, remember the time zones when setting global announcement times. U.S. publicly owned companies must release all material news before the stock market opens or after it closes. It often is best for global companies to set announcement times in the very early morning, before the market opens, so the fewest possible journalists, financial analysts, staff and other key members of your global audiences are asleep when the news first comes out. Seven a.m. Eastern time works well for U.S. companies because when it is 7 a.m. in New York it is 8 p.m. in Hong Kong and 10 p.m. in Sydney. Look on the Internet for a selection of international electronic news distribution services to help send your news to the areas of the world you want to target.

Translate your materials. While many international journalists speak English well, they often prefer written material to be in their local language. This is important to remember when sending out media kits or preparing for international trade shows.

When preparing a document for translation, it is best to skim the copy for ambiguous word clusters of the type "modifier + noun + noun" (e.g., "plastic widgets and fasteners"). These are commonplace for English but for languages like Spanish and French, where modifiers must follow their nouns, it is critical that the translator know whether "plastic" refers to both the widgets and the fasteners or only to the widgets. Also, when you send photo captions for translation include the photo itself. Without seeing the visual, a translator does not know whether "widget assembly" means the actual "widget unit" or the process of "widget being assembled." In Spanish, for example, widget would be translated as *conjunto* in the first case but *ensamblaje* in the second.

Also, remember that most translations "grow." The translated version may take anywhere from 125 to 150 percent of the space of an English version. Indonesian can take as much as 200 percent. Chinese, on the other hand, with a writing system in which nearly every character represents a complete word, will frequently be shorter than the English version.

Watch those words! There are classic examples of product names that result in embarrassment when pronounced or when translated into another language. Internet scribes and comedians have a field day with these mistakes, especially if they are risqué. Example: The people who named Wii must not be familiar with the fact that British speakers, and many others in the Commonwealth, refer to urine as "wee." As a result, "Let's play with our Wii" takes on a whole new meaning when you speak British English.[5]

Check, recheck and then check a third time before introducing a name into a country. These multiple checks can save embarrassment — not to mention lost sales and wasted advertising and promotion efforts.

Scenario #1

You are the media relations director in the corporate offices of a giant U.S.-based multinational company that is composed of highly autonomous business units. They are supposed to coordinate with your office any major announcement that will generate international public attention or media coverage — and expansion into new markets falls under that umbrella. The problem is that the definition of "coordinate" is rather vague and your corporate culture strongly supports divisional autonomy, with little interference from headquarters as long as sales and profit goals are achieved.

You and Gary, the investor relations director, have been talking about concerns you both have relating to your company's alliance and new market announcements. You usually hear the plans at the last minute, with little chance for input relating to timing or positioning of the announcement, and lots of scurrying is required to get the message out on time. Also, lack of coordination between business units results in two or three announcements coming from the company in some months, followed by a long dry spell of five or six months with no significant public news. On one occasion, an Asian new market announcement requiring the CEO's attendance had been scheduled in Hong Kong for the same day as the company's annual meeting in Chicago until you caught the conflict and got it fixed.

You and Gary believe that the individual business units as well as the overall corporation would greatly benefit from a more coordinated and systematized new market announcement planning process. How do you proceed?

Scenario #2

You are attending an interdepartmental update, which the international group president holds quarterly for all senior managers in his organization. You notice the agenda includes an item, "New product announcement," being given by Julie, one of the company's most highly regarded managers. As her presentation progresses, you realize that the planning is very far along. In fact, a joint venture partner already has been selected, and some of the advertising placements have been booked by your New York agency in media in the U.K., France, Germany, Scandinavia, Hungary and Italy.

You are surprised, since you are the PR director for the division, and furthermore, you thought you had a pretty good working relationship with

Julie. Yet, here she is, giving details of a highly confidential (and newsworthy) expansion of her product line into major European markets to a room full of 60 of your colleagues. You also note that the only consumer research she cites was done in Atlanta, New York, Chicago, Denver and Washington, D.C.

Toward the end of her talk, Julie turns to you and says in front of the whole group, "John, we are counting on you to get us lots of positive media coverage not only in Europe but also worldwide." You are upset because the date she mentioned is right in the middle of a long-planned vacation with your wife. Furthermore, you know, on a confidential basis, that there is a good chance that a highly restrictive European Union directive, relating to her product line, will come down about a month before Julie's planned announcement date. What do you do … now at the meeting? Later?

Be respectful of the local culture and observant of local customs. This is good business as well as good manners. Business customs differ worldwide. North Americans want to get down to business right away, while other cultures — notably Asian — prefer to get to know you first. It is mainly only in big cities like New York that "power breakfasts" are an accepted fact of life. When "early birds" phone Mexico, Spain or Portugal, for example, in the early morning or early afternoon and find only empty offices, they need to remember that the locals will make up for the late start and long lunch by working well into the evening.

In China or other countries where language may become an issue, offer to use an interpreter. To avoid offending others' pride, point the responsibility back at you. Say, "Please allow me to have an interpreter here to assist me in making sure I understand your needs." Also, when speaking through an interpreter, it is important to look at and speak to the individual you are communicating with and not the interpreter.

Retrain your speakers. While you probably already have put your key spokespersons through public speaking and media interview training, they will need special training for interviews in non-English-speaking countries. For many reporters, English will be a second language. That means that the easygoing banter of North American news conferences probably will not come off elsewhere. Also, if your spokesperson is answering questions at a news conference with a simultaneous interpreter, it is essential to speak in short sentences or phrases and then wait for the interpreter to catch up.

 News conferences using simultaneous interpreters require special spokesperson skills.

Industry or technical jargon, business or government acronyms and non-English English ("actualizing your parameters" probably won't translate anywhere!) also can cause great confusion.

One of the easiest ways to retrain a spokesperson is to set up a mock interview with a "reporter" who does not speak English and must use an interpreter. The interpreter, only school-trained in English, will interrupt to ask the spokesperson to explain jargon or the meaning of such words as "reprioritization." It's a disconcerting experience for a spokesperson — and a dramatic way to learn to state your case simply and clearly.

Check for local taboos before deciding on giveaway items for trade shows, news conferences or other events. A small digital clock might be perfect in the United Kingdom but received with dismay in Asia. Colors could have religious connotations in several countries. Key chains are of little use in lesser-developed countries. Two good resources for advice are in-country public relations agencies and protocol officers at your embassy.

Ten Takeaway Tips for Doing Business around the World

The Reader's Digest Association established new companies and launched local editions of Reader's Digest magazine in Russia, Hungary, the Czech Republic and Poland while the communist empire was disintegrating and capitalism was beginning to flourish. We learned many lessons as we planned and implemented our media relations and publicity for these launches. These lessons provide useful hints for others moving into today's international marketplace:

1. **A "back to basics" approach is essential to success.** Don't be misled by the visibility of McDonald's, Subways and Pizza Huts

around the world. Most North American companies and products are nowhere near as well-known. In fact, journalists and consumers may have little or no knowledge of your brand — or your company. Take time up front to work with your operations colleagues to develop detailed business, marketing and communications plans. Do market research early so you have time to recover from surprises. You cannot assume your target audience knows what your company stands for and what you are trying to sell. In Eastern Europe, for example, consumers thought the Energizer Bunny commercials were selling little pink toy bunnies for children.

2. **Study the competition and others' perceptions of you.** As companies do business around the world, it can be useful to communications and marketing strategies to understand how your organization is perceived relative to your competitors in each country. A social media audit for your brand can be a useful tool. It also is helpful to know how your home country is perceived in new markets. Anti-American sentiment, for example, can have a profound effect on your company. Harris Interactive and its London subsidiary HI Europe regularly conduct research on how various companies and brands are perceived and how other countries' citizens see the United States.[6]

3. **Make sure your positioning is right.** Basic positioning questions that are key to success in home markets are even more crucial when you start communicating in new markets. Is your product or service clearly defined? Is it differentiated from the competition? Does its performance match the promise? Can you play up the emotional benefits? The world's greatest marketers sell on emotions. Disney sells magic, not theme parks or movies. Nike sells performance, not sneakers.

Think through your positioning carefully. Then pick one or two simple messages and repeat them over and over again. You want potential customers, journalists and opinion leaders to see your brand name and your key messages in everything you produce — on your website, in news media materials, advertisements, promotional and point-of-sale pieces, VIP mailings, on billboards — everywhere.

Never miss an opportunity to picture your product and your logo. Frequency, focus and consistency are key to making them familiar to your potential customers.

4. **Even more than you do in your home country, pay relentless attention to details.** Take a leadership role in planning the timing, location, messages and spokespersons for major announcements. You can expect complications because you are operating somewhere other than on familiar ground — and frequently in a language other than English.

> *Take a leadership role in planning the timing, location, messages and spokespersons for announcements.*

Make sure the translations of your news releases, media kits, speeches and other materials are impeccably accurate. Choose translators or interpreters with experience — and an understanding of the local idiom. Hire several if they will be working long hours — tired people may overlook possible misinterpretations that can cause embarrassment and inaccuracies. Provide them with copies of your presenters' speeches in advance so they can familiarize themselves with the content, then warn speakers not to *ad lib*.

Be aware that some *translators* translate literally, which can result in crazy wording. *Interpreters*, on the other hand, work to put your key message in appropriate language or symbols so that it will be received the way you intend it to be. Make sure you know which skill you're buying. We've had the greatest success hiring interpreters with experience in high-level government events where nuances matter a great deal. Refugees returning home after living many years outside their home countries may not be the best translators if they are out of date on some of the current word usage and phraseology.

Hold your news conferences at business centers with experience in and equipment for simultaneous translations. Print captions in both English and the local language at the bottom or on the back of your press photographs. Watch for misunderstandings if you are not used to working in the metric system. Get advice from local experts on the correct protocol for invitations, seating and toasts at banquets.

The food for banquets needs to be carefully chosen with an eye to dietary restrictions, factoring in the tastes and cultural diversity of all the participants.

Pay even more attention to money and bills than usual. To protect yourself from inflation and currency devaluations, negotiate so your bills are paid in local currency. In some cases we have found it cost-efficient to prepay local agencies the amount of their budget so they can buy space and purchase other services as the dollar fluctuates. Check the local country's laws if there is a value added tax (VAT); ordering and paying your bills through your local subsidiary can result in large savings. Don't be surprised if there is an ulterior motive to generate hard currency when some of your suppliers or partners make recommendations.

5. **Most media relations techniques that work at home will also work well in other countries as their business practices become more universal — and more Western.** You may be asked to advertise or get involved in a business venture by journalists. In some countries there is no clear separation between business and editorial, and it is common to pay a "publishing fee" to get your news release printed. But most professional news media relations techniques work around the world — when they are based on real news announcements and practiced with respect for journalists' needs as well as your own organization's objectives. In Mexico the local Reader's Digest company's media relations director helped get the "pay for press" practice stopped by refusing to participate. Her office supplied real news and got it treated like real news.

6. **Even universal media tools often require local touches to be successful.** We hosted news conferences for all the Reader's Digest magazine launches. The Eastern and Central European events followed our Western format fairly closely. In Moscow, however, presentations were expected to be significantly longer — 40 to 60 minutes rather than our more normal 20 to 30 — and if you could incorporate a historical perspective about your company and product, so much the better. In Poland they liked numerical research from a reputable outside firm to support product and consumer claims. Most reporters asked their best questions at the news conference, not waiting to do so in private after the general Q and A session, as is true in North America. On the contrary, as

soon as the news conference was over, everyone rushed to the food — traditionally a full meal consumed at record speed. To make your meals memorable, ask the locals what are the most desirable dishes for a party and try to serve at least one of them.

Giveaways are eagerly received and it is worth your while to make them special. Knowing the long lines that Russian citizens were enduring in those days, we gave each journalist a very large tote with a shoulder strap — featuring our new magazine's logo in English and Russian. Inside was a "traveling office" with a wide variety of office supplies in a leather case, also featuring our logo — just the items that were so hard to get in Moscow. In Hungary our giveaways also matched the market: another tote, with our logo in Hungarian and English — plus a business card holder, again featuring our bilingual logo. We were told executives were getting and giving business cards for the first time and had nowhere to keep them. These giveaways were popular because they were so useful. The totes became very visible "moving billboards" for our brand long after the news conferences were over.

Our bilingual invitations to the news conference also were special. We engraved them, pictured both countries' flags and individually wrote in the reporter's name in fancy script. We were told these touches made our event stand out in journalists' minds.

To attract media and consumer attention, we used large hot-air balloons and billboards. The balloons drew a crowd and the one in Moscow made the front page of Advertising Age magazine. Our Moscow billboards were unusual enough that they were mentioned on the "NBC Nightly News."

Direct mail also can be effective if you can purchase accurate lists. But in formerly communist countries, you might initially face suspicion and concern. Privacy is a major issue in countries like Poland. "Where did you get my name?" consumers want to know. After all, for years they lived in a police state where anonymity was the best way to survive.

7. **Always remember your objective and your primary audience.** In Moscow we got pressure from suppliers to invite government officials and other so-called VIPs (mostly politicians) to the news conference. We refused, saying the news conference was for working journalists and its objective was solely to generate media coverage

about the launch of our new magazine and local Russian company. In most markets you lose focus when you begin to mix messages and target audiences. The one hundred-plus journalists who attended seemed to appreciate our concentrating on them alone — and the extensive positive coverage around the world about the new magazine and our local company reinforced our belief that we'd made the right decision. In fact, media coverage was so extensive and our magazine so popular in the republics of Russia, Ukraine and Belarus that we sold out within days. So we scaled back plans for significant additional promotions, relying primarily on mailings of each issue of the magazine to key journalists every month.

In Asia, however, the situation is different. There they expect many local dignitaries to be on the stage with your company's presenters. The more VIPs in attendance, the more important your organization must be.

8. **Choose your speakers based on your business and marketing strategies.** As discussed previously, the balance between global and local speakers and content should depend on your organization's business strategy and organizational structure. Multinational companies with autonomous subsidiaries and independent strategies in each market likely would want to feature local executives as spokespersons. Global companies, on the other hand, probably want to showcase both global and local spokespersons at news conferences and other announcement events. You also could provide a copy of your corporate annual report to journalists even if it is in English, while augmenting it with fact sheets in the local language showing the number of in-country employees, facilities, products, contributions to the local economy, etc.

 The balance between global and local speakers and content should depend on your organization's business strategy.

9. **English is the universal language of global business ... but, be careful!** Don't underestimate the language barrier. Most of the people you are dealing with will be listening and speaking in a second language, so each conversation takes place on two planes. You are thinking and speaking in English but your colleagues probably

have to do the translation in their heads before they can comprehend and respond.

People sometimes pretend to understand, not wanting to interrupt the flow of the conversation for clarification. Maybe they think they do understand, but subtleties are lost. It is important to state things as simply as possible and be crystal clear in your communications. Get agreements in writing to see if your expectations match theirs. Interact frequently to be sure there's an easy avenue for questions. Get on a plane, make yourself available and find out firsthand what's going on. It is called "management by traveling around."

On the other hand, be wary of businesspeople who have traveled in the United Kingdom or North America saying they speak no English. Even if they require an interpreter, they may understand more English than they let on and you should be careful not to discuss your negotiating strategy with colleagues in asides, thinking no one else understands.

10. **Take advantage of local resources to help you achieve your objectives and avoid cultural gaffes.** Look for PR firms with proven experience and knowledge of local media — plus a staff that speaks the local language and understands the local culture.

You need someone who will catch you if your ad looks like it was created from a North American perspective, like the Coke print ads showing a glass filled with ice, when every North American who travels to Europe knows that Europeans don't use ice in their drinks; to alert you that Ukrainians want their country to be called Ukraine, not *the* Ukraine; or to remind you that in Hungary last names come before first and in Russia people wear their wedding rings on their right hand. That was important to a U.S. baby-care company that offended consumers when it pictured a young girl with a baby in their product promotions; scandalized viewers thought she was an unwed mother because she wore no ring on her right hand.

Another valuable contact is the U.S. Embassy — especially the press attachés at U.S. Information Service offices around the world. They have daily dealings with journalists and are pleased to give you advice and practical counsel on how to conduct business in their countries.

Social Media Tips by Market

In a white paper titled, "The Global Social Media Challenge: A Social Marketer's Guide to Managing Brands Across Borders," LEWIS PR offered this advice for social media by market:[7]

- **Australia** — Australia has one of the highest Internet penetration rates in the Asia Pacific region and one of the largest Facebook user bases per capita in the world. Content must be relevant locally, not replicated from the U.S. or Europe.

- **Belgium** — Belgians use Dutch, French, German and English to communicate online; know which your audience prefers. Also, data privacy is a big issue in Belgium.

- **China** — If you want to reach journalists in mainland China, use Mandarin. For people in Hong Kong, Cantonese is best. A local counterpart exists for every well-known Western social media channel. This creates audience fragmentation so you need to research your target markets carefully.

- **Czech Republic** — Czech companies are starting to use social media for marketing. Facebook is a popular platform.

- **France** — Always communicate in French. Social networks and sharing sites are more popular than blogging. Consider using Twitter and Facebook to nurture and retain customers.

- **Germany** — Although most Germans understand English, they appreciate your using German. They are extremely focused on data privacy. Make sure you know the rules for company use of social media and explain why exactly you need any user data.

- **India** — More than 30 million Indians use social networking sites and 60 percent of those are open to being approached by brands. English is the language of business, but to connect with wider audiences incorporate Hinglish (combination of Hindi and English).

- **Italy** — All content and social media communications must be in Italian. Religion, crime and sexuality are taboo subjects.

- **Netherlands** — There are a lot of widely read collaborative blogs here. Most of them are open to new contributors, so consider joining forces to reach a large audience instead of building your own blog.

- **New Zealand** — Be sure to have a clearly defined strategy for New Zealand that is separate from Australia. They are separate markets with unique demographics and business challenges.

- **Poland** — Local language and references are essential. Monitor grassroots initiatives in social media that are already popular; identifying with one that is relevant to your brand is more likely to be successful than building a community from scratch.

- **Portugal** — Many brands are successfully using YouTube. Avoid standard corporate videos. Videos that demonstrate a brand's personality and encourage interaction resonate best.

- **Singapore** — The population is made up of people from India, Indonesia, Malaysia, China and Singapore, so you need to be mindful and respectful of different races, beliefs and religions. Ensure that local statistics and facts relevant to Asia are included in your content.

- **Spain** — Companies serious about engaging Spanish audiences must have Spanish language social media programs. Remember, Catalan is a separate language.

- **United Kingdom** — U.K. audiences are extremely skeptical. Make sure you have your facts in hand and can back up any claims you make. U.K. audiences react well to content that is humorous and witty, as long as it is not offensive.

- **U.S.A.** — Don't worry about tagging content to a specific location. Where something took place isn't as important to U.S. audiences as why something is compelling and relevant.

For more information from this white paper, go to www.lewispr.com.

Advice from PR Pros on How to Succeed in Their Markets

Here are some suggestions passed on by PR professionals, editors and business executives, all of whom are practicing PR in their local markets, to help you get the best possible results from your efforts as you go global:

Asia

A major difference is the way news conferences are handled in Asia. For example, in Hong Kong and Taiwan it is a real show with all the key people sitting at the head table wearing corsages. The more senior people you have on stage, the more important the event. The setup is also very different. Theatre style is not very popular. Small tables for four where journalists can lean on something and have tea or coffee (obviously not served during the program) works very well, particularly in Taiwan. Because of their culture, Chinese journalists will rarely ask questions as a group, preferring to talk one-on-one with the speakers before or afterward. In Thailand a product launch involves two separate functions in one day, one for VIP guests with lunch, followed by the news conference. The odd thing is that all the journalists gather in a separate room at the same time as the VIP guests arrive and seem to enjoy themselves immensely at this informal gathering before the news conference. Again, the more keynote speakers the better. It may also be useful to know that the media here say they far and away prefer dealing with a company PR manager than an agency in most cases, because they feel they are getting directly to the source.

— Liz Dingwall Mueller, Hong Kong

Australia

Even though Australia and the U.S. may appear to be very similar in terms of culture, there are some key differences. Aussies are not as intense when it comes to business presentations and face-to-face contact. That doesn't mean we're not serious about doing a great job. But we find some of the "show" associated with U.S. fanfare rather false instead of involving. So despite the fact that we follow the U.S. very closely in many trends, we tend to look to our English heritage for what is stylish, frowning upon flashy trappings. Also, American business people are much more direct about what they want and what they expect. Aussies, on the other hand, don't like to be seen as too bossy and we like to be friends with our business suppliers. So what we *don't* say may be as critical as what we say. We'll just not use your services again if we are unhappy rather than complain and cause a fuss. So you need to find the proper balance between not frightening us but also giving and getting useful feedback. As well, while Americans tend to idolize heroes, Aussies are known to "cut down tall poppies." So, for example, when Bill Gates was here there was as much talk about his being a boring speaker as there was about his brilliance in making Microsoft a worldwide brand name.

— Jo Roper, Sydney

Canada

Consider whether your PR program or campaign is national or regional. We have a huge country and your approach would be different for each region. Nationally, you would aim at the larger media outlets (the networks and syndicated press), which are predominantly centered in Toronto. If you are looking at effectively reaching the entire country, you'll want someone with regional contacts to do the legwork for you. Use your professional network — the International Association of Business Communicators or Public Relations Society of America — to help you find them. Is it a national campaign only to the English-speaking public, or to the French as well? If so, you will have additional costs for translation, a francophone spokesperson and perhaps an agency that has experience in providing services for both the English- and French-speaking markets. The cultural tastes of Quebeckers, for example, are very different from the rest of the country and, as a result, the way you communicate with this group might be quite different from how you present your story in the west. Also, Canada in recent years has become a nation of nations, with a great many people now speaking a Chinese dialect or Hindi.

Social media has greatly changed the way we communicate. In today's world, our relationships with our audiences are instantaneous and interactive. It will be important for you to clearly understand your objectives and include social media as part of your overall strategy, where it makes sense. If you are looking for feedback, wanting to build relationships or change behavior, you need to carefully consider how to incorporate social media into the overall mix. In fact, in some instances it may be the key factor. Websites, Facebook, YouTube, blogs and Twitter all give you the powerful potential to create relationships with your audiences in a way that would have been unheard of just a few years ago.

— Bonnie Venton-Ross, Whitehorse, Yukon

France

If you want more media coverage in France about your company, provide journalists with background information on the history of your company and also how you are sharing the financial results of your business not only with shareholders but also with employees and society. Journalists here are very interested in cultural as well as economic success. So it is a good idea to brief them on how the company was built and what it is contributing to society overall — for example, establishing a foundation to support young artists.

— Henri Capdeville, Paris

The language of PR is highly culturally dependent. Any American operating here would have to be competent enough to read and write in French — or hire it done locally. Industry and government rules are quite different from the American scene, and for broadcast in particular the regulatory environment is very different. As a result, the rules and recipes valid in America have to be drastically adapted to fit the context here. Rules governing social and personal relations in France also are different from what an American is accustomed to. For instance, giving out one's home address or phone number would be misunderstood and it is not information expected on a news release. PR people here have many virtues but suffer from a lack of professionalism compared to their American colleagues. So as long as you adapt to "the French way," your ideas and talents would be welcomed and very useful here.

— Benedicte Barre, Paris

Hungary

It is important for PR professionals to gather and weigh all advice from their clients and local colleagues — but then take care not to be overly influenced by such advice. The locals often try to manipulate journalists from behind the scenes rather than invest the time, energy and money that a professional campaign requires. Their results understandably often are mixed at best. U.S. PR professionals should make sure they are aware of relevant local laws, customs and attitudes but make their own decisions according to their best professional judgment.

— Peter Keresztes, Budapest

175

Mexico

Before contacting the media, learn how it works in Mexico. It is very different than in the U.S. or Europe — much more personal interaction and less technology and specialized services, for example. If you cannot afford the time for this relationship building, get local help. Try not to go on your own "the American way." Also, always say no to media people who ask you to pay to get your news release published. It is much less common than it was, but it still exists — and if you do it once you'll have to do it forever.

— Ligia Fernandez, Mexico City

South Africa

It is advisable to collaborate with a local PR firm who understands the media and how they work. If you want to conduct a major media campaign, which may include above- and below-the-line elements, it is imperative you join forces with a PR firm experienced in the kind of campaign you want. Contact an ad agency, many of whom have PR divisions, your local attorney, even the local office of a multinational company to ask for their recommendations. Bigger is not always better. Small consultancies are known to go the extra mile. There are 11 official languages and nine provinces in South Africa, which means that sometimes stories will be covered regionally rather than nationally. Mainstream news coverage is mostly still conducted in English and Afrikaans.

Since the first democratic elections in 1994, the media landscape has changed and the country has seen the introduction of tabloid newspapers as well as a big shift to social media. Newsrooms have become "juniorized" and have very few dedicated beat reporters. So developing relationships and contacts and having a good angle or hook to your story is all the more important. For this reason, you will also need to add context to your story to ensure accuracy when dealing with inexperienced journalists. Pick up on some topical news and research the issue so that you offer something newsworthy. Shortage of staff in the newsroom can work to your advantage, as a well-written story is appreciated and often used in its entirety. It also is important to bear in mind that a significant percentage of the consumer market is functionally illiterate and/or doesn't spend money on newspapers, which makes radio and TV important outlets. As well, there is a plethora of smaller community-based radio stations and free issue newspapers, colloquially called "knock 'n' drops," that are widely consumed.

Media tend to focus extensively on politics, crime and the economy, leaving little space for "soft news." Press releases and story angles need to be strategic and not seen as pushing a brand. However, a cleverly presented human interest story will find space. Corporate social responsibility remains of paramount importance, and the media are sympathetic to empowerment stories and extraordinary achievement. They will readily carry stories, events and activities of nonprofit organizations.

— Fay Davids Kajee, Cape Town

Switzerland

Although it may sound simplistic, the best tip I can pass on to Americans coming to Switzerland to do PR is to contact a local PR agency skilled in collaborating with American companies. In Europe the best PR approach will differ from country to country. In Switzerland, for example, you will benefit from the local know-how you can get only from a local partner and adviser. Also, language is very important. Although business and media people generally speak English, an effective PR approach in Switzerland could well depend on a competence in French and German.

— Hans Bosshard, Zurich

United Kingdom

Be sure to involve local people in the creative process. When you come over from headquarters and talk about rolling *out* a product or a campaign, the local people feel rolled *over* — like they've been hit by a steamroller rather than involved in a communications partnership.

— Russell Twisk, London

Personal and Professional Growth

Your company or client probably is going or has gone global because expansion into international markets represents the only way

177

to achieve long-term growth objectives. Yet, resources can be scarce in many organizations. So your organization's future in the global marketplace is up to the vision and skills of people like you.

Opportunities can be endless — not only for your firm's growth but also for your own. Immersing yourself in other cultures is a real learning experience. It also is a little like going through Alice's looking glass: You will never see yourself and your own country in quite the same way. With patience, a broad perspective, a willingness to learn and a healthy dose of can-do spirit, you can contribute to your organization's success at the same time you are traveling the world and expanding your professional skills.

CHAPTER NINE

CRISIS PLANNING

How to Anticipate and Manage Emergency Situations

Emergencies. Crises. Catastrophes. Disasters. Terrorist attacks. Mismanagement. Fraud. There was a time when anything that went wrong was called a crisis, from an explosion in a factory to the sudden demise of the CEO to a product recall. Today, the word "crisis" seems insufficient to describe the depth, breadth, scope and ramifications of many bad situations.

Social media have given every critic of your organization the power to instantly trash your brand. Your opponents can blast out blind quotes and negatives that include known inaccuracies on platforms like YouTube, Twitter and Facebook. A popular radio talk show host recently boasted to his listeners that his combination of extremist tweets, live streams of his radio show and on-air diatribes "kicked up a dust storm in the Twitterverse." As political analyst Rob Stein put it: "Web fires are lit every day."[1]

Older readers and journalism historians remember the days when huge events like the assassinations of President John F. Kennedy and Dr. Martin Luther King Jr. and the successful landings of men on the moon brought everyone to their TV sets to have the news interpreted for them by great television anchors like Walter Cronkite.[2] Now news — especially in a crisis — is disseminated differently, as a much less-unified experience. The YouTube audience seems to have no need for establishment figures, whether TV anchors or politicians, to mediate their experience of news.[3]

 "Web fires are lit every day."

Dick Martin, a business writer specializing in marketing and public relations and the former head of PR for AT&T, reminds us, "Word of mouse has become even more powerful than word of mouth." People share online reviews with family and friends. Reporters and financial analysts quote them. "And they live forever in a company's or brand's search results, amplified in power because they are now in front of a highly motivated target — someone seeking information about a specific company or brand."[4] Ari B. Adler, former newspaper reporter and editor and now media relations professional, stresses that because of "electronic formats that are easily reproduced and distributed," it's more imperative than ever that PR pros get their organizations' and clients' stories out quickly in time of crisis.[5] And Richard Edelman, president and CEO of Edelman, the world's largest public relations firm, told the Chicago Tribune: "I just don't think you can advertise your way out of a crisis. I think you have to earn people's respect and trust. [You have to] regain the trust."[6]

London-based LEWIS PR asks: "What happens if a customer in Spain complains on Twitter about your product and no one in that time zone is authorized to act? What if no one is even listening during that time? If your organization is large enough to have listening posts and crisis response processes set up in every time zone, great. But for many that isn't the case and, in the hours between that first complaint and your alarm clock beeping, the situation may have spiraled to much more serious proportions."[7]

Planning for a Crisis

Social media have taken away the ability of many organizations to get in front of a potential crisis situation to manage the media and the message. Communications, always the vital element in any situation, can be wiped out as an earthquake, hurricane or tsunami rips away power lines, cell towers and gas lines or as your country is under attack. This is the world of crisis planning.

The CEO Is Critical to a Successful Crisis Plan

In a workshop on crisis communications, PR consultant Raymond C. Jones said the most important prerequisite for an effective crisis plan is a CEO who understands:

• The serious damage that can be done by a poor public relations effort

• The importance of trusting in and delegating to professionals

• That an organization can actually emerge from a crisis with its reputation *enhanced,* if it responds well

• That honesty is the best policy and that if you engage in gamesmanship with the media, you will lose every time.[8]

While Jones' list is timeless, there are important elements of a crisis plan that need continual updating and rethinking. In the past, for example, crisis plans did not need to take into account the possibility of an entire computer or communications system going up in shreds from a bomb blast. Or having to set up a new business site — from scratch — with no location, no furniture, no computers or telephones, no paper files, no staff.

Plan for Worst-Case Scenarios

The next most important prerequisite for an effective plan is a detailed list of probable and possible events that could become anything from a bad news day to a catastrophe:

- If your business location is near water, natural disasters such as a hurricane or a tsunami, or human disasters, such as an oil spill, should be on your list.
- If your business is in a tower, then fire, terrorism and power outages all should be on your list.
- If you have a manufacturing operation, anything from chemical spills to sabotage to environmental issues should be included.
- If you have operations in Third World countries, possible civil unrest and terrorism should be on your list.
- Also on that list should be the possibilities of a product recall, class-action lawsuit, financial malfeasance, a charge of pedophilia against a volunteer, a federal investigation, or an insensitive remark by a not-thinking-smart executive. Anything that can create a crisis.
- Act as an early warning system by identifying potential problems and working with colleagues in the appropriate departments to fix them before they grow to crisis dimensions. In the Twitter age, when anyone can immediately render swift and harsh judgment, you need to know your organizations' weaknesses and research your vulnerabilities before your enemies do.
- London-based LEWIS PR advises: Whatever your level of commitment to social media, every brand has the responsibility to monitor for potential issues and act on them when necessary. Set up monitoring processes wherever you do business through a combination of "automated monitoring tools, search queries and manual processes."[9]

Develop Individualized Plans

The next step is to develop individualized plans for each eventuality. That may seem like a lot of work, but it is essential as no one plan will work for all situations. Crises don't happen the way you want them to or on your schedule. That carefully constructed scene in your head of having the media meet at a nearby location for briefings doesn't work if the nearby location is also in flames or under water.

Another step is to work in concert with all the other departments who are looking at crises from their points of view. The information technology people are busy building/storing/saving backup systems across town or across the country. Human resources staff are looking at their databases to make sure they can have access to employee names, next-of-kin information, payroll data and benefits information. Corporate safety officers are working with myriad local, state and federal officials on the best evacuation plans and recovery efforts.

 The definition of a crisis is a relative thing.

For your media relations work, you need backup files on media contacts, standby statements and executive contact information. You may need to run the post-crisis media operations from your home or another city or a different company location, so your plans have to account for that and for notifying the media how to find you.

Also, in order to have a successful plan, it must be tested, tried and simulated in order to be the best it can be. As you develop a written cri-

Strategic Questions to Test Your Crisis Plan

The following strategic questions were developed by Canadian publishing executive and Adjunct Professor Ralph Hancox to help boards of directors formulate clear, unambiguous and precise answers as they develop mission statements and strategic plans. They can serve as equally valuable guidelines for media relations professionals and your colleagues as you develop a crisis plan for your organization.[10]

1. What are we going to do?
2. How are we going to do it?
3. How are we going to pay for it?
4. Who's going to do the work?
5. How will we treat them?
6. Who's going to consume what we do?
7 How will we reach them?
8. How will we treat our various publics (customers, clients, employees, industry associates, suppliers, regulators, etc.)?
9 What other people do we need to reach?
10. How will we organize and control all this?
11 What returns do we expect for our activities?

sis communication plan, a key point you will want to make clear to the top decision makers of your company or client is that the definition of a crisis is a relative thing. A few people speaking out to the media over a dress code can be big television news even though you feel the issue is trivial in light of broader, more pressing issues. Your prompt, matter-of-fact management of smaller issues will go a long way toward containing them so they do not develop into major media events.

Guidelines to Follow During a Crisis

While there are countless ways to develop plans for dealing with the media (and other constituencies) during a crisis, you must act — and react — quickly. Jeff Jarvis, who blogs at http://buzzmachine.com, reminds us that these days there is really "only one time zone — now."[11] You must have or know how to get the appropriate information about people, policies and events inside and outside of your organization. You never get a second chance to make a good first impression. You must always be proactive. And, of course, you must always tell the truth.

1. **Make sure everyone knows who is in charge.** Long before any crisis hits, establish a clearly defined chain of command and escalation process.

2. **Know who has the information.** Information exists by department, by type of crisis, by need to know, by the public's desire to know, by federal or state regulations. Make a list of the types of information needed and where it will have been stored in anticipation of a crisis.

3. **Know who will speak on behalf of the organization.** You as the media relations professional should speak on basic matters relating to the crisis. You also will need a senior crisis spokesperson and/or subject-matter expert for more complex matters — or maybe two or three, depending on the situation. Selection of these spokespersons should be done long before a crisis hits.

4. **Understand the feeding needs of the media.** Media reporting on your crisis will want facts when you don't have them, numbers when you can't speculate, estimates of damage that aren't yet available. And they will want them *now*. Give whatever you have:

number of employees, list of products, the count of employees who have checked in, the offers of assistance you've received.

5. **Understand that "first beats better."** In the mad scramble to cover a crisis, reporters sometimes make little effort to corroborate eyewitness accounts, rumors, innuendoes or speculation. Help them get the basic facts right by keeping your website updated.

6. **Monitor the media.** Because reporters are operating at mach speed during a crisis and are chasing all information, however incorrect it may be, you need to pay attention to what is being said. Monitoring both traditional and social media is a key media relations responsibility.

7. **Make a plan for using your website wisely during a crisis.** It is a good idea to create a "dark site," a predeveloped nonpublic website that can be linked to your main website if a crisis develops. Dark sites are typically developed for areas of known risk or vulnerability.

8. **Communicate with employees.** Employees can be your best line of defense and/or offense. Frequent updates from top management will help keep employees from speculating and spreading rumors.

 In a crisis, the relationships you have built with journalists will pay dividends.

9. **Be accessible.** As counterintuitive as it may sound or feel — especially to your management — this is the time to be more accessible than ever with the media. And this is the time when the relationships you have built with journalists will pay dividends. If you have done your job ethically and well, reporters will come to you for information and believe what you say.

10. **Recognize that incomplete and sometimes inaccurate media coverage is inevitable** during a crisis. Perhaps all you can realistically hope for when you are involved in negative news is that the media get most of the facts right and portray your organization as being concerned and actively involved in fixing what went wrong.

PR Week once called James E. Lukaszewski one of 22 "crunch-time counselors who should be on the speed dial in a crisis." Lukaszewski, ABC, APR, Fellow PRSA, is president of The Lukaszewski Group, a division of Risdall Public Relations, management consultants in communications. He advises, coaches and counsels senior management through extraordinary problems and critical high-profile circumstances. His extensive experience and expertise makes his advice well worth heeding:

The Perfect Apology
The most powerful action in reputation recovery and rehabilitation is to apologize. If you want or need forgiveness, you'll need to apologize. The perfect apology has three components: First and foremost, the perpetrator has to have an attitude of humility; then an apology strategy, which leads to sincerity of action. Here are the elements of an apology strategy:

- Ongoing expressions of regret and empathy
- Continuous explanation of how behavior will change
- If serious enough, third-party oversight of new behaviors, reported independently, to the public
- Encouragement of public discussion, especially by the victims, about the perpetrator's mistakes and callousness
- Commitment to overcompensate and complete restoration of damages and injury
- Resolve to maintain contact with the victims and survivors until *they* lose interest

The biggest problem with apology is the attitude among leaders and their attorneys that apology is "sissy" stuff. My advice is, "Get over it." There's mounting statistical evidence that apologies, even if they are required by insurance companies (which they more frequently are), are having a dramatic affect on reducing litigation.

When the lawyers say you can't apologize because it's an admission of something (which it is), you can tell them (with nearly absolute certainty) that an apology will, at a minimum, mitigate and, at a maximum, eliminate litigation. An apology may be the trigger to settlement. Failure to apologize is always a trigger for litigation.[12]

Seeking Forgiveness
Obtaining forgiveness involves completing the nine steps below. To achieve success in the shortest possible time, these steps must be com-

pleted in the order presented, as quickly as possible. Seeking forgiveness is society's requirement for relationship, trust and credibility restoration. Adverse situations handled this way cost a lot less, are controversial for much shorter periods of time, suffer less litigation, and help the victims come to closure more quickly.

1. **Candor:** Outward recognition, through promptly verbalized public acknowledgement, that a problem exists; that people or groups of people, the environment, or the public trust are affected; and that something will be done to remediate the situation.

2. **Empathy/apology:** Verbalized or written statement of personal regret, remorse and sorrow, acknowledging personal responsibility for having injured, insulted, failed or wronged another, humbly asking for forgiveness in exchange for more appropriate future behavior and to make amends in return.

3. **Explanation** (no matter how silly, stupid or embarrassing the problem-causing error was): Promptly and briefly explain why the problem occurred and the known underlying reasons or behaviors that led to the situation (even if you have only partial early information).

4. **Affirmation:** Talk about what you've learned from the situation and how it will influence your future behavior. Unconditionally commit to regularly report additional information until it is all out or until no public interest remains.

5. **Declaration:** A public commitment and discussion of specific, positive steps to be taken to conclusively address the issues and resolve the situation.

6. **Contrition:** The continuing verbalization of regret, empathy, sympathy, even embarrassment. Take appropriate responsibility for having allowed the situation to occur in the first place, whether by omission, commission, accident or negligence.

7. **Consultation:** Promptly ask for help and counsel from "victims," government, the community of origin, independent observers, and even from your opponents. Directly involve and request the participation of those most directly affected to help develop more permanent solutions, more acceptable behaviors, and to design principles and approaches that will preclude similar problems from re-occurring.

8. **Commitment:** Publicly set your goals at zero. Zero errors, zero defects, zero dumb decisions, and zero problems. Publicly promise that to the best of your ability situations like this will never occur again.

9. **Restitution:** Find a way to quickly pay the price. Make or require restitution. Go beyond community and victim expectations, and what would be required under normal circumstances to remediate the problem.[13]

Behavior Patterns that Perpetuate Trouble

Sometimes the only way to help organizations avoid embarrassment, humiliating visibility, enormous litigation, and just plain stupidity is to illustrate dramatically the pattern of behaviors and attitudes that lead to catastrophic reputational trouble. These behaviors can be easily recognized and their impact predicted. If you are looking for trouble, here's the way to quickly multitask your way into long-term difficulty.

- **Denial:** Refuse to accept the fact that something bad has happened and that there may be victims or other direct effects that require prompt public acknowledgement.

- **Victim confusion:** Irritable reaction to reporters, angry neighbors and victims' families when they call asking for help, information, explanation or apology. "Hey! We're victims, too."

- **Testosterosis:** Look for ways to hit back, rather than to deal with the problem. Refuse to give in, refuse to respect those who may have a difference of opinion or a legitimate issue.

- **Arrogance:** Reluctance to apologize, express concern or empathy, or to take appropriate responsibility because, "If we do that, we'll be liable," or, "We'll look like sissies," or, "We'll set a precedent," or, "There will be copycats."

- **Search for the guilty:** Shift blame anywhere you can while digging into the organization looking for traitors, turncoats, troublemakers, those who push back, and the unconvinceables.

- **Fear of the media:** As it becomes more clear that the problem is at least partly real, the media begin asking, "What did you know, and when did you know it?", "What have you done, and when did you do it?", and other humiliating, embarrassing and damaging questions for which there are no really good, truthful answers anymore because you have stalled so long.

- **Whining:** Head down, shuffling around, whining and complaining about how bad your luck is — about being a victim of the media, zealous do-gooders, wacko-activists, or people who don't know anything; about how people you don't respect have power; and, that you "don't get credit" for whatever good you've already contributed.

Execute these behaviors in any order and I guarantee trouble, serious reputation problems, and brand damage. By the time you recover — if you do — some career-defining moments and a new team may replace you and yours.[14]

Repetition and Frequency Are Valuable Tools

Research shows that overcommunicating pays off — and nowhere is this principle more applicable than when you are in a crisis situation.

In his newsletter "Cutting Edge PR e-News," Australian Kim Harrison cites the 2012 Edelman Trust Barometer survey that found PR messages need to be repeated at least three–five times to gain traction with recipients. The repetitions can be in the form of variations on a theme and in different channels rather than the exact message being repeated.[15]

In their book "News Reporting and Writing," The Missouri Group advises that the more media you use, the better chance you have to succeed. They counsel you to think in terms of campaigns and strategies. A campaign assumes that you can't just tell an audience once what you want them to learn, retain and act on. You need a strategy to reach a goal that may take days, weeks, months or even years to attain. Which media do you use to introduce your subject? Which media for follow-up and details? What aspects of your message are best suited for which media? It's far more effective to send your message in a mix of media in a carefully timed and orchestrated way.[16]

Use Twitter to Communicate Quickly

Chris King, a New York-based PR professional and social media specialist, points out that there are many ways you can use Twitter effectively in a crisis situation. "Twitter allows you to do damage control if your brand is taking a beating by correcting misinformation and keeping a strong flow of positive communication flowing from you — the source," King said.[17] He advises you to use Twitter to:

- **Provide valuable *real-time* updates** and critical information when other communication vehicles are too cumbersome to use or have failed, and

- **Put the word out quickly and widely** not only to reporters but also to customers and your internal communications constituencies. They in turn can re-tweet your information to their audience of followers (and so on, and so on), allowing for instant viral spreading of your side of the story. Hopefully, some of those people also will pass your position on via word of mouth or their websites or blogs.

Similar to the way a traditional telephone tree works when a school needs to spread the word quickly that classes have been cancelled due to weather or a campus safety issue, so Twitter can be used in a crisis to disseminate information quickly to reporters and your other key stakeholders. Twitter becomes an invaluable tool when more complex avenues of communications you have in place can't be accessed or updated. Perhaps the servers that host your website are down. Or the resources that do your website updating don't have the time or access to perform those functions. With Twitter, your news gets out instantaneously to your audience in the time it takes to type out 140 characters or fewer on your mobile device.

Lesson learned: King cautions that you need to make sure only one "mouthpiece" is doing the tweeting, so that only accurate and approved information is coming out — from one vetted source — to serve as the official information you want circulated during the crisis. You can't have a satellite office making tweets, for example, about the situation that might conflict with what your senior management wants communicated.

Three Case Studies: How *Not* to Handle Sensitive Situations

Frequently the way a sensitive situation is handled will determine whether it goes away quietly or becomes a self-created crisis generating unnecessary and unwelcome visibility. Here are three examples of how *not* to handle sensitive situations. Ask yourself: Would you have anticipated these strong negative reactions? Would you have counseled other actions to avoid these crises? Are you well enough positioned in your organization that your counsel would have prevailed?

Target Inadvertently Offends Gays

Target is widely admired for its ability to spot trends and capitalize on them by leveraging the creativity of a wide array of talented designers and manufacturers around the world. But in his book, "Other-Wise," Dick Martin, offers an analysis of what went wrong at the Minneapolis-based retailer relating to a political donation:[18]

> In 2010, Target made a contribution to the political campaign of a candidate for Minnesota governor because he was "business friendly." The donation was legal and aboveboard. But this candidate was strongly opposed to same-sex marriage, a hot issue in the campaign. Target — which had long provided domestic partner benefits to its gay and lesbian employees and was widely seen as a pro-

gressive company — appeared to be taking sides on the issue. Within days there were calls to boycott the retailer and demonstrations in front of its stores. At first, the company tried to defend its donation, pointing out that it did not oppose same-sex marriage. Eventually, though, Target's CEO felt it necessary to issue an apology and promise to review the process it uses for making political donations. Target had put its corporate reputation in the center of its own famous bull's-eye logo. The retailer learned the hard way that in an age of angry minds and single-issue politics, no institution can afford to underestimate the power of small groups with a belief in their cause.

Labatt Reaction to Photo Gives It More Visibility

While the case around suspected murderer Luka Magnotta continued to grab media attention in Montreal in 2012, it was an offshoot story that quickly rose to the top of Twitter trends. In its digital access version, The Montreal Gazette ran a photo of Magnotta holding a bottle of Labatt Blue. In an effort to distance its brand, Labatt Brewers of Canada's legal team threatened legal action unless the photo was taken down, sparking a rash of discussion on social media.

This incident provides a glimpse into how quickly social media can shape the opinions of millions of people, and highlights key things organizations and brands should be thinking about from a communications perspective. It may be crisis communications 101, but given how easy it is to fire off a tweet, you should take a deep breath before you respond. Think through your response, no matter how small, and make sure you've considered all perspectives before acting. Sometimes the best way to protect your brand is to do nothing at all. Labatt later dropped its threats of legal action — but it was too late. It was their response that fueled the story.[19]

Catholic Church Boosts Sales of Book It Wanted to Ban

Catholic theologian Sister Margaret Farley's book "Just Love" was languishing at No. 142,982 on Amazon in 2012 when the Vatican censured it. Within days, the book hit No. 16 on the best-seller list.[20] Bottom line: The resultant coverage in both traditional and social media caused the 77-year-old author's book to shoot from obscurity to best-seller status six years after it was published.[21] And the church's heavy-handed and poorly thought-out tactics brought ridicule to its leadership.

CHAPTER TEN

MEASUREMENT/ EVALUATION

How to Know if Your Program Is Working

Globally, the number of websites, blogs, Twitter accounts, live feeds and posts used as part of organizational communications increases exponentially every day. In addition — in spite of the pundits' prognostications — there remain hundreds of thousands of daily, weekly and Sunday newspapers, and trade and consumer magazines worldwide. Add to this, thousands of public and subscriber-based television and radio stations, and you can begin to see the scope of measuring and evaluating a media relations program for your company or organization.

While it probably is not the intent of your media relations efforts to reach all of these media outlets, it should be your intent to know, insofar as possible, how many of your targeted media responded to your efforts to communicate about your organization and in what way and, more important, what action the targeted audience took in response to your message.

 Measurement should be well planned and executed.

Measurement of the various media relations activities is generally the forgotten element of most programs. In fact, some handbooks on publicity do not even include a section on measurement or evaluation. Measurement should be as well thought out, as well planned and as well executed as the rest of your media relations program. You should know if you want/need to measure:

- **The relationships you have** with reporters, editors, bloggers, columnists and freelancers. Do you detect any negativity?

- **The effect your messages have on the publics you are attempting to reach.** Do they react to your messages the way you/your client want them to? Do they understand your messages? Do they buy your products/use your services?

- **The way your message is perceived by the public.** Do they feel about your organization, product or service the way you want them to?

- **Which media used your message.** Traditional and social media? Local and global media? All print/no electronic? All electronic/no print?

- **The results of your efforts.** Was a boycott avoided? Did the public vote to support your organization? Did your program receive positive editorials?

An organization that has had a disaster also needs to consider evaluating the spillover effect of that disaster onto subsequent media relations activities. Bad news stays in the public mind for many years — even generations — and can heavily influence how the public feels about your company, organization, management or campaign. Innocent attempts at new, positive media campaigns can revive old, bad memories.

For example, a story of a new method of cleaning up oil spills will trigger an editor's — and the public's — memory of the oil spill in the Gulf of Mexico that severely damaged several coastal states, inevitably linking a good story to a bad one. A long-term, professionally administered measurement of current levels of this "guilt by association" attitude can help you determine when, how and where to launch social media campaigns.

The Goal of Measurement

No matter how large or small your operation may be, every well-run media shop should have some method of monitoring and evaluating the results of its *output* in order to know its *outcome.*

For many years, the rule of thumb on media measurement was counting clips, hits, column inches, circulation numbers and mentions. Then "air time" was added to the mix along with "impressions," which is another way to describe circulation and viewing audience numbers. Others added "output" as a measure, but that's just manual labor. All of these might have been sufficient at the time, but they don't work in a world of fragmented media and even more fragmented audiences. Even size and reputation of the medium have been used as measures of success. Perhaps the worst, and yet most used, "measurement" has been the "advertising value equivalent." There is *no* equivalent between earned media and paid media in print, broadcast or social media forums.

 True measurement focuses on outcome, not output.

True measurement will show how a designated audience responded or how an activity changed as a result of your media relations efforts. Measurement begins with setting measurable objectives that are based on your organization's business goals and not on the process of media relations. If your media relations objective is "to get 1.5 million impressions," then you are measuring your process, not the company's goal of "increasing sales in the Southwest market by 10 percent."

What to Measure

Finding and clipping stories, citing television or radio references and creating quarterly clip reports have been for decades the number one "measure of success." But all of these efforts are outputs ... not outcomes. Of concern to many professionals is the measurement of electronic media. The number of "eyes" and "ears" for television and radio can be determined but the all-important measurement of outcome remains a challenge.

What you want to measure are outcomes: What happened as a result of your media efforts? Did more people attend your event? Did sales on that product pick up? Did student enrollment increase? Did donations increase? Did your candidate get elected? Did more people sign on to your website(s)? Did your website visits increase? Was there a change in how the public views your company?

When planning a major news announcement you should always consider first what you want the outcome of that announcement to be: What are the measurable objectives? For some companies the desired outcome might be an uptick in the stock price/value. For others, it might be a decline in customer complaints. Colleges and universities want an increase in enrollment; nonprofits want increases in donations and volunteers.

How to Measure

There generally are two ways to measure how effective your media campaign is: quantitative and qualitative.

- **Quantitative measurement** is focused on numbers: the total reach of your media campaign in terms of how many people saw/read/ heard your message and/or how many times readers clicked on your company's news site to read the article. One of the challenges with using quantitative measures for social media is that not all social media can be tracked. Of perhaps greater import is that quantitative measures lack descriptive information: You know how many are in your audience, but you don't know who your audiences are.

- **Qualitative measurement** considers categories such as these, listed by PaperClip Partnership in England:
  - **Tonal bias:** Does the article have a positive, neutral or negative slant?
  - **Target publication tracking:** Is there coverage in the target publications?

— **Press release tracking:** How much of your press release has been published verbatim?

— **Sector analysis:** Measuring your industry sector's media coverage as a whole.[1]

Also, there are ways to both calculate the number of responses to your posts or articles and capture quantitative data, as noted by Bill Bradley, principal at Bottom Line Communications. His Media Branding Analysis includes criteria such as: the importance of the media outlet, are the key messages included in the article, and is the article a stand-alone or part of a roundup.

Bradley's measures of responses to a published story or article are based on practicality:

• Lower than expected queries, e.g., less that 5 percent spike in Web, phone and/or email activity

• Encouraging response: 5–15 percent spike in Web, phone and/or email activity

• Strong response: more than 15 percent spike in Web, phone and/or email activity, and additional media opportunities created from the reporting[2]

Only by linking media measurement to some activity, such as a spike in Web, phone or email activity, attendance at an event, number of new customers, etc., can you truly draw a correlation between your work and the results.

In "4 Ways to Measure Your Social Media Success," writer and PR Director Alex Honeysett recommends four tools to aid in measurement:

1. **Google Analytics** provides the number of visits to your site, demographics of users, how long users stay on your site and the most/least favorite content pieces.

2. **Klout:** The Klout Score focuses on measuring influence, described as "your ability to drive action on social networks."

3. **Wildfire's Social Media Monitor** offers a free social media monitor to help you understand your Twitter and Facebook presence.

4 **My Top Tweet by TwitSprout** provides rankings on your tweets.[3]

LEWIS PR, a global PR and digital communications agency headquartered in London, offers advice on how to find your most active audiences to learn what they are saving about your organization or brand. You may find that they coalesce around specific topics rather than language or geography — useful information when you are creating a communications strategy.

- Set up monitoring tools and search queries to watch who is mentioning your brand. Tools like Radian6 and SocialMention enable you to search social sites to find mentions in multiple languages.

- Facebook Insights shows which regions your fans are in. Find out how many people in your target audience are using Twitter by using sites like Sweepsearch and TwitterGrader. Filter results by specifying the location you are targeting.

- Use Google Trends to see how people are searching for your brand or topics relating to your brand.
  - Identify forum communities by using tools like Boardreader and filter your results by language.
  - Check your own website analytics for signs of significant traffic from specific markets.

- Study the results to identify any differences in the way markets respond to your brand. Do you see more engagement in certain regions or countries? More negativity in others? You can use tools like Sysomos to analyze sentiment within online conversations.

LEWIS PR also recommends that you first establish outcomes that reflect your business goals, then key performance indicators to show progress toward those outcomes.

Other suggestions:

- Your most important goals should focus on your hub channel. If that's your organization's blog, showing continued growth in subscribers and links will be key. If your focal point is a website geared to lead generation, the number of conversions to sales on that site will be your top metric.

- Review Web Analytics and Platform Analytics for each of your channels. They can be helpful for refining tactics. But bear in mind that you are working toward your key outcomes, so the most important thing to establish is whether your channels are contributing to those outcomes.

- Be careful about comparing metrics across markets because social media adoption can vary. Instead, focus on qualitative metrics: What is the overall tone of the conversation? Which messages gain the most traction? What is the level of engagement in proportion to the audience in each market?[4]

Where to Get Help

For many organizations, measuring and evaluating media relations activities and outcomes is best left to the professionals — companies that specialize in media measurement. PR Newswire is a good example of a global organization that offers focused distribution and evaluation capabilities. But if you can't afford to hire a professional service, at least learn from what and how they measure, and create your own program.

CHAPTER ELEVEN

THE FUTURE

Expanding Your Counselor Role

The evolution from communicator to counselor is so natural and so subtle that you may not be aware of the metamorphosis until it has occurred. One day you are responding to a journalist's question on why your organization has a certain policy on drug abuse in the workplace. While your lips are providing the answer, your mind is asking, "Why indeed?" Or you might be briefing a spokesperson for your organization before a major media interview, when suddenly it becomes obvious to both of you that a particular corporate practice is woefully out of date. So together you work out a plan to change it. Or perhaps you are writing

201

remarks on your organization's global marketing strategy for your CEO to deliver at a news conference when you cross the line from simply articulating someone else's policy to actually participating in policy formation yourself.

Your role has changed. Your responsibilities expand. As a stained-glass window diffuses the light that passes through it, enhancing the light by the addition of myriad beautiful colors, you find yourself contributing to your organization's policies and helping to shape its future. You have become an entrepreneur in the broadest sense, whether or not you run your own company, because you are breaking new ground. You have become a public relations counselor.

You still will spend time answering questions from reporters and preparing media plans. But more and more you will find yourself focusing on communications strategy, being a champion and agent of constructive change, and giving advice — on issues as complex as your CEO's responsibilities, as broad as your organization's business, as fundamental as its culture and values.

Avoiding Surprises

There is an old saying among CEOs — and media relations counselors — that there is no such thing as a good surprise. The objective of effective counseling is to anticipate and identify developing issues early so your organization can help shape those issues instead of just react to them. This proactive posture guarantees a minimum of surprises, good and bad.

Important issues may surface in the community, in the industry or within the ranks of your own organization. They can have a local, nationwide or global impact. They might involve employee matters, politics, health care, privacy or the environment. The possibilities are endless. Many are fundamentally "wallet issues," affecting people's financial and emotional well-being.

 Think of yourself as an ombudsman.

If an issue has the potential to someday affect your organization, it is your job to understand that issue and share your knowledge with the decision makers of your organization. PR counseling, though, goes beyond sharing information. As a PR counselor, you also should help your organization develop a position on emerging issues, as well as manage the business to avoid negative situations and capitalize on opportunities. Think of yourself as an ombudsman. In addition to being the eyes and ears of your organization, you sometimes have to be the conscience as well. Being an effective counselor is one of the most important and demanding roles of the media relations professional.

As a counselor, you need to be part of the decision-making process in your organization. You must:

- Have constant access to the CEO and other key executives.
- Be part of the strategic planning team for your organization's business activities.
- Have "a seat at the management table" when debate is underway and decisions are being made.
- Help management consider the long-term strategic implications of your company's response to an issue.
- Ensure that your company's policy-formation process gets the benefit of a broad perspective and variety of opinions, both inside and outside the organization.
- Have media relations and other communications functions included in your organization's business plans.

If you are being called in only after decisions are made, you are not practicing PR counseling.

Lessons to Be Learned

Corporate reputation and governance issues offer significant opportunities for counselors because the solutions cross disciplines from public relations and legal to investor relations and finance, and they affect virtually all the organization's target audiences. They also remind us that integrity now stands high on the list of attributes people consider important as they evaluate organizations and their leadership.

What lessons can we learn from recent abuses of power and the failure of those in responsible positions to speak up — especially when we appear to have been conspicuously quiet in our role as advocate for the corporations' stakeholders during the financial meltdown that left Wall Street essentially immune from punishment while Main Street suffered incalculable losses?

Even years after massive corporate scandals first surfaced, many public companies continue to use legal accounting actions to smooth earnings and meet analyst estimates. Average citizens may not understand the intricacies of accounting ploys, corporate corruption and insider trading. But they know what it means to the lives of employees and their families when corporations deliberately take money out of pension funds to puff up corporate profits and inflate management pay. They understand the pain to the typical family when health benefits are curtailed — or cut altogether. And they know that mutual funds, once considered the quintessential good investment for the small investor, have been stained by improper trades by some of the industry's most prominent and richest managers.

Public relations people do not have the option of operating in a moral twilight. How could we have continued to write news releases, annual reports and CEO speeches when their content was as much fiction as fact?

Symbols Communicate Loudly

Sometimes it is the relatively small things like corporate jets that disgust and infuriate the public, causing extraordinarily passionate responses. After all, PR people learn from the earliest stages of our careers that perception is reality and symbols have exceptional power.

The symbols keep communicating: The big guys take care of themselves while average workers and small shareholders lose. This dire situation can be a defining moment for media relations. We are not alone in missing opportunities to right what is going wrong. Many legal, accounting, brokerage and banking firms act no better. But pointing fingers at others does not lessen our responsibility.

Speaking Up for What Is Right

It is one thing to navigate our way through blurred ethical boundaries. It takes guts, family support and a solid bank account to confront senior management when we might be committing job suicide.

Recent actions in corporate America — most especially in the financial sector — were blatantly and obviously wrong. We ask for the proverbial "seat at the table," wanting to be involved in decision making and considered as respected counselors to management. Along with rights, that seat brings responsibilities: to speak up when things are wrong; to act to get them changed.

If it is an auditor's job to catch malfeasance at the companies they oversee, then it is our role to help keep it from happening in the first place — or to work to get it stopped if it starts. Weren't there opportunities to pass on concerns to the corporate auditor or outside counsel during working sessions on the 10K, on a road show or at the annual meeting?

Accepting Responsibility

A shocking number of firms have paid multimillion-dollar fines that sound enormous until you remember the huge profits, pay and perks of the organizations and people involved — and the fact that many are permitted to "neither admit nor deny wrongdoing." Hardly a reassuring message about their sense of individual responsibility.

What happened to the fundamental premise of crisis management (and decency) that we admit error and say what we're doing to fix the situation? Obviously there still is a large leap between accepting punishment and accepting accountability. It will take much more than new accounting standards, independent boards of directors and corporate oversight laws to fix what's wrong in too many executive suites today. Actions speak louder than words.

Social Media as a Watchdog

Ongoing research by Dr. Donald K. Wright and Michelle Drifka indicates PR and media relations practitioners believe social media have improved each year in terms of accuracy, credibility, honesty, trust and truth telling. Significantly for the future, they also think social media "effectively serve as a watchdog for traditional news media, impacting corporate and organizational transparency and advocating a transparent and ethical culture."

Not surprisingly, this research shows PR leaders believe the current use of social media does not come close to matching how important these media should and will be in the future. That makes the research finding that communications or public relations departments are most likely to be responsible for monitoring and managing an organization's blog and social media communications an important responsibility for our profession. A key area for improvement in the future: Wright and Drifka found that most measurement research today focuses on outputs such as the amount of information being disseminated rather than "outcomes such as the impact these messages have on the formation, change and reinforcement of attitudes, opinions and behavior."[1]

Returning to the Fundamentals

Performance is what counts. We need to help our organizations return to the fundamentals of right and wrong, fairness and decency that most of us were taught by our parents years ago. We need to adhere to the basics of trust, honesty and genuine concern for customers, employees and shareholders.

Harold Burson, founder of Burson-Marsteller, once described the evolution of public relations this way: When PR was in its infancy, clients called on us to ask, "How should I *say* it?" As the profession became more sophisticated, the question evolved to, "*What* should I say?" At the next level it became, "*How* should we *do* it?" And at the highest level it is, "*What* should we *do*?" As that question has changed over the past few decades, so our function has changed and broadened as well. Such breadth requires that we have a thorough understanding of our organization's business strategy and marketing plans, internal challenges and future opportunities, customers and competitors. We must regard ourselves as counselors and general managers, not just communicators.

 "PR is 90 percent doing and 10 percent talking about it."

In the end, Arthur W. Page had it right all along. He was an AT&T vice president from 1927 to 1946, the first person in a PR position to serve as an officer and member of the board of directors of a major corporation, and the founder of corporate public relations as a strategic management function. Page believed that while well-thought-out communications programs are vital to an organization's success, they must be based on the reality of its performance and not on Madison Avenue slogans. Page summed up his philosophy in a single sentence: "Public relations is 90 percent doing and 10 percent talking about it."[2] This is wise counsel for CEOs and public relations counselors as well.

Building Your Credibility

While media relations professionals generally are well informed, you can increase your chances of recognizing important issues early by paying careful attention to all media, traditional and social. As a media relations professional, you should:

- Read a wide variety of media — not just the business and trade press but also "alternative" press and publications devoted to subjects and ideologies outside the scope of your industry. Do key word searches on the Internet and visit opinion-leading websites and blogs.

- Read editorials consistently to be alert to new subjects and shifts in the opinions of thought-leaders.

- Monitor letters-to-the-editor sections in newspapers and magazines, especially in the more prestigious publications, and follow blogs, tweets, newsgroups, chat rooms, user groups and forums on the Internet. Emerging issues or changes in viewpoints on old ones often get their first public exposure in these arenas.

- Pay attention to better-quality TV and radio talk shows and interview programs, which are good sources of perspectives on issues.

- Maintain informal contacts with key media people. Seek their opinions. Get them to share their experiences with you.

- Build internal alliances and a strong informal network of source people within your organization. They can alert you to developing trends within your industry and markets, and changes in courses of action that are needed.

An Expert's Advice on How to Offer Counsel

James E. Lukaszewski, ABC, APR, Fellow PRSA, is president of the Lukaszewski Group, a division of Risdall Public Relations, management consultants in communications. He counsels companies facing serious internal and external problems involving activist counteraction, community conflict and grassroots campaigns, corporate relations failures, reputational threats, employee relationship building, ethics/integrity/compliance, litigation visibility, Web-based attacks and threats to corporate survival. Over the years, he has developed what he calls the "Executive Decision Model: Three Minutes to Strategic Executive Decision Making" that provides wise advice as you expand your counselor role:

"One crucial reality of being a trusted advisor is that the best and most useful advice is often needed in a brief period of time (on-the-spot) under the pressure of events. The Executive Decision Model is a compact, direct process for giving those you help focused, accurate and complete information — framed in a strategic way — from which to choose a course of action.

"The discipline is to use this highly focused, structured, time-sensitive approach to get your recommendations promptly put forward. This allows the balance of discussion time, meeting time or face time with those you advise to be productive and directed toward helping them make better decisions. The six steps of the process:

Step 1: Situation description (60 words). Briefly describe the nature of the issue, problem or situation. This is the factual basis for "what we know now," "why we need to take your time, now, to discuss this," or "This is a new and important topic we need to talk about, now."

Step 2: Analysis (60 words). Briefly describe what the situation means, its implications, and perhaps, how it threatens or presents opportunities. Include one or two key assumptions that validate the analysis. Managers always need to know why, but not in great detail. They're also interested in the intelligence you've gathered or know about that supports your analysis, assumptions and recommendations.

Step 3: The goal (60 words). The clear, concise statement of the task to be accomplished. Goals keep everyone focused forward.

The goal should be stated as the behavioral, emotional or intellectual change in your target constituencies. Useful goals are understandable, brief, achievable, positive and time/deadline sensitive.

Step 4: Options (150 words). Always present at least three options for action. You can suggest more, but three is optimal for management to choose from. The goals you suggest are to "do something," "do something more," or "do nothing." Having multiple options keeps you at the table and avoids the "death by question" syndrome that often strikes should you have only one recommendation. Lose that single recommendation through a crucial unanticipated question, and you'll be out of the discussion for the duration.

Step 5: Recommendation (60 words). Be prepared to say what you would do if you were in your boss' shoes, and why. The recommendation is usually selected on the basis of which option will cause the least number of negative unintended consequences. This is where you earn your paycheck and a place at the table. Be prepared to walk through a similar sort of analysis for each of the options proposed.

Step 6: Justification (60 words). Identify the negative unintended — but fully predictable — consequences of each option, including the option to do nothing. These are the reactions or circumstances that could arise resulting from the options you suggest (including to do nothing). Every management decision or action has consequences that can be forecast. Each also has unintended consequences that can be forecast. Inadequate provision for consequences is what can sabotage an otherwise useful strategy.

"Striving to provide advice in this 450-word format (three minutes) is powerful, conserves management time, and — coupled with the discipline of suggesting three action options every time — will get you invited back to the table again and again. Anyone who can spontaneously provide three decision options, on-the-spot, every time, is an extraordinarily valuable individual. If you want to be where the important decisions are made, when important decisions are being made, the three-minute strategy process will help get you there."[3]

Behind every high-powered technology company and executive you'll find a man or woman — and often a team — making sure the company's message is being communicated correctly and strategically. In an article for Business Insider, Matt Lynley rated the top 50 PR professionals in the tech industry in 2012 using three measures — influence, effectiveness in dealing with the media and networking with other people in technology.[4] A look at the education and experience of some of Lynley's chosen PR leaders in the most successful high-tech companies can be instructive as you plan your career and expand your counselor role:

- **Teri Daly, Samsung:** Daly, APR, is head of PR for Samsung Telecommunications America and plays a major role in aligning corporate communications with overall business strategies. Previously she had 20 years of communications industry experience including supporting global clients in technology, telecom and wireless and founding her own agency. She has a B.A. in journalism from Texas State University.[5]

- **Hani Durzy, LinkedIn:** A former reporter and graduate of Bates College, Durzy and his communications crew work tirelessly with reporters and the public to make sure LinkedIn remains in the same conversations with the likes of Facebook and Twitter. Lynley observes that LinkedIn is seen as a sexy social media company thanks to the efforts of its communications team.[6]

- **Erika Brown Ekiel, Freelance:** Some of the best PR professionals spend a long tenure as a reporter before shifting over to media relations. Ekiel spent a decade as associate editor at Forbes covering venture capital before moving on to marketing with Greylock Partners, and Matrix Partners before that. Now she's one of the top independent consultants on branding and marketing in Silicon Valley.[7]

- **Lynn Fox, Klout:** Fox joined the tech PR scene during Silicon Valley's first bubble. Now leading communications at Klout, she has worked at Apple, Google, Palm and Twitter. With such an extensive background comes what Lynley calls "a staggeringly large network and a wealth of experience working with some of the most famous tech executives in the valley, including former Apple CEO Steve Jobs." Fox's career started as one of three people to lead the PR launch of DIRECTV. She earned a B.A. in communications with high honors from Loyola Marymount University.[8]

- **David Kane, Google Ventures:** Kane was Google's first PR official, and he's had a hand in almost every public launch of a Google product since the debut of Google.com in 1999. He led the financial communications involved in Google's IPO and served as the voice of Google for a wide range of inquiries. He also founded Google's international communications function. He has a B.A. in journalism from Indiana University-Bloomington where he serves on the Dean's advisory board for the IU School of Informatics and Computer Science.[9]

- **Brian O'Shaughnessy, Skype:** Now head of global communications at Skype, O'Shaughnessy has more than 20 years of experience in global media relations, crisis communications, executive communications, integrated marketing, branding and legislative affairs in Washington, D.C., Silicon Valley and international markets. He has a B.A. in political science from Merrimack College and an M.P.S. from New York University.[10]

- **Carolyn Penner, Twitter:** Formerly with Google, Penner was tasked with altering Twitter's media strategy, which in the past used to rely on reporters writing articles based on blog posts rather than working closely with the media. Lynley says the new strategy has worked. Penner has a B.A. in human biology from Stanford.[11]

- **David Swain, Facebook:** Lynley says that the Facebook Platform it is arguably the most important part of Facebook, given that you can build an entire business on top of it, and it's equally important that reporters understand how to adequately explain it. Swain works night and day to communicate with reporters and Facebook platform users, ensuring that its message gets across correctly and any complaints are handled speedily. He graduated from St. Lawrence University.[12]

Involvement Brings Responsibility

The access that our media relations responsibilities gives us — not only to top management but also to the decision-making processes of our company or client — brings with it a great obligation. We can take apparently random sequences of events and help translate them into an actionable agenda. We can ensure that our organization's decision makers have access to public opinion and attitudes so they can evaluate their actions against perception as well as reality. After all, every misconception begins with a certain element of truth. Much like products, public issues also have life cycles. We can help identify emerging issues early enough so our organizations can shape and manage them rather than merely respond.

Counseling is much more than offering advice. It acts as a strategic glue, bonding input from all available external and internal sources to ensure a holistic rather than a partial view. It is selectively sorting information and focusing only on events that are important and contribute to understanding. A good counselor will relate and interpret the facts; a great one will understand and enhance the meaning. Harold W. Burlingame, a retired executive vice president at AT&T, advises:

> You should try to get yourself positioned as one who has a special sensing system and thus can anticipate problems in time to solve them before they erupt publicly. Public relations people need to be an integral part of the planning process if you are to help your organization anticipate and prepare for change. To be credible, however, you have to demonstrate a solid understanding of the business and appreciation for its operations problems. Without that knowledge you will have great difficulty being accepted as an equal member of the management team.[13]

Business Problems Are PR Problems

Almost all the critical problems facing your organization are public relations problems in the broadest sense of the term. Like Rubik's Cube, the solutions can be deceptively simple in appearance. But the cosmetic touches of a publicity program cannot obscure deeper blemishes in organizational policy or practice for long. You can help your top management look at each problem strategically, searching for well-thought-out actions that contribute to permanent resolution. You can reflect shareowner sentiment, customer concerns and employee expectations, for you are their voice within your organization just as you are its ears and eyes in the community and the marketplace.

 Use the unique window you have to public opinion.

You have an opportunity to use the unique window you have to public opinion — those constant contacts with the news media — to

212

act as an early warning system for the decision makers of your organization, to perceive not only what is going on around you but also what is coming. You can become a catalyst for change.

Case Study:
For P&G, Social Media Is the Problem and the Solution

Author and former AT&T PR executive Dick Martin offers his analysis of how a global consumer products company missed an opportunity to involve its customers in a product enhancement.[15]

Procter & Gamble is one of the savviest companies in the world. Just as it was a leader in advertising techniques in the 20th century, it has pioneered new technologies of the 21st century. But even P&G can drop the ball.

Thanks to its invention of disposable diapers, P&G sells more baby products than any other company in the world. The company has maintained a position of product leadership by investing millions in research and development. For decades, its diaper scientists were obsessed with one thing: dry bottoms. In 2010, the diaper lab came up with what the marketing people considered a major innovation — printing absorbent gel onto the diaper rather than pouring it into a bulky pulp material. That made the diaper 20 percent thinner and reduced the amount of material used. But it would take three months to get new packaging into full distribution, so P&G started putting the new Pampers into old packaging and prepared for a big launch later in the year.

Some mothers noticed the difference in the diapers almost immediately. Since 2.5 million babies develop diaper rashes every day, it was inevitable that some of the babies in the thinner diapers would get red bottoms. And it was just as predictable that their mothers would blame the reengineered diapers. They started a Facebook page to detail their complaints and press P&G to bring back the old diapers. Their claims quickly attracted media attention, as well as the plaintiff's bar, and ultimately led to 12 lawsuits and inquiries by product safety regulators in the U.S. and Canada. When the company settled the case in 2011, it was on the hook for about $3 million.

The great irony of this situation is that Pampers had a Facebook page with 250,000 members, far more than the opponents of the new diapers ever attracted. It could have announced the new diapers there even before they went into distribution, preparing their customers for "new and improved" diapers. It could have interviewed its employees, many of whom had used the new diapers on their children, and posted the videos to YouTube and its existing Pampers Village forum. It could have shown that the changes were based on customer feedback and met a clear customer need. It could have documented the extensive testing the new design went through. And it could have done more to educate its customers on the real causes of diaper rash, which ended up as one of the requirements of its settlement.

P&G didn't do any of this because it considered its customers an "audience" for its product announcement rather than a community of users who had a stake in its products. And that may be the difference between social media and traditional media relations. The goal of traditional media relations was to deliver a message to an audience. The goal of media relations through social media is to participate in a community.

You can't build an online community. You can only seek to join one. You can give it a place to meet, as P&G did — but you'll never own it, as P&G also learned. The trick is to become a full participant, listening to the chatter, encouraging discussion and acting on feedback. Above all, recognize that social media is about customers helping each other. When big changes are coming, a company owes it to the community to involve them from the earliest practical point.

Case Study: Domino's Harnesses the Power of Social Media

In contrast to P&G, Martin cites Domino's Pizza as an example of a company that stuck with the same recipe for 50 years, even as sales were declining and focus groups were describing its pizzas as "ketchup on cardboard."[16] Given the company's history with social media, no one would have guessed that it would go online to solve its problems. Here is Martin's analysis of this case:

Just a year earlier Domino's suffered the mother of all social media disasters. Two employees videotaped themselves doing all sorts of disgusting things to pizzas and sandwiches about to be boxed and taken to customers' homes. Then they posted the videos to YouTube. Domino's delayed making a public statement for 24 hours for fear of drawing even more attention to the videos. In the meantime, YouTube counted nearly a million viewings of the video, the conversation spread to Facebook and the blogosphere was in full Twitter.

When the company did respond, it did all the right things. Its president posted an apology on YouTube, thanking the online community for bringing the issue to the company's attention. He separated the company from the wrongdoers and announced their prosecution. And he outlined the steps being taken to make sure it would never happen again. Most of all, he learned an important lesson about the power of social media — a lesson he remembered when he read those disturbing focus group results.

Instead of rationalizing that the research was flawed or reflected a minority opinion, Domino's decided to take the radical step of changing the ingredients for all its pizzas. And instead of waiting to announce a "new and improved" product, the company decided to own up to its shortcomings and involve its customers in the re-launch through social media. Domino's reached out to food bloggers and others who had criticized the brand in the past and asked them to comment live on the company website about the new taste. It put up PizzaTurnaround.com, a social micro-site which documented the whole reformulation. And it encouraged people who liked the new pizza to tweet their endorsements.

The results? Television host Stephen Colbert devoted an entire segment on his "Comedy Central" show to the new pizza, and taste tests were performed all over, from social commerce sites to news stations to CBS's "The Early Show." More important, sales increased 14 percent just months after the introduction of the new pizza and the company's stock price shot up 50 percent.

Earning the Right to Counsel

An increasing number of organization leaders have given their public relations people a status in the corporate and nonprofit worlds comparable to operations, marketing, human resources, legal and finance staffs because our skills are recognized as vital to setting sophisticated strategies and meeting ambitious objectives. Indeed, wise leaders take advantage of the broad expertise of their PR departments, using the staff not only as communicators but also as counselors.

But the right to offer candid counsel and expect confidence in your advice does not flow automatically from your role as the media relations spokesperson. It must be earned. To be credible you have to demonstrate a solid understanding of the business and appreciation for its operations problems. You must do as good a job of preparing a case to persuade your management, board of directors and other decision makers as you do when you are preparing a case to persuade the public.

When you make a presentation to management or the board of directors, support your position with opinion poll or research results, news media reports, speech excerpts from opinion leaders, and your operations colleagues' evaluation of its relevance to the business. Important issues — especially emerging issues — usually have many interpretations. Your own interpretation is part of the value you contribute as a counselor. To protect your credibility, though, you should make your management aware of other views on the same issue by different interest groups.

James E. Lukaszewski, president of The Lukaszewski Group, a division of Risdall Public Relations, suggests the following questions to test yourself on how well you know your CEO and understand your counseling role within his or her context:[17]

- Do you know your CEO's favorite business book?
- Do you know your CEO's top priority every day?
- Do you know whom your CEO quotes as a business thought leader or model?
- Do you know what's on your CEO's desk?
- Have you met other CEOs your CEO admires?
- Can you help your CEO meet other CEOs?
- How frequently do you read publications like the Harvard Business Review, Sloan Business Journal, Fortune, Barron's and the Berkshire Hathaway annual report?

It also can be helpful to pre-sell your programs to others in the organization who will benefit from them. They then are likely to support you in their own interest. All too often media relations people are in the position of selling not only their programs but also the need for them. Make sure your priorities are the same as your top management's. Then work with others in your organization whose needs you are attempting to meet, and turn your recommendation into a joint solution.

 Reporters are a window to the world's view of our organizations.

Only then will you have completed the circle that is — or should be — your job description: to work professionally with the media to *tell* your organization's story, and to take advantage of your daily contacts with reporters by listening not only to what they are *asking* but also to what they are *saying*. Whether you believe the media leads public opinion or reflects it, the opportunities are the same: Reporters are a key window to the world's view of our organizations, our products and our people. Reflecting their interests, anticipating their concerns, adapting our media relations efforts and suggesting new courses of action as a result of their input — that is what makes us valuable to our companies and clients. That is also what makes us true media relations professionals.

You should help ensure that your company or client has long-range plans reflecting both economic and social objectives, just as you provide guidance and discipline for making better decisions today. You should take care that your plans are operating like an architect's drawing: Changes can be made and arrangements altered while the basic structure remains a strong, workable blueprint for action.

Beyond that, you should put the same effort into the long-term "storm warning" job as you do into the short-term activities. You must

Checklist: How Involved and Valuable Are You to Your Organization?

Following is a checklist that the public relations directors of The Reader's Digest Association's worldwide subsidiaries were given at their Global Public Relations Conference in New York City to help them evaluate their value as communicators and counselors to management. Test yourself to see how you measure up:

❏ Recognized by colleagues as having excellent communications skills

❏ Knowledge of the company — mission, strategies, products, people, competitive strengths — to be a competent counselor to management

❏ Member of significant committees and task forces within the organization

❏ Close relationships with decision makers in all departments so your advice is sought by them

❏ Always know of major news long before it breaks

❏ Involved in counseling and planning as well as communicating

❏ Offer advice — sometimes on own initiative — to CEO and other members of senior management

❏ Advise senior management of upcoming PR opportunities and anticipate potential problems

❏ Work with CEO and affected departments to create "just in case" communications plans when necessary

gain the confidence of the top management of your organization or client so that when you disagree with them they know it is because you feel you would be abdicating your responsibility if you were to remain silent while they launch an unguided missile. You must gain their confidence so that you earn the right to offer counsel by persuasion, negotiation or exhortation. You need to be an expert in influencing behavior. The trick is to rock the boat without making everyone sink.

 We need to be experts in influencing behavior.

Above all, you need to return the values most of us were brought up with. For years we have advised our clients (and ourselves) not to say or do anything that we would not be comfortable seeing on the front page of The Wall Street Journal, www.cnn.com or any of the prominent online or broadcast media. Now we think there's an even more fundamental test of acceptable behavior: Just ask ourselves if we would be happy if our parents or our children knew what we were

What Keeps CEOs Up at Night?

Consulting firm Accenture surveyed 425 senior executives at the world's largest companies in all major industries and geographies in 2011. Here are the issues identified by senior executives as their top priorities — the issues where your communications and counseling skills should be making a contribution:[18]

1. Attracting and retaining skilled staff
2. Changing organizational culture and employee attitudes
3. Acquiring new customers
4. Developing new processes and products to stay ahead of the competition
5. Increasing customer loyalty and retention
6. Managing risk
7. Improving workforce performance
8. Increasing shareholder value
9. Using information technology to reduce cost and create value
10. Being flexible and adaptable to rapidly changing market conditions

doing. We should be concerned not just with what is legal but also with what is right — in the service of all the organization's stakeholders.

It gets down to individual behavior and responsibility. Every action you counsel, every thing you do and every word you write is a litmus test of your integrity. Not your employer's or your client's integrity, but your own. You would never let your executives walk into a news media interview without preparing them for tough questions you expected from the reporter. By the same token, you cannot let your organization move unprepared into next year — or into the next decade.

Advice from Top Executives, Consultants, Academics and Agency Heads

We asked experienced public relations executives, consultants and academics and agency heads the question, "What skills and qualities are the most valuable for media relations professionals to develop in order to become an effective counselor to management?" Here are their replies:

> Management today is seeking out and depending upon public relations professionals who can see down the road and point out the likely outcomes of a course of action. This requires good risk management skills. It also is increasingly important to know both the business you are working in and the language of that business in order to understand the unspoken motivations and the backdrop for decisions that need to be made. As you learn to "read" the management group you are counseling, you need to understand the peer group of each executive, who she/he respects, etc. This will add rich perspective to the counsel you give. Today's public relations professionals need solid skills in working with the media and being able to build ongoing strong media relationships. This clearly is on the list of top concerns of corporate management — and can be the ticket to credibility as a counselor to management.
>
> —Ann H. Barkelew
> Senior Counselor
> Fleishman Hillard, Inc.
> Minneapolis, Minnesota

> Anticipating and managing issues that are pertinent to the viability of the business and can impact the corporate reputation

are the proving grounds. Having a voracious appetite for knowledge about the company and its market will help you better identify ways to manage these issues and force those in public relations to demonstrate value in language and context common to business leaders. This is job one, and by performing it well we gain credibility to protect and enhance reputation in other ways.

—Matthew P. Gonring
Vice President, Corporate Communications
Jackson National Life Insurance Company
Lansing, Michigan

The counselor learns to listen. Listen, interpret, initiate. That's the essence of counseling. Consider publics — employees, the news media, stakeholders of all stripes — to be "customers" who must be created and re-created constantly. You can only sell to customers your product, service or message if they understand, want and are ready to deal with you. You can only sell when you understand them. To understand them you must listen to them. That's why public relations begins with research. It is the listening strategy. Listen a long time before you talk.

—E. Bruce Harrison
CEO
EnviroComm International
Washington, D.C.

PR professionals first and foremost need to be businesspeople who understand corporate finance, operations and strategic planning. It is not enough to be an accomplished practitioner of any one public relations skill, such as media relations, employee communications and the like — those skills should be a given for any senior professional. But, reading a balance sheet, understanding cash flow and why it's important, knowledge of SEC regulations that apply to your business/industry and the like will convey to your colleagues and to senior management that you are their peer and speak their language. Add to this, an understanding of issues that affect or might affect your business and your industry, experience in operating divisions, broad and deep knowledge about what's going on in the world as well as in the business world, the ability to listen and to articulate complex ideas in understandable language, and the ability to inspire trust and support from your colleagues and your subordinates, and you will have at least a reasonable

221

chance of achieving that enviable position of *effective* counselor to management.

—Carol B. Hillman
Strategic Planning Consultant
Framingham, Massachusetts

Good listening skills, courage and confidence are critical qualities of a PR person who is counseling senior executives. I've found that it is most important to be able to recognize the underlying concerns or issues (not just what's said out loud), not only from the CEO but from employees, customers and shareowners. Then, you need to have the courage to bring these perspectives or issues, good or bad, to the forefront. And, you've got to be confident enough to take executives out of their comfort zones by really serving as the voice of your constituencies. Don't think of communications as reporting on an organization. Think of it as driving the organization.

—Maril MacDonald
CEO
Gagen MacDonald
Chicago, Illinois

In my experience, what a CEO looks for in a PR counselor boils down to three things: judgment, creativity and integrity. Judgment based on deep business knowledge, not political correctness. Creativity applied to solving business problems, not to crafting nifty slogans or cheap publicity stunts. And integrity to stand up for what is right, even at high personal cost. The PR counselor's role is to help the CEO bring the company's policies and practices into harmony with its stakeholders' needs and expectations. Sometimes that means winning agreement or, at minimum, acceptance. At other times it means getting the company to change its plans. But it always means having acute antennae and anticipating where corporate and public interests might collide. One of my colleagues called it "seeing around corners." It's an apt description because for the senior PR counselor the world is all corners, all roads are narrow, and all bridges have tolls.

—Dick Martin
Business writer and former
executive vice president of public relations
AT&T
Summit, New Jersey

In my many years in media relations consulting, I've generally found three types of executives — those who revile and avoid media contact, either delegating the responsibility to others or forbidding contacts altogether; those who are uncomfortable with media, but see it as a necessary evil that is part of their lives in management; and those most enlightened ones who view the media as a conduit to amplifying their organization's brand, connecting their values to those of their constituents, and explaining their challenges and problems with a human face on them. A crucial role of today's communications executives is to guide your organization's management towards the latter category by helping them recognize that media relationships and contact, while not without some risk, offer clear rewards in terms of public understanding and acceptance, rewards that are hard to deny. A successful media relations counselor must do more than offer the strategy and words needed in a given situation. You must barrage management with best practices of other organizations, training that ensures increasingly positive results in communications settings, and frank evaluation of the executives' experiences with the news media.

—Art Merrick, Fellow PRSA
Senior Counsel
Hill and Knowlton Strategies
Santa Fe, New Mexico

Counseling is more than just being a professional communicator, although that's an important prerequisite. It requires always being on top of your game, both internally and externally, anticipating the good as well as the bad and being able to offer constructive advice in a timely manner. You must also have the ability to earn the trust and confidence of those in senior management who may look to you for sage counsel in achieving the goals of the company. Without that trust and confidence, your message, no matter how good, will likely fall on deaf ears.

—Edwin F. Nieder
Partner
Nieder & Nieder Associates
Los Angeles, California

When CEOs are asked who they listen to on important issues, there is a great deal of consistency. They tell me they want people who deal well with ambiguity. They want an individual who, while having a balanced approach to a problem, sees both sides — and has a point of view, with the confidence to back it up. At the top of our profession, we have moved from a skill-based profession to a strategic seat at the table, and now we are being forced to view our jobs from a policy platform. Business-people first — and then communications becomes one of the tools to solve the issue. The ability to know what is possible, and probable, comes from experience and practice. Basic skills will always be necessary to get in the door.

—Kurt P. Stocker
Associate Professor, Emeritus
Northwestern University
Dean of NYSE Directors' Institute
New York City

Strong writers must have a good understanding of how research can be used to develop and evaluate consistent, integrated and accountable strategic communications campaigns. They also must possess the ability to develop and nurture professional relationships with internal and external customers; have the knowledge to align senior management's goals with external and internal communications needs; and have the talent and abilities to integrate public relations measures with the organi-zation's business objectives. I'll take one additional step and suggest all of this will require solid undergraduate-level educa-tion — and perhaps graduate-level study backed up with appro-priate professional development training — that focuses upon (a) a solid understanding of practical and theoretical aspects of communications and public relations; (b) a thorough back-ground in liberal arts and sciences; (c) an awareness and under-standing about technology, diversity, politics and culture; and, (d) an appreciation of the global business environment, ideally including the ability to read and speak foreign languages.

—Dr. Donald K. Wright
Harold Burson Professor and Chair in Public Relations
Boston University

To bring real value to senior management, public relations counselors must be logical thinkers who can analyze issues, anticipate problems and communicate their recommendations in a rational, well-thought-out process. This kind of thinking is a trait particularly valued by technology managers here in the Pacific Northwest who by nature are exceptionally logical. Effective public relations counselors know that the solutions to most problems are not simple black and white answers, especially in the realm of media relations. They have a keen understanding of the big picture and present recommendations to management that include an analysis of the possible outcomes of alternative courses of action. They counsel senior management to have realistic expectations — that there are no guarantees in media relations. Focus on doing your best to communicate in an honest, forthright manner while respecting the needs of the media and their audiences.

—Candy Young, APR
Principal
Synchro Creative Communications
Bellevue, Washington

The Future of PR

As president and CEO of Edelman, the world's largest PR firm, Richard Edelman has a unique view of our profession. Here is an edited version of a message he posted on his 6 a.m. blog on October 1, 2012, the 60th anniversary of the firm founded by his father Dan with three employees and one client. His observations are insightful for expanding your role as a media relations specialist from communicator to counselor:

"At that time, PR was viewed merely as an add-on and something used primarily for corporate reputation or publicity for celebrities. Over the last 60 years, that has dramatically changed, as has the world. The classic pyramid of influence with elites at the top and mass audiences at the bottom has been supplanted by an inverted pyramid with passionate consumers, empowered employees and social activists. They are the new opinion formers.

"Our profession is uniquely suited to help business engage in this new world. We help companies decide on policy, then explain the rationale. For our industry, this changed dynamic presents a new role and opportunity.

"As I look to the future, I see five behavioral changes that will be required of us as an industry:

- **Provide clients with advice on what to do, and then how to communicate** around the "media cloverleaf" (social, hybrid, owned and traditional). Business must go beyond the minimum standard, leading and taking on the major issues of the day, proving performance through transparency.

- **Aim to have the dominant creative idea.** The stranglehold of advertising on the marketer is now loosened.

- **Be comfortable with interpreting data and insistent upon using it.** Offer clients fresh discussions and learn from communities of shared interest. Find the new opinion formers in the inverted pyramid of influence. Use search insights and web analytics to tailor the delivery of content based on time of day.

- **Show, don't tell.** In a world of increasingly limited attention spans, harness the power of video and photos because they are more emotive and sharable. Provide deeper, more informative visuals such as infographics.

- **Find the right balance between global and local.** Help clients shape global reputations, but at the same time remember that PR is inherently local.

"PR, at its best, can help move business and society forward in a complex world. Simply put, it's PR's time to lead."[19]

ENDNOTES

Chapter 1

[1] Dr. Amanda Hamilton-Attwell, CPRP, "Developing a Communication Strategy," client presentation, Magalieskruin, South Africa 2003.
[2] Materials from the Arthur W. Page Center, Penn State University.
[3] Debra Gelbart, writer and editor, Phoenix, Arizona, emails with the authors, September 2012.
[4] Dick Martin, business writer and former executive vice president of public relations, employee communications and brand management at AT&T, white paper prepared for the authors, "Social Media and Media Relations: From Pushing Out News to Building Relationships," September 2012.

Chapter 2

[1] *The Harvard International Journal & Press/Politics*, Volume 6, No. 3 (2000), and, *Nieman Reports*, Volume 60, No. 4 (Winter 2006).
[2] Tony Rogers, "What Makes Something Newsworthy: Factors Journalists Use to Gauge How Big a Story Is," journalism.about.com. http://journalism.about.com/od/reporting/a/newsworthy.htm.
[3] http://merriam-webster.com/dictionary/news.
[4] "What News Is — From the Reporter's Point of View," © 2012, James E. Lukaszewski, ABC, APR, Fellow PRSA, emails with the authors, November 2012.
[5] Brian Solis, *The End of Business as Usual* (Hoboken, NJ: John Wiley & Sons, 2012).
[6] Tiffani Frey, "6 Social Media Best Practices for Business," July 22, 2012, *Craft, Creative Marketing* (blog). http://www.craftcreativemarketing.com/social-media-best-practices-for-business-infograph.
[7] Quoted in Mitchell Osak, "Social Media Best Practices," September 26, 2012, *Mitchell Osak online* (blog). http://www.mitchellosak.com/2012/09/26/social-media-best-practices/.

Chapter 3

[1] Strauss Radio Strategies, Inc. http://www.straussradio.com.
[2] Charles Marsh, David W. Guth, and Bonnie Poovey Short, *Strategic Writing*, 2nd ed. (Boston: Pearson/Allyn & Bacon, 2009), 108.
[3] "Media Tip — Visiting an Editorial Board," Wisconsin Clearing House for Prevention Resources. http://www.tobwis.org/_Media/Content/Editorial-Board-Visit-Tips.pdf.
[4] Dr. Anthony Curtis, "How to Write a Feature Story," 2011. http://www.uncp.edu/home/acurtis/Courses/ResourcesForCourses/WritingFeatureStories.html.

[5] Dr. Tom Seekins and Dr. Stephen B. Fawcett, "A Guide to Writing Letters to the Editor: Expressing Your Opinion to the Public Effectively. RTC Rural. http://rtc.ruralinstitute.umt.edu/advocacy/editorials.htm.

[6] Marsh et al., p. 34.

[7] Marsh et al., p. 37.

[8] "Writing and Formatting Tips for News Releases," iReach. https://ireach.prnewswire.com/tips.aspx.

[9] Marsh et al., pp. 35–36.

[10] Dick Martin, business writer and former executive vice president of public relations, employee communications and brand management at AT&T, white paper prepared for the authors, "Social Media and Media Relations: From Pushing Out News to Building Relationships," September 2012.

[11] John McClain, "How to write an Op-Ed," All About Public Relations. http://aboutpublicrelations.net/ucmclaina.htm.

[12] Katya Andersen quoted in Joanne Fritz, "Pitching Nonprofit Stories to the Media," About.com Nonprofit Charitable Orgs. http://nonprofit.about.com/od/nonprofitpromotion/a/pitching.htm.

[13] Susan Young, "How to Pitch Your News Story to the Wall Street Journal," Get in Front Communications. http://www.getinfrontcommunications.com/how-to-pitch-your-news-story-to-the-wall-street-journal.php.

[14] Ibid.

[15] Wikipedia, "Public Service Announcement." http://en.wikipedia.org/wiki/Public_service_announcement.

[16] Mike Periu, "How a Satellite Media Tour Can Boost Business," October 26, 2011, Open Forum. http://www.openforum.com/articles/how-a-satellite-media-tour-can-boost-business.

[17] "Standby Statements for Leaders," *Public Relations Strategist*, Summer 2012.

[18] Katie McMurray, "So You Think You're a Subject Matter Expert?" January 6, 2012, FlyingSolo. http://www.flyingsolo.com.au/marketing/public-relations-pr/so-you-think-youre-a-subject-matter-expert.

Chapter 4

[1] Andy Oliver, "Public Relations in the Digital Age," July 17, 2012, *LEWIS 360* (blog). http://blog.lewispr.com/.

[2] Amy Chozick, "Time Inc.'s New Chief Rethinks Magazines for a Digital Audience," *The New York Times*, July 29, 2012.

[3] The Missouri Group, *News Reporting and Writing*, 10th ed. (Boston: Bedford/St. Marin's, 2011).

[4] Charles Marsh, David W. Guth and Bonnie Poovey Short, *Strategic Writing: Multimedia Writing for Public Relations, Advertising and More*, 2nd ed. (Boston: Pearson/Allyn & Bacon, 2009).

[5] Scott Bourne, "Seven Basic Steps to Posting Video to YouTube," July 3, 2010, *Photofocus.com* (blog). http://photofocus.com/2010/07/03/seven-basic-steps-to-posting-video-to-youtube/.

Chapter 5

[1] Mike Bruno, "Oscars 2011 Winners: 'King's Speech' Rules the Night," Inside Movies, February 27, 2011. http://insidemovies.ew.com/2011/02/27/oscars-winner/.

[2] Wikipedia, *The King's Speech*. http://en.wikipedia.org/wiki/The_King's_Speech.

[3] Materials from the Arthur W. Page Center, Penn State University.

[4] *The Diane Rehm Show* from WAMU and NPR, June 7, 2012.
http://thedianerehmshow.org/shows/2012-06-07/gary-knell/transcript.

[5] Chris King, new media specialist, Brewster, NY, emails with the authors, September 2012.

[6] Don Crowther, "Public Relations: The Press Conference: When to Hold it and How to Do It Right," 101PublicRelations.com. http://101publicrelations.com/sr27.html.

[7] Dan Rather with Digby Diehl, *Rather Outspoken: My Life in the News* (New York: Grand Central Publishing, 2012).

Chapter 6

[1] Duane Lester, "How to Assert Copyright Over Your Work When It's Been Plagiarized (Video)," *All American Blogger*. http://www.allamericanblogger.com/21327/how-toassert-copyright-over-your-work.

[2] Wikipedia, "Plagiarism." http://en.wikipedia.org/wiki/Plagiarism.

[3] Andrew Beaujon, "Jayson Blair on the First Time He Plagiarized: 'I Can't Believe No One Caught That,'" October 22, 2012, Poynter. http://www.poynter.org/latest-news-/mediawire/192383/jayson-blair-on-the-first-time.

[4] http://www.huffingtonpost.com/2012/08/10/fareed-zakaria-plagiarism.

[5] Mary Elizabeth Williams, "A Plagiarist's Lame Excuse: Addiction Made Me Do It," SALON, December 2, 2011. http://www.salon.com/topic/quentin_rowan/.

[6] Miranda Brookins, Demand Media, "Examples of Plagiarism in the Workplace," Chron. http://smallbusiness.chron.com/examples-plagiarism-workplace-11971.html.

[7] Wikipedia, "List of Plagiarism Incidents: Journalism," October 19, 2012. http://en.wikipedia.org/wiki/List_of_plagiarism_incidents.

[8] Student Technology Services, "Safe Computing: Copyright Infringement," Washington University in St. Louis. http://sts.wustl.edu/copyright-infringement.

[9] http://www.copyright.gov/help/faq/faq-definitions.html.

[10] "Connecting with Our Values — Code of Business Conduct," © 2007 Cisco Systems, Inc. See http://files.shareholder.com/downloads/CSCO/1483197776x0x387353/97e5e9eb-b4e4-472c-8bc6-9241cc73be5c/Cisco_2010_COBC_external.pdf.

[11] "Case of Copyright Infringement by Zee Khana Khazana," March 30, 2012, Social Samosa. http://www.socialsamosa.com/2012/03/case-of-copyright-infringement-by-zee-khana-khazana.

[12] Paul J. Friedman, "The Troublesome Semantics of Conflict of Interest," *Ethics Behavior*, Volume 2, no. 4 (1992): 245–251.

[13] "Code of Business Conduct on Ethics: Conflicts of Interest," Tootsie Roll Industries, 2006. http://www.tootsie.com/comp_ethics.php.

[14] "Conflict of Interest: A Matter of Judgment, Objectivity," SRP. https://www.srpnet.com.

[15] "Connecting with Our Values."

[16] "Off the record," The Phrase Finder. http://phrases.org.uk/meanings/263350.html.

Chapter 7

[1] "How to Use Social Media to Interact with Subscribers," July 25, 2012, RJI. http://www.rjionline.org/news/how-use-social-media-interact-subscribers.

[2] Melissa Munroe, senior editor and graphic designer, CHNU, Surrey, B.C. Canada, emails with the authors.

[3] Michael Fanning, director, sustainable development, Michelin Group, Clermont-Ferrand, France, emails with the authors, September 2012.

[4] John Colapinto, "Undercover with a Michelin Inspector," *The New Yorker*, November 23, 2009.

[5] Dick Martin, business writer and former executive vice president of public relations, employee communications and brand management at AT&T, white paper prepared for the authors, "Social Media and Media Relations: From Pushing Out News to Building Relationships," September 2012.

[6] Jackie Welch, director, Ruby Sisson Library, Pagosa Springs, Colorado, conversations and emails with the authors, October 2012.

Chapter 8

[1] "Living in the EU," European Union. http://europa.eu/about-eu/facts-figures/living/index_en.htm.

[2] "World Press Encyclopedia a Survey of Press Systems Worldwide," Amanda C. Quick, project editor, Miami University Libraries. www.lib.muohio.edu/multifacet/record/mu3ugb3505760.

[3] "The Global Social Media Challenge: A Social Marketer's Guide to Managing Brands across Borders," LEWIS PR, 2011. http://publish.lewispr.com/whitepapers/globalsocialchallenge/LEWIS_whitepaperEN.pdf.

[4] Ibid.

[5] "Top 10 Unfortunate Product Names," October 27, 2007. http://listverse.com/2007/10/27/top-10-unfortunate product names/.

[6] "The 2012 Harris Poll EquiTrend Study on Brands of the Year" and "The 2012 Annual RQ Study on Corporate Reputations." www.harrisinteractive.com.

[7] "The Global Social Media Challenge."

Chapter 9

[1] Jane Mayer, "Bully Pulpit," *The New Yorker*, June 18, 2012.

[2] Douglas Brinkley, *Cronkite* (New York: HarperCollins, 2012).

[3] "What Makes YouTube's News Audience Click?" *storyful.blog*. http://blog.storyful.com/2012/07/16/what-makes-youtube-audience-click/.

[4] Dick Martin, business writer and former executive vice president of public relations, employee communications and brand management at AT&T, white paper prepared for the authors, "Social Media and Media Relations: From Pushing Out News to Building Relationships," September 2012.

[5] The Missouri Group, *Telling the Story: The Convergence of Print and Online Media*, 5th ed. (Boston: Bedford/St. Martin's, 2013).

[6] Robert Channick, "Public Relations Scion Richard Edelman, Subject of an Upcoming Book, Shares His Take on the Business in the Digital Age," *Chicago Tribune*, November 7. 2012.

[7] "The Global Social Media Challenge: A Social Marketer's Guide to Managing Brands across Borders," LEWIS PR, 2011, p. 7. http://publish.lewispr.com/whitepapers/globalsocialchallenge/LEWIS_whitepaperEN.pdf.

[8] Raymond C. Jones, PR consultant, remarks given at PRSA Crisis Communications Workshop, May 8, 2001.

[9] "The Global Social Media Challenge."

[10] "From the Chair of the Board to the Shipping Room Clerk," paper presented by Ralph Hancox, adjunct professor and professional fellow, The Canadian Centre for Studies in Publishing, Simon Fraser University, Vancouver, Canada, to the 3rd McMaster World Congress on Corporate Governance, January 23–27, 2006.

[11] Jeff Jarvis, associate professor and director of the Two-Knight Center for Entrepreneurial Journalism at the City University of New York's Graduate School of Journalism, speaking on CNN's *Reliable Sources* program, August 5, 2012.

[12] James E. Lukaszewski, ABC, APR, Fellow PRSA, "Tip Sheet: The Perfect Apology," *PR News*, June 2011.

[13] © 2012, James E. Lukaszewski, ABC, APR, Fellow PRSA, emails with the authors, November 2012.

[14] Ibid.

[15] Kim Harrison, "Repeat Your Messages to Gain Greater Cut-Through," *Cutting Edge PR e-News*, Issue 112, September 5, 2012. http://www.cuttingedgepr.com.

[16] The Missouri Group, *News Reporting and Writing*, 10th ed. (Boston: Bedford/St. Martin's, 2011).

[17] Chris King, new media specialist, Brewster, NY, emails with the authors, September 2012.

[18] Dick Martin, *OtherWise: The Wisdom You Need to Succeed in a Diverse and Divisive World* (New York: ANACOM, 2012).

[19] Mia Pearson, "PR Lessons from Labatt Reaction to Magnotta Photo," *The Globe and Mail*, June 7, 2012.

[20] Ron Charles, "The Futility of Banning Books," WashingtonPost.com, quoted in *The Week*, June 22, 2012.

[21] Maureen Dowd, "Is Pleasure a Sin?" *The New York Times*, June 10, 2012.

Chapter 10

[1] "Media Evaluation," PaperClip PCS Ltd. http://www.paperclippartnership.co.uk/media-evaluation.html.

[2] "Scorecard: Give Your Media Coverage the 'MBA' Test," *PR News*. http://www.prnewsonline.com/digitalpr/15081.html.

[3] Alex Honeysett, "4 Ways to Measure Your Social Media Success," *Forbes*, August 22, 2012. http://forbes.com/sites/dailymuse/2012/08/22/4-ways-to-measure-your-social-media-success.

[4] "The Global Social Media Challenge: A Social Marketer's Guide to Managing Brands across Borders," LEWIS PR, 2011, http://publish.lewispr.com/whitepapers/globalsocialchallenge/LEWIS_whitepaperEN.pdf.

Chapter 11

[1] Donald. K. Wright, Ph.D. and Michelle Drifka Hinson, "Examining How Social and Emerging Media Have Been Used in Public Relations Between 2006 and 2012: A Longitudinal Analysis," *Public Relations Review*, June 2012 and http://www.prsa.org/Intelligence/PRJournal/Documents/2012WrightHinson.pdf.

[2] Materials from the Arthur W. Page Center, Penn State University.

[3] "Executive Decision Model: Three Minutes to Strategic Executive Decision Making," © 2004, James E. Lukaszewski, ABC, APR, Fellow PRSA, emails with the authors, November 2012.

[4] Matt Lynley, "The PR 50: The Best Communications Pros in Technology." *Business Insider*, July 24, 2012. http://www.businessinsider.com/the-pr-50-the-most-effective-communications-professionals-in-technology-2012-7?op=1.

[5] Ibid. See also *Global PR Summit 2012*. "Speaker Bio: Teri Daly." http://events.holmesreport.com/gprs-2012/speaker-teri-daley.aspx.

[6] Ibid. See also Linkedin. Hani Durzy. http://www.linkedin.com/in/hanidurzy.

[7] Ibid.

[8] Ibid. See also Arik Hanson, "Working in PR for Klout: An Interview with Lynn Fox." *Communication Conversations*, October 17, 2012. http://www.arikhanson.com/2012/10/17/working-in-pr-for-klout-an-interview-with-lynn-fox/.

[9] Ibid. See also *Google Ventures*. David Krane, General Partner. http://www.googleventures.com/team/david-krane.

[10] Ibid. See also Linkedin. Brian O'Shaughnessy. www.linkedin.com/in/brianoshaughnessy.

[11] Ibid. See also Linkedin. Carolyn Penner. http://www.linkedin.com/pub/dir/Carolyn/Penner.

[12] Ibid.

[13] Conversations with the authors.

[14] Kim Harrison, *Cutting Edge PR e-News*, Issue 113, October 10, 2012. www.cuttingedgepr.com.

[15] Dick Martin, business writer and former executive vice president of public relations, employee communications and brand management at AT&T, white paper prepared for the authors, "Social Media and Media Relations: From Pushing Out News to Building Relationships," September 2012.

[16] Ibid.

[17] James E. Lukaszewski, "Inside the Mind of the CEO," *Public Relations Strategist*, Summer 2004, p. 17.

[18] Lisa Petrilli, "Four Priorities Keeping CEOs Up at Night," *C-Level Strategies*, May 23, 2011. http://www.lisapetrilli.com/2011/05/23/four-priorities-keeping-ceos-up-at-night/.

[19] Richard Edelman, "The History (and Future) of PR." *6 A.M.*, October 1, 2012. http://www.edelman.com/p/6-a-m/the-history-and-future-of-pr/. This edited extract is used by permission of Richard Edelman.

INDEX